☐ QUESTIONNAIRES: DESIGN AND USE

second edition

by
Doug R. Berdie
John F. Anderson
Marsha A. Niebuhr

The Scarecrow Press, Inc.
Lanham, Md., & London

Library of Congress Cataloging-in-Publication Data

Berdie, Douglas R.
  Questionnaires : design and use.

  Bibliography: p.
  Includes indexes.
  1. Psychometrics.   2. Questionnaires.   I. Anderson, John F.
II. Niebuhr, Marsha A.   III. Title.
BF39.B445   1986   001.4'222   86-1783
ISBN 0-8108-1884-1

dedicated to

Ray Berdie,

Dr. William W. Anderson,

and

Ben & Helen Niebuhr

CONTENTS

FOREWORD TO FIRST EDITION

We have recently completed a study at the University of Minnesota that used six different questionnaires and surveyed more than 3,000 people [10]. During the course of this study, we were faced with many of the problems that confront anyone who uses questionnaires.

Prior to designing our study, we reviewed literature pertaining both to past works on how questionnaires can be used most effectively and to opinions regarding the methodology involved in the use of questionnaires. We were unable to find any single, concise, yet complete source describing how to conduct a study using questionnaires. What we did find were abundant articles and books dealing with various aspects of questionnaire research, many of which presented conflicting advice.

From close to two hundred sources, we were able to glean enough information to carry out our study and also convince us that a complete and readable book about questionnaires and their use was needed. The purpose of this book is to help you learn to design and use questionnaires. We believe the answers to many of the questions concerning questionnaire use depend on "study-specific" variables and differ from one study to another. Consequently, the goal of this book is to enumerate these issues so the reader will be aware of them and consider them in a manner appropriate to a specific project. Our book may appear to raise more questions than it answers; the most important point, however, is that these questions be known beforehand so that they can be intelligently considered.

Our intent is not to defend questionnaires and their use against legitimate criticism, although we do suspect that most criticisms of studies using questionnaires should be directed against poor research design or poorly constructed instruments rather than against the use of questionnaires per se. Hopefully, users of questionnaires who are aware of the issues raised in this book will control many of the problems that in the past have discredited many studies that used questionnaires.

Numbers in square brackets throughout this work refer to entries in the Annotated Bibliography.

Jack Anderson
Doug Berdie
September 1973

FOREWORD TO THE SECOND EDITION

In the twelve years since the first edition, interest in survey research has mushroomed. The bibliography in the first edition contained 137 entries and, although it did not cover all relevant work prior to 1974, most of the important work conducted during the preceding 50 years was annotated therein. The current edition contains an *additional* 357 entries, which indicates the growing interest in the topic and the need for a revised, second edition of the book. The current annotated bibliography contains its own index to facilitate its use. Reference numbers cited in the text of the book refer to the entry numbers in the bibliography.

Following publication of the first edition in 1974, we opened a research firm, now known as Anderson, Niebuhr & Associates, Inc., that specializes in survey research. For the last twelve years, we have been "practicing what we preached" while conducting mail, telephone, and personal surveys in the private, public, and nonprofit sectors of society.

Based on twelve years of experience, we are pleased to report that careful adherence to the principles described in the first edition *does* result in surveys that

- obtain response rates in excess of 90 percent;

- obtain reliable and valid data;

- provide the basis for confident decision making; and

- do not alienate respondents.

These results can be, and should be, obtained in surveys regarding all topics and addressed to all types of people.

The primary emphasis of the first edition was directed toward mail questionnaires. Through years of experience in business conducting telephone as well as mail surveys, we realized the need for more thorough coverage of interviewing. This edition has been expanded to address that type of survey in more detail.

Ralph Schmoldt worked conscientiously over long months to help compile the updated, annotated bibliography. To Ralph, our warmest thanks!

The staff at Anderson, Niebuhr & Associates, Inc. continually contribute to the improvements in our survey systems by conscientiously working with us to provide the highest quality research possible.

Jack Anderson
Doug Berdie
Marsha Niebuhr
September 1985

The time of busy people is sometimes wasted by time-consuming questionnaires dealing with inconsequential topics, worded so as to lead to worthless replies, and circulated by untrained and inexperienced individuals, lacking in facilities for summarizing and disseminating any worthwhile information which they may obtain.

—*John K. Norton*

CHAPTER 1: OVERTURE

A questionnaire is a series of predetermined questions that can be either self-administered, administered by mail, or asked by interviewers. Some questionnaires consist of only one or two questions, while others include more than fifty pages bound together. Questionnaires may be printed, mimeographed, dittoed, or written by hand. They may be reproduced on colored or white paper. Questionnaires may even include photographs or charts. Questionnaires can be fun or boring.

Questionnaires are used by marketers, educators, managers, physicians, clergy, social service agencies, hospitals, government, and you the reader.

The purposes for which questionnaires are used, and the type of information sought, vary from study to study. Business firms frequently attempt to determine consumer preferences whereas politicians might try to ascertain the opinions of voters concerning political issues. Those receiving questionnaires may be asked to give opinions ranging from world affairs to religious issues, or they may be asked to supply factual data concerning marital status or family income.

The use of questionnaires in research is based on one basic, underlying assumption: Each individual question will work. This means the respondent will be both *willing* and *able* to give truthful answers [7, 169, 231, 258, 262, 353].

Consideration of this assumption is vital throughout any study using questionnaires. For example, some questionnaire items may require respondents to rummage around in file cabinets to find the requested data. Are people willing to take time to do this? If not, they should be asked only questions to which

1

they can respond from direct knowledge. Subjects should not be given too much credit for good memory [169, 235]. Furthermore, ". . . recall may differ from fact, and therefore should not be taken as fact" [345, p. 29].

One study [216] concluded that even when factual numerical data were requested, the responses from study participants were often incorrect. This type of inconsistency is usually the result of vaguely worded questions and undefined terms.

Accurate factual data can often be obtained from record searches or other direct sources of information. For this reason, the use of questionnaires should be limited to asking for information that is not directly available from other sources.

Research concerning the use of questionnaires often reports seemingly inconsistent results. These reports usually have not been based on an experimental design chosen exclusively to test questionnaire methodology; typically, they are offshoots of surveys designed for other purposes. Consequently, the inconsistent findings concerning questionnaire methods are not surprising, as they are based on results from different questionnaires used for different reasons with different people at different times. The prime theme of this book is that *each study using questionnaires is unique and must be tailored to fit the individual circumstances of that study.*

I. RELIABILITY AND VALIDITY

Suppose you undertook a study using questionnaires, planned it carefully, designed a beautiful and precise questionnaire, and analyzed the results with super human diligence. How do you know that the questions you so painstakingly sculptured actually elicit the information you want? How do you know that respondents will interpret a question on a given day the same as they might interpret it on another day? These questions deal with the issues of validity and reliability [169, 229]. Many people are quick to criticize the reliability and validity of all questionnaires; these criticisms are only legitimate when directed at poorly designed questionnaires. Well-designed questionnaires are reliable and valid.

A reliable questionnaire is one which consists of *reliable items.* A reliable questionnaire item is an item that consistently conveys the same meaning to all people in the population being surveyed. Will a respondent interpret the question the same way each time the question is administered? If the question does not present a single meaning for a given person, we cannot be sure which meaning the respondent had in mind when answering the question. [See 169, 390, 445 for further discussions of reliability.]

A valid questionnaire is one that consists of *valid items.* A valid questionnaire item is one that stimulates accurate, relevant data. A questionnaire item cannot be valid unless it is also reliable. Question selection and phrasing both influence validity. If questions are asked that the respondent is unqualified to answer, the responses may be purely guess work and almost certainly invalid. The authors of one study concluded that the truthfulness of responses is "peculiarly vulnerable when employed for the collection of personal information or when used with subjects who see (or who imagine they see) an opportunity to advance their personal interests by means of the returns made by them" [427, p. 436]. Our experience, however, shows that properly phrased and administered questions overcome this problem. [*See* 169, 390, 445 for further discussions of validity.]

Many people design questionnaires by borrowing questions from other people's questionnaires. This is often done to save time or out of pure laziness. The problem with this practice is that it assumes that people are all the same. Questionnaire items that are reliable and valid for one group of people are often not so for those in another group, who have different experiences, different levels of knowledge, or different world view. For example, a question containing the word "gastroenteritis" would be understood by your family doctor, but would you understand it? Most people would understand the question better if the term "stomachache" was used.

II. REPRESENTATIVENESS

The value of results, in terms of their generalizability, depends on the representativeness of the sample of respondents [353]. The main issue here is the percentage of people who respond to the items contained on the questionnaire, assuming randomness of sample. If only a handful of those surveyed respond, a replication of the study could produce a different handful of respondents having a different set of perspectives and opinions. In such a case, the results would not be representative of the entire sample. Therefore, sample representativeness is uncertain without high response rates.

Surveys that we conduct achieve response rates that routinely exceed 90 percent. Such high response rates are not magic, but result from careful planning and hard work. Further aspects of the problems associated with low response rates and ways to address them are extensively discussed in Chapter 5.

III. LIMITED FUNDS?

Most questionnaire studies are designed with a specified budget. Some of the suggestions throughout this book may prove too expensive for studies with limited funds. However, certain aspects of questionnaire research need not be monetary matters; a good questionnaire can be constructed with limited funds. The merits of various suggestions throughout this book should be compared in an effort to find formulas for best using available funds.

CHAPTER 2: SOME THOUGHTS ABOUT STUDY DESIGN

How does one begin a study that uses questionnaires? Begin constructing possible questions? Draw a random sample? Have a stiff drink? All of these may become a part of your study, but several considerations should receive prior attention. Perhaps the first issue to resolve is whether the study is worth doing [169, 329].

A good starting point is to decide upon goals for your study [22]. "If you're not sure where you're going, you're liable to end up someplace else" [287, p. 13]. If you are doing the study for other people, you need to know exactly what information they want. However, do not assume that what others initially say they want is the information they truly need. If you are initiating the study yourself, think carefully about what information you need to gather [345]. The kind of information you gather will be determined by the purpose and objectives of the study [150]. Many well-meaning investigators neglected to specify their goals and designed broad questionnaires that collected abundant data, only to find that most of the resulting information was not related to the issue at hand. As one writer notes,

> A questionnaire is not just a list of questions or a form to be filled out. It is essentially a scientific instrument for measurement and for collection of particular kinds of data. Like all such instruments, it has to be specially designed according to particular specifications and with specific aims in mind. . . . We cannot judge a questionnaire as good or bad, efficient or inefficient, unless we know what job it was meant to do. This means that we have to think not merely about the wording of

5

particular questions, but first and foremost, about the design of the investigation as a whole. [335, pp. 2–3].

Explicitly formulate the study goals [150, 329] and go over them with other people involved in the study to make certain all agree on what the study is to accomplish. Consider the following possible goals:

(a)   To find out how much employees earn

(b)   To compare by job title, age, and sex the average salary paid to employees during the fiscal year, 1984–85.

The first goal certainly tells us something; i.e., it puts us in the right ball park; but the second goal also tells us which teams are playing. Even more specific objectives surely could be devised that would provide even clearer direction for the study in the example above.

Precise goals facilitate clearer communication and under-standing of purpose among all involved with the study. They also help make the basic decision regarding whether a study is worth the time, effort, and money required to conduct it.

The best way to specify goals is to identify decisions that will be made based on the information obtained from the survey. Once it is clear exactly what decisions need to be made, the types of information needed to make those decisions usually becomes obvious. Goals as specific as (b) above only become obvious once the decisions to be made have been identified.

I. KNOW YOUR TOPIC

One important step is to become thoroughly acquainted with the topic of your study before actually commencing the questionnaire design (22, 169, 231, 275, 353, 373]. Those conduct-ing the study should gather as much information about the subject matter as realistically possible. One source is relevant literature: research journals, books, newspapers, and government reports frequently are useful. People experienced in the area of your study, the so-called "experts," are other sources of information which are often overlooked. If you are conducting a survey for a client in a field about which you know little, don't be dismayed. In most cases, the client is highly familiar with the topic and can provide all the background information you will need.

II. KNOW YOUR PEOPLE

One of the persistent themes of this book is to adapt your research design to the people you will survey. Consider the unique characteristics of those who will be asked to complete the survey. The careful researcher will make every possible effort to know the population to be surveyed and will design the study accordingly [18].

Work diligently to insure that only those with information to give are asked to give information. People may be hesitant to admit ignorance when a question assumes they know the relevant background information. For example, if a random sample of the general population were asked, "Do you agree or disagree with yesterday's Supreme Court decision regarding pornography?" they might be reluctant to admit they were not aware of this Supreme Court decision and might randomly choose an answer. For such a sample, it would be better to preface this question with one asking whether they know of the Supreme Court decision. If, on the other hand, a sample of managers at movie theaters showing pornographic films were asked the original question, there would be better reason to assume they were familiar with the recent decision. The discussion above shows only one of the many problems encountered when people are asked questions regarding issues about which they do not know.

A step in "knowing your people" is to solicit input from potential respondents and other knowledgeable persons regarding the topic of the survey, their reaction to the method you will use, and their opinion on other study design considerations. You will avoid becoming a "scientist in a vacuum" by such interactions. These people can help you decide whether the study is appropriate for the population and whether respondents will be able to supply the requested information.

One additional caveat—although it is important to consider the possible emotional effect of your questionnaire upon persons receiving questionnaires, also keep in mind that watered down surveys gain little useful information. Occasionally, an important question may offend some people. Knowing what items your questionnaire should include clearly depends upon knowing what information you want and how it will be used.

III. HOW MUCH?

A minimum of four "how much" questions must be answered during the early phase of each study design.

1) An obvious consideration is, How much money is needed? Underestimation of costs can easily occur, resulting in an incomplete or inadequate job when money runs out. When estimating costs, be sure to include all phases of the study. Most people remember to estimate the cost of printing the initial questionnaires, but what about extra forms that will need to be sent with follow-up reminders in mail surveys? What about the extra cost associated with interviewers calling more than once to reach people who are not available when initially called? How much will it cost to process and analyze the data? What about printing a final report of the results?

2) Another key "how much" question deals with time. Establishing a time table for the *entire study* is important. Many studies begin with a commitment to obtain a high response rate and end up with only enough time for one follow-up and a resulting disappointingly low response rate. When establishing a time table, don't overlook time needed for pretesting the question-

SOME THOUGHTS ABOUT STUDY DESIGN

naire, following up nonrespondents, editing and coding responses, processing and analyzing the data, and presenting the results. The best way to establish a realistic time line is to work backwards from the anticipated date of completion. Establishing such a time line will allow you to decide whether you can complete the study as you plan within the time available, or whether you will need to modify your plans.

3) The amount of endorsement is another "how much" question that must be considered [142, 353, 371]. Most investigators agree that the endorsement of key individuals or organizations has a major effect on the attitude of people being asked to participate in the survey and is helpful in achieving a high response rate [124, 274, 415]. For example, people are not likely to be impressed by an unendorsed questionnaire, but they might enthusiastically complete the same form if it is endorsed by a person or organization with whom they identify favorably. "To obtain a respondent's involvement and cooperation, it is necessary to impress him with the seriousness and importance of the project. . . . They [potential respondents] must be assured that the results will justify the time and effort expended in filling out the questionnaire" [275, p. 569].

4) Finally, early in the planning stage of a study, a decision must be made concerning how much effort will be needed to obtain a high response rate. Also, what will you do if you fall short of your desired response rate? Should you disregard the data? Should you go ahead and report your findings anyway and merely caution the reader? These are important considerations, which should be thought about early in the study's development.

IV. SAMPLING

Three good reasons exist for utilizing sampling procedures when conducting surveys of large populations: the survey can be done for less expense, the survey can be done in less time, and the quality of the data will usually be better. The first two reasons are obvious; the third reason, less so. The basis of why sample surveys can yield higher quality data than population studies is because it is easier to obtain a high response rate from a smaller sample than from a large population. This fact, coupled with the fact that nonresponse bias (the result of not getting a high response rate) can introduce more bias into a survey than sampling error (the result of surveying a sample rather than an entire population), indicates that well-designed sampling procedures should be used whenever possible.

Two issues underlie all sampling designs: the manner in which the sample is selected and the size of the sample.

The manner in which a sample is selected determines how *representative* the sample is of the population of interest. The purpose of sampling is to obtain information from a "representative" sample (i.e., a sample that mirrors the population in terms of the characteristics being studied). Samples are either "random" or "nonrandom." The benefit of random samples is that their representativeness can be mathematically determined; the representativeness of nonrandom samples is never known and can only be guessed.

Different types of random samples include equal probability random samples (i.e., "simple random samples"), systematic (i.e., "nth-select") random samples, stratified random samples, cluster random samples, and various multistage combinations of these designs. Commonly used nonrandom samples include convenience samples and quota samples.

In survey samples drawn from a telephone directory, there is a danger that bias exists because first, not all people live in households that have a telephone, and second, not all telephone numbers are listed in the directory. In situations where the former is a problem, the use of telephone listings must be supplemented with other sources, such as city directories that list population members. The use of telephone interviewing in these cases would need to be supplemented with other techniques to survey people who do not have a telephone. In the case of unlisted numbers, the use of "random digit dialing" can be effective as a means of including in the sample people whose telephone number is not listed in the directory [41, 85, 93].

The size of sample needed is related to how accurately the sample data need to represent the population. "Sampling error" is related to the sample size, so one needs to determine how much sampling error can be tolerated and then choose a sample size that is appropriate. Other factors that influence sample size include the extent to which variables measured by the survey are homogeneous within the population, the population size, and the statistical confidence level desired.

Formulas exist for calculating sample sizes based on the issues mentioned above. Different formulas exist for different types of questions [81, 299, 449].

The intricacies of selecting samples that are representative have been discussed in great detail elsewhere. The reader is encouraged to consult these other sources for guidance regarding the proper use of sampling [81, 256, 299, 437, 478].

V. A CHECKLIST

Careful study design and early planning can prevent later headaches. Have you considered the following:

- Can you clearly and explicitly state the specific goals of your study? Try it!

- Do these goals describe a study that is really worth doing?

- Have you made an effort to become thoroughly acquainted with the topic of your study? A sincere effort?

- Have you become familiar with the characteristics of people you will survey? Can you anticipate reasons why they may be "nonresponsive"?

- Have you estimated the cost of your study and the time it will take to conduct it? Many people under-estimate both of these factors.

- Have you decided how you will select representative samples for your study?

- Have you determined a sample size that will provide the accuracy you need?

CHAPTER 3: INTERVIEW OR MAIL?

People often ask, "Are mail surveys better than in-person or telephone interviews, or are interviews better?" Many people who conduct research are prejudiced in favor of one of these data collection techniques and recommend their "favorite" in all situations. Our experience, as well as the experience of others [280], has convinced us that some surveys are uniquely suited to mail, whereas others are more appropriately conducted by interview.

Mail surveys and interviews each have unique advantages and limitations [4, 80, 202, 465]. The choice of which method to use in a particular situation should be made by considering the overall nature of the survey, rather than because of preconceived notions regarding which technique is "better." Consider each of the following factors related to your survey and select the data collection technique that best fits the unique characteristics of your study.

I. AVAILABLE RESOURCES

How much money, time, and personnel do you have at your disposal? Almost always, in-person interviewing is more expensive than either telephone interviewing or the use of mail surveys [18, 29, 195, 215, 314]. This is especially true in cases where the sample size is large and/or spread out over a wide geographic area [80, 169, 382]. The need to pay for travel time associated with in-person interviewing is the main reason for this cost disparity. Many writers [18, 29, 215, 314, 391] insist that the use of mail surveys is less costly than is telephone interviewing, especially when sample sizes are large. This is only true, however, when the mail survey does not involve extensive follow-up activity to promote a high response rate. Our cost analyses of hundreds of mail and telephone surveys over the last twelve years show that mail surveys with effective follow-up cost about the same as do telephone surveys.

Telephone surveys can usually be conducted in less time than can either of the other two methods. High quality mail surveys generally take the longest, given the usual need to extend the follow-up phase over a period of several weeks. To obtain a high (i.e., 90 percent or higher) response rate, a "typical" mail survey will need to be in the field for four to six weeks, depending on the motivation of people to respond.

If you have a limited number of people available to work on the survey, the use of mail works quite well. One or two people can manage the data collection phase of even fairly large (e.g., sample of 3,000) mail surveys. Obviously, conducting interviews (either in-person or telephone) of many people requires a large staff of interviewers.

It is wise to acknowledge the relationship between money, time, and personnel. If you have a lot of money, you can reduce the time needed to collect data by increasing the personnel who work on the project. This is especially true of interview projects. Conversely, if you have limited funds and a limited number of people to work on the project, you can still conduct a high quality study by extending the project timeline. It is a rare situation to have unlimited money, no deadline, and as large a work staff as you desire. Be realistic and utilize your resources effectively by accurately assessing them and by coupling them in a manner that best fits your situation.

II. ESTABLISHING CONTACT

Think about the environment where your survey participant will be found when you initiate contact. Some people are rarely at home, and those at work are not often in an office or by a telephone. Traveling sales representatives and factory assembly line workers are examples of these types of people. It is difficult to utilize interviews in these cases because it is difficult to determine when the person has free time to be interviewed. Mail surveys work well when scheduling an interview is difficult because the mail survey can be completed at the convenience of the respondent.

In other cases, it may not be clear who should, indeed, be surveyed. For example, an industrial survey designed to obtain data about a manufacturing process may be appropriate for one job title at one plant and a different job title at another plant. In this situation, it is hard to know the person to whom a mail survey should be sent. Telephone interviewing is very effective in studies like this because a skilled interviewer can fight through the red tape at a firm to identify which employee has the needed data. Once identified, this person can usually be interviewed at that time.

III. EASE OF COMPLETION

Mail surveys have the advantage of allowing people to complete them at their leisure and in an environment of their choosing [65, 235]. They also allow people the time to search through personal records (if they desire) to find information needed to answer the questions.

The use of mail surveys, even ones clearly designed, assumes a minimal level of literacy on the part of respondents; in cases where this assumption is not valid, the use of interviews will be easier for respondents to complete and they should be used.

IV. BIAS

"Interviewer variability" refers to the different voice inflections, pronunciations, mannerisms, and gestures that are used by different interviewers during an interview. This variability can affect the responses given to survey questions [21, 29, 65, 80, 148], especially if the respondent is more concerned with pleasing the interviewer than with giving accurate responses [159, 231]. Interviewer variability is an especially serious problem in large surveys that require many interviewers. Even with careful training and monitoring, it is hard to insure consistent presentation of survey questions in these large surveys.

The stimulus presented by a mail questionnaire is the same from respondent to respondent [235]. In this sense, the interviewer is removed as a possible contaminating factor. However, if the questionnaire format of a mail survey is poorly constructed, it will be interpreted differently by different respondents, leading to biased responses. The bias resulting from questionnaire formats should be avoidable in interview settings because the interviewer training sessions should suffice to make the question formats clear to all interviewers.

V. METHOD FAMILIARITY

Depending on the study sample, the fact that some people have had frequent experiences with one type of data collection method may be either an advantage or a disadvantage as far as using that method again. Mailed self-complete formats are easy to execute for people with "pencil and paper" experience, and unless they have received so many mail surveys that they resent them, the use of mail works well with these types of people. Although some people who receive many mail questionnaires have come to loathe them [329], this is usually because they have received many poorly designed mail questionnaires, not merely many [98].

The key here is to use a technique that people understand (which usually means with which they are familiar), and to use that technique in a manner that makes it easy for people to respond (i.e., do not abuse the technique by imposing unreasonable demands on people).

VI. RESPONSE RATE

The most widely voiced criticism of mail surveys is that they often achieve poor response rates [29, 353, 374]. Low response rates are the results of poorly conceived and poorly implemented mail surveys. During the last twelve years, we have conducted hundreds of mail surveys that have obtained response rates exceeding 90 percent. So, low response rates are *not* an inherent shortcoming of mail surveys.

Equally important is the realization that in-person and telephone interviews are as susceptible to response rate problems as are mail surveys. The fact that this is not widely recognized results from a historical quirk regarding the different ways in which response rate data are reported for mail surveys and interviews.

The nature of the "response rate problem," as well as further discussion about its effects on both mail surveys and interviews, is presented in Chapter 5.

VII. QUESTION LIMITATIONS

Some types of question formats are uniquely suited to mail surveys, whereas other types only work well with interviews. Rating scales that require people to rate items are more versatile in mail surveys than they are in interviews. It is quite easy to ask people in a mail survey whether they are "very satisfied," "satisfied," "neither satisfied nor dissatisfied," "dissatisfied," or "very dissatisfied" with a series of issues about which you might ask. This use of the five response options works well with mail because the respondent can see the options and, therefore, keep them mentally present. In a telephone interview, however, after a few questions respondents are likely to remember only "satisfied," and "dissatisfied." Although they may feel quite strongly about a given response, they are not likely to respond appropriately. Generally speaking, therefore, mail questionnaires work best if it is necessary to use many response options.

Interviews work more effectively than mail surveys when recall and recognition questions are linked together. For example, you might wish to ask, What one factor is *the most* important when you decide which brand of gasoline to buy? and then to follow this open-ended question by asking about several specific factors related to purchase. This type of questioning does not work as well in a mail survey because people may review the specific factors listed before they answer the preceding open-ended question. Hence, their review may influence their answer to that question. Interviews are not susceptible to this problem because the interviewer controls the order in which the questions are presented to respondents.

Also, some questions may require people to look at physical objects as part of the survey (e.g., logo studies, product packaging studies, etc.). Although the object to be examined can sometimes be sent along with a mail survey, it is usually less unwieldly and more effective to conduct these types of studies by in-person interviews.

VIII. IMPERSONALIZATION

Some people are offended by the lack of personal contact inherent in much of modern-day society. To them, mail questionnaires exemplify impersonality. A thorough familiarity with the types of people you wish to survey will indicate whether mail questionnaires will be problematic in this regard. Throughout this book, ways of establishing and maintaining personal contact with people in your study (even in mail surveys) are presented— a reflection of the authors' dismay over the coldly impersonal nature of much traditional research.

IX. WHO COMPLETES THE FORM?

We can rarely be certain who completed a returned mail questionnaire [80, 148, 314, 390]. At times, spouses will have

completed questionnaires sent to their mate; while, in other cases, the questionnaire recipient may forward the questionnaire to a person believed more qualified to respond. One study [390] reports that about 10 percent of returned mail questionnaires had apparently been completed by someone other than the intended person. Sometimes the issue of who completes the questionnaire may be of prime importance. In such cases, interviews are usually preferable to mail surveys.

X. QUESTIONNAIRE LENGTH

Unless a respondent is highly motivated to respond (i.e., is very interested in the topic of the study), the quality of telephone interviews usually starts to deteriorate after about ten or fifteen minutes. For this reason, we recommend that surveys requiring an abundant number of questions be conducted either by mail or by in-person interview. In most cases, a respondent can complete a mail questionnaire more quickly than an in-person interview that contains the same number of questions. This is because people read faster than they can listen to speech.

Given the cost savings of mail over in-person interviews, and given the fact that respondents can answer a lot of mail survey questions in a short period of time, mail surveys are an excellent technique to use when many questions need to be asked. One should not interpret these words as an endorsement of overly long mail surveys. The effect of questionnaire length on response rate is discussed in Chapter 5.

XI. NATURE OF THE TOPIC

The study topic also affects which data collection technique should be used. Topic areas that are sensitive to respondents are especially important to consider. For example, a recent survey we conducted for a police department, which asked people about the types of burglar alarms they have, was successful only because it was conducted by in-person interview—a procedure that allowed interviewers to display appropriate credentials from the police department. A study related to sexual behavior may well be conducted more effectively by mail because respondents may not wish to be personally "confronted" about such topics by an interviewer.

Careful pilot work early in the study will illuminate the extent to which the questionnaire topic influences which data collection technique to use.

XII. ALTERNATIVES TO SURVEYS

In addition to mail surveys and interviews, other methods exist to collect similar types of data. The most commonly used are focus groups, observational techniques, and literature reviews.

Focus groups are, in essence, "group interviews." The main use of focus groups is to create a synergetic effect among a group of people so that ideas are built upon. Although some researchers use focus groups to draw definitive conclusions about people, such conclusions are often not reliable because in real life situations people usually do not make decisions based on the same types of interplay among several people.

Also, focus groups often are not representative of the people in the target population. One reason focus groups are used to obtain final data is because people think it is inexpensive "to get a few people in a room and ask them some questions." However, recruiting representative participants, retaining a qualified focus group moderator and designing a conducive environment for the group are not inexpensive tasks. Often times the cost of a well-done focus group equals the cost of a more widespread survey. Ideally, focus groups should be used to generate ideas for survey questionnaire content or to help frame solutions to problems identified in a survey, although they are not always superior to, or even so effective as, personal interviews in this regard [138].

Observational techniques vary according to the type of data desired and the willingness of subjects to be observed. One investigator [307] suggests the use of the "indirect questionnaire." This method consists of a questionnaire that is completed by the investigator after observing the subject (without the subject's knowledge that the observation is taking place) or after interviewing associates of the subject. Other observational techniques may be instituted with the subject's knowledge and approval. The types of possible observational techniques probably equal the number of studies to which the method is suited [465].

Literature reviews can also provide valuable data. The reason such reviews are not done more often is because the research results available in printed literature are often dated and because the populations studied in earlier studies often differ from those of current interest. Nevertheless, one should not forego an initial examination to determine if data already exist that may eliminate the need to undertake primary data collection.

CHAPTER 4: QUESTIONNAIRE DESIGN— THE SENSUOUS QUESTIONNAIRE

The appearance and arrangement of the survey form itself is vital to a successful study. A well-planned and carefully constructed questionnaire will increase the response rate of your study and also will greatly facilitate the summarization and analysis of the collected data.

Questionnaires used for mail surveys differ in many ways from those used for interviewing. For example, questions that ask people to rank ten things by assigning each of them a number from 1 to 10 work better on mail surveys because the respondent can see all ten at once. They do not work as well on an interview because the respondent sees no list and would have to remember all ten items to be ranked. Also, some questions that read well on a mail survey can be tongue twisters for interviewers.

The physical appearance of mail surveys is more important than that of interview forms because the respondent sees the actual questionnaire. Regarding mail surveys, one author believes that "the appearance of the questionnaire frequently determines whether it is read or discarded. Once the respondent takes the effort to read it, he has some psychological commitment to complete it" [275, p. 571]. A more detailed discussion of the relation between response rate and specific aspects of questionnaire appearance, such as length and color, is included in Chapter 5.

When you actually begin to construct a questionnaire, embroider on the face of your mind the specific goals and objectives of the study, which by now should have been formulated, destroyed, and carefully reformulated numerous times. Remind yourself throughout this process that your purpose is to gather specific information that will shed light on your topic. Be critical! Don't ask questions because you think the answers would be "interesting" or because "you always wanted to know that" but, rather, because the resulting data will be directly related to your stated purposes.

Thinking up questions for a questionnaire is not a problem; coming up with the *right* questions is. Usually a literature review, preliminary interviews with potential respondents, and discussions with experts provide a multitude of possible questionnaire items. The difficult task is selecting only those items that are really needed in the questionnaire to accomplish the purpose of the study.

I. GENERAL FORMAT CONSIDERATIONS

When designing a questionnaire, always consider the people who will be asked to respond. Completing a questionnaire is an imposition. If one approaches questionnaire designing with this in mind, the finished product will be an interesting form that can be efficiently completed. Format considerations make a great difference in the final product. Poorly constructed formats influence not only response rates, but also the quality of responses obtained [2, 5, 24, 153, 163, 381].

The format of a questionnaire refers to the physical arrangement of questions on the page. Questionnaires are often designed as though there were no difference between the format of a mail questionnaire and that of an interview questionnaire. Some format considerations apply to both mail surveys and interviews, but others are unique to either mail or interview questionnaires.

The following procedures should be followed in designing both mail and interview questionnaires:

- Begin with a few interesting, "nonthreatening" [124, 374, 414] questions because introductory questions that are either "threatening" or "dull" may reduce the likelihood of the subject's completing the questionnaire [275].

- Group items into logically coherent sections [275, 374, 391]—i.e., those that deal with a specific topic or those that use the same response options should go together [150].

- Make smooth transitions between sections, avoiding the appearance of a series of unrelated "quiz" questions [169].

- Do not put important items at the end of a questionnaire [275].

- Number questionnaire items so the respondent or interviewer will not become confused while completing the form.

- Put an identifying mark on each page of the form so that if one page should get separated from the rest, it can be reattached.

- Put the study title in bold type on the first page of the questionnaire.

Because the response rate to mail questionnaires is affected by the visual appearance of the questionnaire, particular attention should be paid to the following format suggestions:

- Make the questionnaire as "appealing to the eye" and easy to complete as possible [373, 374, 414, 448].

- Include brief but clear instructions for completing the form. Construct questions so they do not require extensive instructions or examples. Print all instructions in boldface or italics.

- If questions appear on both sides of a page, put the word "over" on the bottom of the front side of that page.

- Avoid constructing sections of the form to be answered only by a subset of respondents—such sections may lead respondents to believe the form is not appropriate for them or it may cause frustration and result in fewer completed forms.

- If you have sections that consist of long checklists, skip a line after every third item to help the respondent place answers in the appropriate spaces.

- Avoid the temptation to overcrowd the pages of your questionnaire with too many questions. Many people squeeze every possible question onto a page, which can cause respondents to mark answers in the wrong place.

- Arrange the questionnaire so that the place where respondents mark their answers is close to the question, which encourages fewer mistakes.

- Avoid using the words "questionnaire" or "checklist" on the form itself. Some people may be prejudiced against these words [326] after receiving many forms not designed with the care of yours.

- Put the name and address of the person to whom the form should be returned on the questionnaire even if you include a self-addressed return envelope since questionnaires are often separated from the cover letter and envelope [326].

A good summary statement is this:

> Common sense dictates certain practices about the design of
> the mail questionnaire. The mail questionnaire should be at-
> tractive, easy to fill out, have adequate space for response, be
> legible. A neat, well-organized, attractive questionnaire should
> increase the response rate. This assumes people associate ap-
> pearance with quality and are more willing to complete and
> return the form. Conversely, a sloppy, crowded, or poorly re-
> produced questionnaire will have an adverse effect on response
> rates. [143, p. 43]

The following are format considerations unique to interview
questionnaires:

- Print questions on only one side of each page of the
  questionnaire because it is cumbersome for interviewers to turn to the reverse side of pages during the
  interview.

- Clearly distinguish between what the interviewer
  should read aloud and other things printed on the
  questionnaire that should not be read. Different type
  styles can be used to make this distinction unambiguous.

- Provide clear instructions so that the interviewers
  will know exactly which questions to ask after each
  response is made. This means "skip" patterns should
  be clearly indicated.

- Arrange questions so that interviewers don't have to
  refer back to earlier parts of the questionnaire.

- Limit the number of response options so that respondents can remember them all.

- Do not end an interview with an open-ended question

because the interviewer will have a harder time controlling when the interview ends.

- Leave enough space on each page so that interviewers can record any additional important information obtained from the respondent.

- Anticipate responses to open-ended questions and provide a list of these on the interview form to help the interviewer mark responses. This will speed up the interview.

II. FORMAT CONSIDERATIONS RELATED TO MACHINES

In today's high-tech world, there is an increasing tendency to design formats of questionnaires so that they accommodate the needs of machines used to tabulate responses rather than the people who are asked to give the responses. This is dangerous because if the needs of people are ignored, they may choose not to respond. If a choice has to be made between pleasing a machine or pleasing respondents, the respondents should be considered first. If the needs of machines can be met without compromising the respondents, then do so.

Optical scanning is often used to process data from questionnaires. An optical scanner functions by reacting to the amount of light that passes through a specially constructed sheet of paper. This sheet of paper may be a separate answer sheet on which responses to questionnaire items are made, or it may contain both the questionnaire items and the response options (*see* Appendix A). If optical scanning is to be used, the people who will print and score the scanning form should be consulted prior to designing the questionnaire. Optical scanning restricts the format possibilities the questionnaire may take and those who work with specific scanners know best how to design appropriate questionnaire formats for their machines.

Another commonly used procedure for processing data from questionnaires involves transcribing the responses made on the questionnaire by use of a keyboard device. Different types of machines commonly used to do this include keypunch machines, key-to-disk machines, and key-to-tape machines.

Because many questionnaires are poorly formatted, data processing personnel often have requirements that detailed keying instructions be printed on every copy of the questionnaire. These instructions are often confusing to respondents and to interviewers. Before assuming these instructions are necessary, show a draft of your well-formatted questionnaire to the data processing personnel. We have conducted hundreds of surveys that did not contain these instructions and have had no complaints from data processors. A well-designed questionnaire can meet the needs of both respondents and data processing people without causing either confusion or unhappiness.

Computer assisted telephone interviewing (CATI) is a procedure whereby responses to questions are entered directly into a computer by the interviewer who conducts the interview while seated at a computer terminal keyboard [218, 219]. The questions to be asked are displayed on the screen for the interviewer to read. The proper display of questions requires that the programmer who sets up the system understand the desired formats and sequencing of questions. If CATI is used, be sure you carefully test the system with your questionnaire to make certain all happens exactly as you wish it to.

III. QUESTION CONSTRUCTION

Writing a good questionnaire item is probably the single most difficult task involved in the entire study. "The formulation of good questions is a much more subtle and frustrating task than is generally believed by those who have not actually attempted it" [169, p. 132]. Why? The purpose of any item is to communicate a certain exact meaning. The meaning the respondent gets from an item should be the same as that given it by the question designer [150, 231]. For example, "might," "could," and "should" convey different meanings, yet are frequently used interchangeably [345], leading to confusing interpretations of the data. Clear communication is essential to a good questionnaire study. One writer warns,

> Each question should be so clearly worded that all respondents will interpret it the same way. It is only by the most painstaking efforts, preliminary trials and revisions, that questions can be prepared which are entirely clear, and which will mean the same to all respondents. Such an ideal is hard to achieve, but the value of the results of the study will depend largely on this factor [329, p. 21].

Some people believe that achieving absolute clarity of meaning isn't always necessary because interviewers can provide additional information or clarification. However, allowing interviewers such latitude during interviewing can result in substantial bias due to interviewer variability. What must be done is to exert great effort in constructing items that are unambiguous and self-explanatory. Norton warns that "no respondent should be expected to puzzle out a questionnaire. One should be able to make his wants known in simple language" [329, p. 20]. The more effort a respondent must exert to figure out the meaning of a question, the more doubtful is the validity of the response made to the question. We do not mean such legitimate efforts as recalling information or mental calculations, but rather the unnecessary mental gymnastics that too often are required just to understand what the question is asking.

Many excellent books and articles deal with communication, meaning, and question phrasing which would certainly benefit the questionnaire designer [314, 325, 335, 345]. The effects on responses of all the following factors have been studied: question order [47, 68, 327]; wording of question [15, 27, 37, 350]; question length (270, 290]; and questionnaire length [209]. The remainder of this chapter will present some standard recommendations that too often are neglected.

A. What Type of Question. . . ?

Different types of questions are useful for obtaining different types of information. For example,

> The free-answer [open-ended] question is useful in setting up the issue but may need to be asked of only a small number of respondents. The multiple-choice question . . . brings all sides of the issue to each respondent's attention. [345, p. 77]

Before writing a question, consider the variety of question types available and choose the one most appropriate for eliciting the exact information you need. Among the most common question formats are these: dichotomous questions (those allowing the respondents only one of two possible responses, e.g., a "yes or no" question), open-ended questions (those where respondents are asked to express answers in their own words), fill-in-the-blank questions (those where the respondents are asked to supply a missing word or number), multiple-choice questions (those where the respondents choose from more than two response options), and ranking questions (those that ask the respondents to rank given response options according to some specified criterion). A variety of these types of questions is displayed in the questionnaires included in Appendix A.

B. What Questions Should I Ask?

Obviously, decisions regarding what questions you ask are based on the goals of your study; what do you want to know? However, another issue is involved as well: What will be the effect of your question on the respondent? Will it offend anyone? Naturally, the degree to which a given question will offend depends upon who is asked. A question about venereal disease might shock the average citizen but not upset a physician. Questions about sex, violence, race and minority groups, politics [268], religion, family finance, and patriotism [33] have a certain offensive potential. Moreover, questions about such areas are often asked when the information is not essential to the study purpose. At other times, however, questions that deal with such potentially offensive topics may be crucial to a study and therefore must be asked. When such a need arises, there are several different ways these questions can be asked, some of which are less offensive than others. The trick is to phrase questions in the least offensive manner possible without appearing clandestine. Some writers [33, 314] suggest that many questions, when phrased in the third person, may be less threatening than when asked in the second person. By asking questions in the third person (e.g., "How do your neighbors feel about abortion?") you will get information different from that gained by phrasing the question in the second person ("How do you feel about abortion?"), but in some cases information from the third person may suffice. The danger with this technique is that in some cases people will tell you how others feel and not how they themselves feel. Another technique for asking threatening questions is the "randomized response technique." This technique, based on mathematical models of probability, is described in several sources [26, 266, 491, 492]. Because of the guaranteed anonymity of responses associated with the technique, it is probably best suited to personal interview settings where follow-up of nonrespondents is not required [63].

C. How Do I Ask a Question?

Generally, the most effective questions are worded as simply as possible [345]. Questions should communicate something specific, so don't try to impress respondents with fancy vocabulary at the risk of confusing your meaning. Use language that is familiar and appropriate to the population for whom the questions are intended [150, 314]. If the questions are designed for a specialized group, you may wish to use the language or jargon of that group. However, to get the same information from the general public, the question will have to be reworded [373]. For example, you might ask physicians about gastroenteritis, but the general public about a stomachache. Slang and colloquialisms should be avoided, as they are frequently ambiguous [345].

Also, avoid using stuffy bureaucratic words or phrases (e.g., "data base" or "ad hoc"). These types of words bore respondents and detract from clarity of meaning.

Do not write loaded questions that suggest a response [230, 275, 353]. For example, a sales representative who wants you to purchase a product might ask you, "What will you have?" This, of course, assumes you will have something. The careful question designer might ask, "Will you have anything?" Consider the following examples:

A.   Is it desirable to socialize medicine?

B.   Is it desirable or undesirable to socialize medicine?

Question A suggests an affirmative answer. However, question B does not suggest an answer and gives the respondent a freer choice. One author points out this:

> Sometimes the questioner assumes that the negative side of the question is so obvious that it need not be stated. He may simply ask: "Do you think most manufacturing companies that lay off workers during slack periods could arrange things to avoid layoffs and give steady work right through the year?" Sixty-three percent said companies could avoid layoffs, 22 percent said they couldn't, and 15 percent had no opinion. The alternative here seems to be so implicit in the question that it need not be stated. Either companies could avoid layoffs—or they couldn't. No other interpretation seems possible. But what happens when we take the trouble to state an alternative to another carefully matched cross section of respondents? "Do you think most manufacturing companies that lay off workers in slack periods could avoid layoffs and provide steady work right through the year, or do you think layoffs are unavoidable?" Thirty-five percent said companies could avoid layoffs, 41 percent said layoffs are unavoidable, and 24 percent expressed no choice. So, a few words changed here and there and explicit statement of the other side of the picture results in a 28 percent falling off from the affirmative side of the question! [345, p. 7]

Here are other examples of questions that suggest answers:

a) All politicians are dishonest, aren't they?

b) Environmental concern is a good thing, isn't it?

c) "Does small business need a government wet nurse in all its daily activities?" [345, p. 180]

Bias resulting from loaded questions such as those above is a particularly serious problem in interviews because respondents find it more difficult to disagree with an interviewer than with a self-complete questionnaire.

Furthermore, avoid asking questions that assume that a certain state of affairs existed in the past. For example, how would you answer the following questions?

a) Have you stopped beating your children?

b) Do you still design bad questionnaires?

Regardless of whether the respondent answers "yes" or "no," such questions imply previous participation in the activities about which the person has been asked.

The following are additional suggestions that should be considered when writing questionnaire items:

• Before asking a question, be sure the respondent is capable of giving an accurate answer [22, 329].

• Be sure the question clearly indicates whether it requires a factual answer or an opinionative answer. A difference is likely to exist between what is and what should be; unless you are precise about which information is wanted, the respondent can easily confuse the two [22].

* Avoid writing "double" questions that ask for more than one piece of information per question. Trying to squeeze too much into an item may confuse the respondent or may actually make the question impossible to answer. Consider the following example: "Do you like dogs and cats?" This question asks whether respondents like both dogs *and* cats. Suppose they like one but not the other? Ask instead two questions: a) Do you like dogs? b) Do you like cats?

  Furthermore, a question with more than one adverb or adjective is likely to be either a double question or an overly wordy question. Consider: "Is the text informative and interesting?" If "informative" and "interesting" are taken to mean the same thing, they are redundant and one of them should be eliminated. If their meanings are taken as different from each other, the question becomes a double question. Some people will actually answer poorly worded questions such as this double question. However, when the data are analyzed, it is impossible to know whether the answer given refers to both parts of the question or only one part.

* Exercise caution when using general adjectives and adverbs, such as "several," "significant number of," "most," and "usually." Such words and phrases do not convey the same meaning to everyone [49, 150, 228]. "Vague questions encourage vague answers" [314, p. 323].

* Avoid using words with vaguely defined meanings. Such words as "country," "population," "environment," and "passive" have different conceptual meanings for different people. If a question asked, "Do you believe the country's population should be

less passive about maintaining the environment?" it certainly would be an ambiguous question. Whose country? How much of what population? How passive? What environment?

• Avoid words that have more than one meaning [230]—e.g., "value," "liberal," or "conservative." You will not know which meaning respondents had in mind when they answered.

• Avoid using words that are loaded with possible emotional overtones that might affect responses [142]. Examples of these are "Communism," "divorce," "the FBI," and "the President" [33]. Such words may influence respondents to answer differently than they would have if the same ideas were expressed with unemotional words or phrases. Also, the use of emotional words may cause respondents to skip the item or possibly the entire questionnaire.

• Avoid using double negatives caused by joining a negative response to a question phrased in the negative. Instead of asking questions like "a" below, ask questions directly and concisely as shown in "b."

a)   Do you believe college students should *not* pay tuition?

_____ Yes
_____ No

(b)   Do you believe college students should pay tuition?

_____ Yes
_____ No

- Be careful if you use abbreviations [22]. Be certain the people you ask will know what your abbreviations mean.

- Avoid using "if yes, then . . ." questions on mail surveys. Usually these questions can be asked in an alternative manner. Consider the following example:

Are you married? _____ Yes
                 _____ No
If yes, is your wife
employed? _____ Yes
          _____ No

The same information can be obtained by asking the better question:

Is your wife employed? _____ Yes
                       _____ No
                       _____ I'm not married

- Avoid using hypothetical questions (e.g., "If you win the Irish Sweepstakes, how will you spend your winnings?"). Many people will object and refuse to answer these items because the answers tend to be meaningless. "If hypothetical questions bring hypothetical answers, then the way to obtain factual answers is to ask factual questions. Many hypothetical questions can be recast into a factual mold. . . . [A]ctual experience is often a better guide to the future than present intentions are" [345, p. 199].

- Don't be overly enthusiastic about asking people to rank various things by "assigning a number from 1 to 10 with 1 being the most important and 10 being the least important." This type of question assumes people do not feel the same about two or more of the things being ranked, and this is usually not true. These questions also assume people can rank all the things listed, and often people cannot do so.

- If you want general information from respondents, include an open-ended question at the end of the form [275]. Although such questions are more difficult than objective questions to tabulate [235], they can be a useful supplement. Open-ended questions are useful in a pretest to determine which response options to include in a later, more objective, item for the final questionnaire [345]. Furthermore, ". . . the free-answer question provides quotable quotes which may add sparkle and credibility to the final report" [345, p. 50].

- Make sure you know what use will be made of the responses to each item [22, 150]. Too often, items are included on a questionnaire without a deliberate commitment to analyze them. Many writers suggest actually setting up a "mock" or "dummy" table showing how the data will be summarized before the questionnaire is finalized [169, 235].

D. Response Options

The response options offered respondents can affect their answers. Confusing options lead to unreliable results and, usually, low response rates. The following suggestions will help you design appropriate response options for questionnaire items.

- Make certain one response category is listed for every conceivable answer [22, 275, 374]. Omitting an option forces people either to answer in a way that does not accurately reflect reality or to answer not at all. An example is this question for car owners:

How many cylinders does your car's engine have?

_____ 6 cylinders
_____ 8 cylinders

In this case, people whose cars have four cylinders are unable to answer the question.

- Include a "don't know" response option any time you ask a question to which people may not have the answer. Although a "don't know" option may be viewed as offering respondents an "easy out," it is better to include this option rather than take the chance of getting inaccurate information by forcing people to respond to an item about which they know nothing [22, 235, 345]. When surveys find that many people don't know about a given issue, that information alone is often very valuable.

- Make response options mutually exclusive [150, 275]. Try to answer the following question:

a) Which one of the following are you?

_____ American
_____ Indian
_____ Black
_____ Hispanic

Obviously, many respondents can truthfully check more than one response. An American Indian could check the first two, or an American Black could check the first and third. Question (b) below eliminates these problems:

b) Which of the following are you?

    _____ Black American
    _____ American Indian
    _____ Hispanic
    _____ Other

- Balance all scales used in the response options. Include an equal number of options on each side of a middle position.

Incorrect:	*Correct:*
Very satisfied	Very satisfied
Somewhat satisfied	Satisfied
Not satisfied	Neither satisfied nor dissatisfied
	Dissatisfied
	Very dissatisfied

- Some writers believe that if the midpoint of an agree-disagree scale is labeled "undecided," responses will differ from scales where the midpoint is labeled "neutral" [217]. Therefore, label the midpoint according to the "exact" meaning the scale requires.

- Arrange response options vertically: _____ Yes
                                       _____ No
rather than horizontally: _____ Yes _____ No [326]. This helps reduce errors that occur when people mark the blank after the intended response rather than before it.

- Make certain the respondent knows *exactly* what information should be put in "fill-in-the-blank" items.

For example:

Incorrect: What is your age? _____ years
  Correct: What is your age, at your last birthday?
             _____ years

E. Pretesting

By the time a study has journeyed through the planning stage and reached the stage when the questionnaire is constructed, much effort and money already have been invested. A pretest of the questionnaire at this stage is useful [329, 373, 414] to reveal confusing and other problematic questions that still exist in the questionnaire. We consider pretesting to be essential. We would no sooner conduct a study without a pretest than we would buy a car without taking it for a test drive. Pretesting in either case greatly reduces the chances of getting a lemon.

Pretesting involves administering the questionnaire to a sample of people as similar as possible to those who will ultimately be surveyed. The pretest questionnaire should be an honest representation of your most diligent efforts up to this point.

In the pretest, results of open-ended questions or questions with an "other" response option often suggest response categories to be used in the final questionnaire. Also, encourage those responding to the pretest questionnaire to make comments and suggestions on all aspects of the questionnaire. Regarding pretesting, it is true that,

> The inexperienced researcher is likely to be impatient with this preliminary work, which may seem like hair-splitting over the meaning of words, and other details. But patience and care in this preliminary work may make all the difference between success and failure, both in the cooperation of the respondents and in the reliability and validity of the results. [283, p. 198]

Much useful information can be gained from actually analyzing the pretest results. Such analysis can identify items to which nearly everyone responds identically or items which cannot be summarized in any meaningful way [22]. These items can then be eliminated from the final questionnaire [235].

Appendix B shows the stages through which a series of questionnaire items advanced in a past study.

IV. A CHECKLIST

Test each item in your questionnaire with the following:

- Does the question ask for only one bit of information?

- Does the question assume a previous state of affairs?

- Does the question wording imply a desired answer?

- Are any of the question's words emotionally loaded, vaguely defined, or overly general?

- Do any of the question's words have a double meaning that may cause misunderstanding?

- Does the question use abbreviations that may be unfamiliar to respondents?

- Are the response options mutually exclusive and sufficient to cover each conceivable answer?

CHAPTER 5: HOW TO STIMULATE RESPONSE

Low response rate is one of the greatest obstacles encountered by researchers using questionnaires. *The problem of nonresponse is as serious a problem in studies using interviewing as it is in mail surveys!* This fact is not commonly recognized. The reason the nonresponse problem in interviewing has been successfully camouflaged for so long is because nonrespondents in studies using interviews are often replaced. Typically, contracts for interviewing services call for completion of a specific number of interviews rather than an agreement to select a random sample and obtain responses from as many of that sample as possible. To obtain the required number of completed interviews, interviewing services often replace nonrespondents by contacting additional people not in the original sample, thus magnifying nonresponse bias.

In most studies, the sample chosen for the study has been selected randomly and is, therefore, representative of the entire population. Hence, if responses are obtained from all people in the sample, the resulting data will accurately reflect the characteristics of the population. However, if only a small percentage of those in the sample respond, there is no certainty that the results represent the population. For instance, a survey of a random sample of the general public that asked about criminal behavior might not be completed by most undetected criminals for fear of self-incrimination. The resulting summarized data would be biased because it would underrepresent the criminal element.

Whether low response rates actually do bias questionnaire

data has been extensively studied [109, 116, 159, 176, 215, 302, 311, 312, 365, 373, 423, 425, 429, 447, 448]. Most studies to determine if questionnaire respondents differ from nonrespondents have assumed that a continuum of bias exists from early respondents through late respondents to nonrespondents. This assumption has been questioned in research designed specifically to test it [121].

Furthermore, studies comparing nonrespondents to respondents typically have compared only demographic data. However, these comparisons may not really be relevant to particular instances of the response-rate problem. Most studies are concerned with more than just demographic data, and the fact that nonrespondents may or may not share certain demographic features with late respondents says little about whether they are similar or dissimilar in other ways measured by the questionnaire.

Clouding the issue, further is the question, How do we know who are nonrespondents? A nonrespondent typically has been defined as someone from whom no data are collected, whereas some researchers refuse to count someone as a respondent unless he or she answers each and every question on the questionnaire. More enlightened researchers [32, 146] have concluded that it is much more useful to think about response rates in terms of individual items rather than questionnaires. This approach allows use of all data obtained even though some information comes from partially completed questionnaires.

In certain studies we have little reason to assume that nonrespondents differ from respondents on dimensions relevant to the study. For instance, questionnaires administered to factory workers in June may yield a relatively low response rate because of the many workers who are on vacation and did not receive the questionnaire. Unless we have reason to assume that factory workers who take vacations in June differ from other factory workers in those aspects with which the survey is interested, we could expect their completed questionnaires to represent the sample of factory workers. However, if the questionnaires were administered in December to workers in Minnesota and dealt with attitudes toward skiing, those not responding because of their absence on vacation might be a unique subset of the sample—they might be avid skiers on vacation in December. In this case, responses would not accurately represent the entire sample.

Questionnaire users must consider the response-rate problem as it uniquely applies to their own situation. Careful consideration of the situation will usually show that nonresponse bias *is* a danger. In cases where high response rates are not obtained, researchers should sample nonrespondents to determine the extent to which nonresponse bias is a problem.

What obstacles can be anticipated that lead to nonresponse? One author [268] found that over 40 percent of the nonrespondents in his study had moved, could not be contacted, or were deceased. It is doubtful, therefore, that many of his "nonrespondents" even received a questionnaire. Most of the remaining 60 percent of nonrespondents stated that the political questions on the questionnaire had been responsible for their nonresponse. They felt generally that their political opinions were private and not "fair game" for questionnaires. Other nonrespondents objected to socioeconomic questions and some stated they were not interested in the study or interested in participating in it. This indicates that carefully designed questionnaires may lead to high response rates if alienation due to "personal" questions can be prevented.

Whether nonrespondents differ from respondents will vary from study to study. In some studies, investigators have found that nonrespondents tend to be less involved with the subject matter of the research [109, 429] and less interested in topics addressed by the survey [58, 25]. One author claims, "The less complete the data are, the more likely they are biased in favor of that section of the sample more actively involved in the subject matter under consideration and more likely to give favorable responses" [109, p. 112].

Many investigators [44, 116, 159, 429] have found that nonrespondents are usually the least educated members of the sample. These investigators also support the belief that those most knowledgeable in the subject area of the questionnaire are most likely to respond. One study indicated, "Responses to surveys are in no small part a function of habits and attitudes that are highly personal and deeply ingrained" [378, p. 313; *see also* 132]. Nonrespondents have also been found to differ from respondents in terms of age [464], race [464], marital status [25], I.Q. [285], and overall socioeconomic status [343]. Poor health has also been shown to be related to nonresponse [152].

Merely increasing the sample size will not solve the response rate problem; it will only increase the *number* of respondents and will not increase the *percentage* of respondents. Therefore, it is imperative that response rate be increased, not just sample size.

We have been conducting surveys for years and successfully have been obtaining response rates in excess of 90 percent of the original sample. Such high response rates are routinely obtained by us in mail and interview studies and with diverse populations. Methods to facilitate a high response rate are discussed below.

I. GENERAL TACTICS

"The silent nonrespondent, like the sphinx, is a perpetual question mark harassing the truth seeker" [111, p. 392]. How do we break the stoney silence of this sphinx? Several general tactics should be considered in designing a questionnaire study. Once again, use varying tactics for different samples and studies [11, 18, 398]. Some of the tactics discussed below will not help (and may be a hindrance) when applied in certain settings. Before a specific strategy to increase response rates is chosen, those responsible for each project should try to anticipate all conceivable objections people may have in regard to participating in the study. Plans to increase response rate should be tailored specifically to meet potential objections to the study; all available strategies consistent with financial resources should be implemented. A high response rate should be considered of prime importance, both in study time and funds allotted.

Two basic issues stand out as considerations when deciding on an overall strategy to increase response rates. These issues apply to all aspects of the study and a decision regarding how they will best be utilized is unavoidable if useful response rates are to be obtained.

A. *Personalization—"Dear Sir" or "Hi, Fred"?*

How will you relate to the people in your study? This issue must be decided only after careful consideration of the study purposes and people involved. The authors once found [10] that university undergraduates responded more favorably to a highly personalized relationship during a study. Conversely, professors at the same university responded more favorably to a more formalized approach. These conclusions are based on, among other things, significantly higher response rates from undergraduates who were mailed hand-addressed postcards than from those sent postcards with typed addresses. Professors responded significantly more to the type-addressed postcards.

Other investigators [12, 224] point out that certain people who are highly concerned with the anonymity or confidentiality of their responses will be suspicious of overly personalized correspondence. One author suggests, "When respondents desire anonymity, personalization, by implying decreased anonymity, may actually *decrease* the response rate" [12, p. 277]. Other reports regarding personalization are mixed [43, 69, 87, 101, 130, 144, 277, 293, 294, 312, 413, 418].

Personalization may be accomplished in many ways; however, the important point is be sincere. If you do not feel informal, don't act informally—fake personal approaches are offensive to all in the study. For example, do not address a letter "Dear Fred" and then ask Fred to return his questionnaire to "Mr. Hansen." Ask him instead to return it to "Al." The effect of using a handwritten signature has been studied with differing results [246, 277]. For most surveys, a personal approach coupled with professional quality is best.

B. Anonymity/Confidentiality—"I know you!"

The issues of anonymity and confidentiality of respondents must be decided for all questionnaire studies. The decision you make regarding this issue may affect your response rate [239, 278]. An anonymous study is one in which nobody (not even the study directors) can identify who provided data on completed questionnaires. For interviews, anonymity is usually impossible, and for mail surveys anonymity is not practical because of the need to send follow-ups to nonrespondents. When response rate may be seriously impaired without anonymity, the use of mail surveys is recommended. In such cases, follow-up will be sent to *all* subjects in the study although this may upset some of the respondents who will feel they are being unnecessarily bothered. Another procedure that can guarantee anonymity in mail surveys without hindering follow-up strategies is to include a postcard with each questionnaire. Those receiving questionnaires are then asked to return this postcard (which already has their name on it) as soon as they have mailed back a completed questionnaire [44]. A possible problem with this technique is obvious. Some nonrespondents might mail back a postcard just to avoid being contacted by follow-up techniques. As with most follow-up strategies, this procedure is more suited to some studies than to others.

It *is* usually possible to guarantee confidentiality to people in mail surveys and in interviews. A study is confidential when the project directors and interviewers know who has responded to each questionnaire and promise not to reveal this information. If you guarantee confidentiality, do not call it "anonymity."

It helps to use identifying numbers on questionnaires instead of using names or asking the subjects to fill in their names. In mail surveys, be sure to mention the fact that this number is being used and exactly why it is being used so people will not think you are trying to "pull a fast one" on them by slipping an identifying number past them. Avoid the use of invisible ink numbers and other clandestine techniques, which can alienate people in your study. Do not forsake the trust of your subjects— without their cooperation, your study is doomed to failure.

In all correspondence with people participating in your study, include a note instructing them to call or write (give a name and phone number or address) if they have any problems or questions. Encourage people to communicate because it is necessary to establish two-way communication to determine why they are reluctant to respond so that remedial measures may be taken.

II. SPECIFIC TACTICS—INITIAL CONTACT

Many opportunities to help increase response rates occur when people are initially contacted in the study. Of prime importance is recognition that some tactics are appropriate and others are inappropriate, depending on the particular sample and study. Evaluate the appeal of each in relation to each sample before including it in your "increasing-response-rate arsenal."

Discussed below are some initial tactics that should help increase response rates in most studies. These tactics apply to contact with people before and during the actual survey. The general theme of each of these tactics is the importance of impressing people with the professional nature of the study.

A. *Printing and Paper*

All correspondence should be reproduced in the most professional manner possible, commensurate with available funds. Ditto and mimeograph correspondence should be avoided if possible. Photo-offset printing is recommended for its professional appearance as well as for such benefits as ease of print reduction

preletters and cover letters is to say only what is necessary and to say it briefly. The chances are that people do not enjoy reading more than they must and long letters may "turn them off."

The following issues related to cover letters and their effect on response rates have all been studied, often with different results: individually signed letters vs. reproduced signatures [246, 362]; use of postscripts [77, 149]; status of person signing cover letter [151, 222, 265]; use of flattery [203]; appeal to social utility of the study [277, 368]; appeal to altruism [277, 490]; color of ink used for signature [417]; and offers to share results with respondents [315, 483].

Appendix B contains a sample cover letter.

F. The Questionnaire Itself

Questionnaire design can increase response rates:

1) *"How long?"*—For years, questionnaire users have assumed that long questionnaires receive lower response rates than do shorter questionnaires [56, 274, 340, 371]. More recent studies [31, 74, 75, 112, 272, 293] have shown that questionnaire length itself need not interfere with response rates. Four-page questionnaires can receive response rates as high as do two-page ones. However, this does not mean that 60-page questionnaires will obtain response rates as high as two- or four-page ones. Seemingly more important than length is question content. People do not like to be asked irrelevant, uninteresting questions. One or two irrelevant questions are bad enough but to deluge people with a long, boring questionnaire is inexcusable. Therefore, rather than the usual edict issued to keep questionnaires short at all costs, the authors believe that questionnaire items should be interesting to the respondent, obviously relevant to the purpose of the study, and limited to absolutely essential items. Adherence to these guidelines will make the questionnaire more meaningful to people, and their view of how *meaningful* the questionnaire is, more than how *long* it is, will determine whether they choose to respond.

2) *"White space"*—Do not crowd items together on the questionnaire. Mail questionnaires with much "white space" are likely to achieve higher response rates than ones which have crowded pages. White space on interviews prevents interviewer confusion. Also, white space on questionnaire pages allows respondents or interviewers adequate room to enter verbatim comments to either specific items or the study in general.

3) *Starting the questionnaire*—The first impression of the questionnaire is all important; based on this impression people decide whether or not to complete the questionnaire. Therefore, start the questionnaire with interesting, yet nonthreatening, items [275]. Traditionally, items asking such things as age, sex, occupation, etc., have been used to start questionnaires because they are believed to be nonoffensive items. These items always offend some people and are certainly not interesting [314].

Some investigators suggest telling people how long it takes an average person to complete the questionnaire. Generally, it is more advisable to do this only in those cases where the questionnaire can be completed in 15 minutes or less [326]. Questionnaires taking longer to complete may well be interesting enough for people to finish, but if they know ahead of time that the survey is long, they may not agree to even start.

4) *"Who responded?"*—For mail surveys, determine how returned questionnaires will be identified. You will need this information to know who to follow up. Use of an identifying number for each person receiving a questionnaire is suggested.

G. *Incentives*

Many studies have found that offering incentives to subjects can increase response rates [42, 136, 184, 253, 358, 370] without leading to response distortion [474]. In mail surveys, the inclusion with the original questionnaire of a pencil, small packet of coffee, or other token gift has somewhat increased response rates [320, 361]. Some studies [259] have used raffles. People have also made contributions to charity in the name of people who respond to the survey [369]. Other studies have shown that paying subjects increases response rates [92, 110, 155, 166, 170, 489], with some researchers [78] suggesting "more pay for more data." The reason offered for the success of monetary incentives is that "the responses of the paid subjects were motivated by a sense of obligation to the task which was not equally present in the non-paid subjects" [92, p. 431]. Greed may also have something to do with this. Most studies using money as an incentive have found that higher response rates are attained when the money is included with the questionnaire rather than offering to send money to people who respond [13, 390, 489], although this has not always been found to be true [161]. The receipt of money with the questionnaire may contribute to the felt "obligation" of the subject. Other researchers have found that the use of incentives did not improve their response rates [54, 107, 267].

Our experience shows that the best incentives are those that are carefully selected to show you understand the needs of people in the study. For example, we recently sent dentists dental instruments as an incentive and were told by many of the 90+ percent who responded that the incentive was "instrumental" in their decision to respond. The use of incentives, as with all the suggestions in this chapter, is not a hard and fast rule—it will need tailoring to fit your sample and study.

III. SPECIFIC TACTICS—MAILING PROCEDURES

Much research exists regarding mailing techniques in mail questionnaire studies. Results of these studies do not always agree as to whether certain techniques are effective in improving response rates. This fact again emphasizes the need to adapt your study to the unique characteristics of the people you are surveying. The function of this section will be to identify a pool of tactics for improving response rates in mail surveys. First, some general observations will be noted that apply to most mail surveys.

The return envelope included with the questionnaire should be a size smaller than the outer envelope, and the questionnaire should be folded so it will not need to be refolded to fit into the return envelope. This is a courtesy extended to people and also helps make the study appear more "professional."

A strategy for locating people who have moved should be planned well before the mailing date and should include several available sources for locating people's addresses. Address lists usually become outdated to some extent because of the lapse of time between assembly of the lists and the mailing dates. Possible sources for address updates include telephone directories, parents, telephone information operators, friends, public utility companies, credit unions, marriage license bureaus, postal record searches, alumni groups, other respondents, and tax rolls [117]. The problem of locating addresses is not to be taken lightly. Design a step-by-step procedure because without such a procedure many envelopes stamped "return to sender," "addressed moved," and "no forwarding address" could find their way back to your office.

Other specific mailing methods need to be individually designed for each study. The following issues should be considered:

1) *Special delivery, certified mail*—Several studies have shown that when reminders are sent to nonrespondents, the use of registered, special delivery [74, 120, 182, 223, 363] and certified mail [116, 415, 442] increases response rates. Other studies have tried this approach for the initial questionnaire mailing and results have been mixed. One writer cautions that ". . . some cattlemen drove 40 or more miles to get a certified letter to find that it contained only a questionnaire and no explanatory letter. They expressed their objections to the use of

certified mail in vigorous language" [415, p. 225]. Let this serve as a caution; consider the trouble a person might have to go through to receive any type of mail that requires a signature. Again, the risks and benefits must be considered for each study.

2) *Hand addressed or typed?*—The use of hand-addressed correspondence is advantageous over typed labels in some cases [242] and, in other cases, makes no difference [252]. Computer-printed labels offend people who are concerned with individuality.

3) *Business reply or stamped postage?*—Most research indicates that the use of regular postage stamps on return envelopes is more effective than business reply postage in producing high response rates [191, 292, 453]. One study [463] received twice as many questionnaires from people who were sent return envelopes with regular postage stamps as from those sent business reply return envelopes. This and other studies [314, 390] suggest that people feel badly about throwing away money (which they would be doing with postage stamps but not with business reply) and will not bother to remove an individual postage stamp for their own use. Furthermore, return envelopes without a postage stamp may suggest advertising to many people [169, 463]. Several studies show a benefit from postage stamps; the authors know of no study showing business reply postage to be more effective than postage stamps in increasing response rate.

4) *Where and when do I send it?*—Certain types of questionnaires may be more appropriately mailed to a place of employment than to a home address [8]. Again, who the subject is and the nature of the questions asked should determine where the form will be sent [159]. Send the questionnaire to the address where it will be completed. For example, do not send a questionnaire to assembly line workers at their place of employment. They are not likely to complete the form at work and will not be inclined to carry it home. Conversely, a question-

naire asking a company vice-president for data pertaining to the company budget should be sent to the office where information needed to complete the form is located.

Think about the environment in which your sample lives and works and design an appropriate mailing timetable. "The most careful mailing system cannot fully compensate for bad timing in respect to the life circumstances of the sample" [371, p. 29]. For example, try to avoid mailing between mid-November and mid-January because people are often preoccupied with holiday activities and inundated with holiday related mail. Also, check with the post office to determine when bills are mailed *en masse* and avoid mailing on those days.

IV. SPECIFIC TACTICS—MAIL FOLLOW-UPS

Follow-ups are an essential phase of any mail questionnaire study [340, 446]. "The use of follow-ups, or reminders, is certainly the most potent technique yet discovered for increasing the response rate" [390, p. 164]. Rarely has a questionnaire survey achieved acceptable response rates without the use of follow-up procedures. Traditionally, between 5 and 65 percent of those sent questionnaires respond without follow-up reminders. These rates are too low to yield confident results.

Many follow-up techniques may be utilized for convincing nonrespondents to respond. Design your follow-up procedures by taking into consideration the unique characteristics of the people in your sample. Above all, be persistent! "No matter how well the researcher does the preparing, packaging, and delivering, good techniques at these stages alone are not enough. Persistence pays off" [100, p. 257]. Remember, persistence does not mean obnoxiousness. Let your nonrespondents realize that their response is missed and really desired.

Be certain to identify all follow-up correspondence with the name of the study. Also, always include the return address and the telephone number of a person who can answer questions concerning the legitimacy of the study and procedural questions regarding participation in the study. Be sure to establish two-way communication with nonrespondents to discover why they are not responding to your questionnaire. Once the reasons for nonresponse are determined, you can usually overcome most of them.

Use well-designed follow-ups and do not spare time or expense; follow-ups are important. Use a high quality paper and don't hesitate to use colored papers or inks.

Follow-ups should be brief and to the point. An excellent idea is to mail an additional copy of the questionnaire to each nonrespondent along with the second follow-up. Typically, response rates to follow-ups that include another copy of the questionnaire are higher than to those not accompanied by additional questionnaires [158, 167, 336, 410].

Several different types of follow-ups should be considered. Formal letters may be tried if humorous pleas have failed. Postcards may be used as alternatives to letters [139, 247, 276]. Telegrams may be used, and phone calls should definitely be considered [377, 398, 423]. One author [446] successfully used "a moralistic story" and "an analysis of objections to replying" as follow-up techniques (see Appendix C). Previous research indicates that the difference in response-rate stimulation between postcards and letters, or between formal letters and humorous pleas, varies from sample to sample.

Decisions regarding the timing of follow-ups should be based on your daily response rates. A good general rule is to send follow-ups when the replies from preceding mailings have dwindled considerably. This point is best determined intuitively by the project directors—after all, by this stage of the study, the directors understand the study far better than the designers of any general rule.

Do not allow excessive time periods to elapse between mailings; however, do not harass your subjects immediately with daily reminders. Busy executives will undoubtedly be offended at receiving a reminder to a 40-page questionnaire only two days after its receipt, whereas they might not be offended by a reminder sent three days after a five-question survey. Be persistent but not obnoxious.

Occasionally, criticism has been raised concerning the effect on responses that may occur from prodding subjects. The argument is that by forcing responses from people who really do not want to respond, one will get invalid answers, which may even be just random pencil markings on the pages. The authors are unaware of any study results that support this contention but are well aware of the ever-present problems inherent in low response rates. One study [116] found that had exhaustive prodding not been carried out, the respondents who returned early questionnaires would have represented a highly biased section of the total sample.

The general issue of follow-up strategy is well expressed in the following:

> The ultimate objective is to obtain as many responses as possible, in the form of completed questionnaires which provide usable data. If questionnaire forms meet criteria of physical attractiveness and obvious consideration for the respondent, it is believed that the percentage of replies will be sufficiently high to fulfill the requirements of the investigator. Every conceivable inducement should be used in the hope of convincing one more potential respondent to take the time and effort necessary to answer the questionnaire. [326, p. 486]

Appendixes B and C include several sample follow-ups.

V. SPECIFIC TACTICS—INTERVIEWING

High response rates in studies using interviewing are influenced by two major factors: successfully contacting people and convincing people to complete the interview. It is naive to think you will reach a large percentage of people in your sample the first time you try. The best way to plan a schedule for contacting people is to learn as much as possible about the people you will be interviewing so you will know when they are most likely to be near the telephone for telephone interviews or, in the case of personal interviews, at the location at which you wish to interview them. For example, when you wish to interview people at their homes, weekends and evenings provide the best chance for successfully contacting them [61]. In other cases, you may wish to survey people who spend most of their time at home. Weekday mornings are best for contacting these people [129]. It is necessary to schedule telephone calls so that people are called at different times on different days to maximize the likelihood of successfully reaching people. Do not forget to take into account the effect of different time zones and daylight savings time when scheduling interview contacts. Our experience shows that almost everyone in the sample can be contacted if up to six or seven carefully scheduled call-backs are made.

A major problem in telephone interviewing is the inaccuracy of lists from which samples are frequently drawn. Almost without exception, the accuracy of any list you obtain will be less than you hope for and also less than the lists' brokers promise. Be sure to allow enough time and money to update lists as needed.

Three factors are vital in obtaining cooperation from people once they have been contacted for an interview. The first of these is the quality of the interviewer. Experienced, professional interviewers know how to establish rapport immediately at the moment of contact, and know how to respond to signals from respondents that they are losing interest in the interview. Good interviewers also convey to people that the interview is important and that their responses are valued. To do this, all interviewers, no matter how experienced, need to be briefed about the study purpose and trained in the precise administration of the questionnaire. Research shows that, in some cases, the age [409], race [467], and sex [26, 103] of the interviewer will also affect the response rate.

The second factor is the critically important introduction, which very briefly tells people the purpose of the study and convinces them it is not a sales call. This information can be, and should be, conveyed in one or two very short sentences.

The third factor is the manner in which the questionnaire is arranged. It is imperative that the interview start with several interesting questions to "hook" the respondent. Avoid using long ranking questions, long rating scales, or other complicated forms that will reduce the likelihood of people completing the interview.

Unless extremely interested in the topic of the interview, many people will not complete a telephone interview that exceeds ten minutes [485].

VI. A CHECKLIST

Information obtained by questionnaires cannot be assumed representative unless a high response rate has been achieved. When designing a study, many considerations arise that will likely affect the response rate:

- How will you relate to the people you ask to complete a questionnaire? Will you be "formal" or "folksy"?

- Are you able to guarantee respondents anonymity, or confidentiality?

- Have you obtained impressive sponsorship?

- For mail surveys, have you considered using different types of printing and paper, and different colors of paper and ink?

- Have you carefully considered the content and approach of your preletter and cover letter, and your interview introduction?

- Would some type of incentive encourage response to your questionnaire?

- Have you identified sufficient resources from which to obtain up-dated addresses and telephone numbers of people in your study?

- For mail surveys, will you use business reply postage or regular postage stamps? Have you considered certified mail, special delivery, and commemorative stamps?

- Will you contact people at their place of work or their home?

- How will you know why people are not returning completed questionnaires or agreeing to be interviewed?

- Have you a follow-up "arsenal" available for use if five or six follow-ups or callbacks are needed?

- Have you considered using the following for follow-ups: telephone calls, telegrams, postcards, raffle notices, formal letters, and informal letters?

- Will your follow-ups be humorous, serious, or a combination of both?

- Are you confident your interviewers are top-notch professionals?

- Is your questionnaire one that you, yourself, would answer?

- Have you sufficiently briefed interviewers about the study and the questionnaire?

CHAPTER 6: ANALYZING THE RESULTS

The questionnaire preparer can avoid many headaches and save much time if some thought is devoted early in the study to deciding on procedures that will facilitate data analysis. These procedures should be kept in mind throughout all phases of the study.

Summarizing raw data from questionnaires requires both time and money. Frequently the cost exceeds expectations; therefore, a good practice is to allow generous amounts of time and money for the data-analysis stage. The following suggestions should help your data analysis.

If possible, involve the person who will be responsible for data handling and analysis early in the study, certainly during the time the questionnaire format is being established. Early involvement of the data analyst eliminates grief at later stages of the study. Lack of such involvement may result in the inability to analyze data from a particular questionnaire item in the way that is desired because the questionnaire format is not suitable for computer analysis. If you are in a situation where a data analyst cannot be involved, then consult with personnel who are knowledgeable about computers.

Computer analysis requires the development of a thorough and precise method of response coding. If you know which computer programs will be used for the analysis, you should devise a coding system consistent with the requirements of both these programs and the computer to be used. These considerations include answering the following questions: Can your program process multiple answers to a single question, i.e., "multiple punches"? Can you use letters and other nonnumerical characters (alpha characters) as well as numbers (numeric characters)? How will you handle unanswered questions (missing data)?

Establish a coding system that enables data analysts who handle returned questionnaires to "edit" ambiguous or hard-to-read responses in a uniform manner. As each form is received, someone familiar with the study and thoroughly familiar with the coding system should carefully examine each questionnaire and check for ambiguous answers which might confound data entry. During this editing stage, responses to open-ended questions can be quantified and coded to allow machine analysis if desired.

Several suggestions regarding data entry were included in Chapter 4; one additional suggestion is appropriate here. Because one possible source of error is the data entry process, be sure to verify and spot check the accuracy of this process. Most errors can be avoided by using a precise coding system and carefully communicating with data entry personnel. However, at times, misunderstanding by data entry personnel can lead to systematic errors. For example, suppose you instruct a keypunch operator to begin punching in column six of a computer card, but the operator begins in column five. This would mean that all data following column four would be in the wrong column. The same type of error can occur with any type of data entry process. To prevent errors of this type, check for data entry errors by proofreading early in the data entry phase. Do not wait until data entry is completed because you may need to have the entire job redone.

Considerable discussion exists regarding whether to verify data entry [321, 335]. Basically, verification consists of entering the data twice and comparing results to make certain the two entries are the same. The advisability of using such a procedure depends upon the clarity of your questionnaire, your editing and coding procedures, the "trustworthiness" of data entry personnel, and the amount of money available.

As mail questionnaires are returned or interviews are completed, have an organized system for keeping track of them

[169]. An example of a "check-off" sheet that can be used for mail surveys is shown in Appendix D. Accurate check-off sheets facilitate rapid and economical follow-up procedures.

Finally, one last reminder regarding time and money allocation. Be sure to allow sufficient resources to cover the possible debugging of any computer programs you might use. Be sure to allow sufficient resources to do an adequate job of data analysis rather than skimping and endangering the quality of your study.

ANNOTATED BIBLIOGRAPHY

This section contains a listing and description of 494 publications related to survey research. The listings are indexed at the end of the book to allow access to references in given topic areas.

The increasing interest in methodological issues related to survey research has resulted in numerous studies being conducted of highly specialized topics (e.g., the refusal rates in sex research) which we have deemed to be outside the scope of the preceding chapters of the book. A perusal of the annotations will provide the reader with a knowledge of the types of research that have been conducted. This will facilitate later use of the bibliography's index.

In the bibliography of the first edition, references to works that describe primary research were denoted by an asterisk. This procedure has been eliminated because virtually all entries in this expanded and revised bibliography do, in one way or another, report research findings.

1. Abrams, Jack. "Evaluation of alternative rating devices for consumer research." *Journal of Marketing Research,* May 1966, 3 (2), 189–193.

    The author compares and contrasts four commonly used rating devices in terms of their ability to predict consumer behavior and to determine attitude change.

2. Ace, Merle E., and Dawis, Rene V. "The contributions of questionnaire length, format, and type of score

to response inconsistency." *Educational and Psychological Measurement,* Winter 1972, 32 (4), 1003–1011.

Questionnaire length (7 vs. 13 items) and format (pair comparison vs. triad) were found to be related to response inconsistency.

3.   Adams, J. Stacy. "An experiment on question and response bias." *Public Opinion Quarterly,* Fall 1956, 20 (3), 593–598.

Respondents in this study failed to inhibit the expression of strongly unfavorable responses as previous research suggested.

4.   Alderfer, Clayton. "Comparison of questionnaire responses with and without preceding interviews." *Journal of Applied Psychology,* August 1968, 52 (4), 335–340.

Alderfer reports the results of a study that suggest an interview preceding administration of a questionnaire requesting data about interpersonal relationships within an organization may reduce distortion of responses to the questionnaire items.

5.   Alexander, Cheryl S., and Becker, Henry Jay. "The use of vignettes in survey research." *Public Opinion Quarterly,* Spring 1978, 42 (1), 93–104.

The use of vignettes—systematically elaborated descriptions of concrete situations—is supported as a means of producing more valid and reliable measures of respondent opinion than the "simpler" abstract questions more typical of opinion surveys.

6.   Allen, Chris T.; Schewe, Charles D.; and Wijk, Gosta. "More on self-perception theory's foot technique in the pre-call/mail survey setting." *Journal of Marketing Research,* November 1980, 17 (4), 498–502.

Pre-calling in general enhances response rate. These results, however, only provide qualified support, for the self-perception foot-in-the-door effect. Alternative explanations are offered.

7.   Allen, I. L., and Colfax, J. D. "Respondents' attitudes toward legitimate surveys in four cities." *Journal of Marketing Research*, November 1968, 5 (4), 431–433.
      Surveys in Hartford, New Haven, Bridgeport and Waterbury show most respondents were favorably impressed by legitimate survey activity. About a quarter were initially suspicious of a sales attempt. Three quarters favor legal restrictions on salesmen posing as interviewers.

8.   Alutto, Joseph A. "Some dynamics of questionnaire completion and return among professional and managerial personnel: The relative impact of reception at work site or place of residence." *Journal of Applied Psychology*, October 28, 1970, 54 (5), 430–32.
      Results of this study indicate that whether or not subjects completed open-ended questions partially depended upon whether the questionnaire was mailed to their homes or places of employment. The recommendation is made to send surveys with open-ended items designed for middle-class males in professional and managerial occupations to their places of employment.

9.   Alwin, D. "Making errors in surveys: an overview." *Sociological Methods and Research*, November 1977, 6 (2), 131–150.
      Alwin presents a summary of the types of errors associated with survey research. He discusses recent literature which defines population and sample errors, different aspects of sample bias, and response errors.

10.   Anderson, John F., and Berdie, Douglas R. *Graduate Assistants at the University of Minnesota.* Minneapolis: University of Minnesota Measurement Services Center, 1972. 243p.

This study of graduate assistants includes useful appendixes containing sample questionnaires and follow-ups.

11.   Anderson, John F., and Berdie, Douglas R. "Effects on response rates of formal and informal questionnaire follow-up techniques." *Journal of Applied Psychology,* April 1975, 60 (2), 255–257.

This study demonstrates that the effectiveness of different follow-up techniques depends upon the groups to which they are directed. Humorous, whimsical, and formal follow-ups, and hand-addressed and typed label-addressed follow-ups were examined.

12.   Andreasen, Alan. "Personalizing mail questionnaire correspondence." *Public Opinion Quarterly,* Summer 1970, 34 (2), 273–277.

As shown by this study, personalization of studies using questionnaires does not always increase response rates—in fact, personalization may decrease response rates. This study surveyed lottery winners who wished to maintain their anonymity and, therefore, did not respond favorably to personalization.

13.   Armstrong, J. Scott. "Monetary incentives in mail surveys." *Public Opinion Quarterly,* Spring 1975, 39 (1), 111–116.

The only type of monetary incentive that has an impact on the nonresponse rate is the *prepaid* monetary incentive. A rule of thumb is offered: There is a one percent decrease in nonresponse rate for each one cent increase in the prepaid incentive up to 40 percent.

14. Armstrong, J. Scott, and Overton, Terry S. "Estimating nonresponse bias in mail surveys." *Journal of Marketing Research*, August 1977, 14 (3), 396–402.

Valid predictions for the direction of nonresponse bias were obtained from subjective estimates and extrapolations in an analysis of mail survey data from published studies. For estimates of the magnitude of bias, the use of extrapolations led to substantial improvements over a strategy of not using extrapolations.

15. Arndt, Johan, and Crane, Edgar. "Response bias, yea-saying, and the double negative." *Journal of Marketing Research*, May 1975, 12 (2), 218–220.

This study with Norwegian subjects indicates that questionnaire wording influences subject response.

16. Astin, Alexander, and Boruch, Robert. "A 'link' system for assuring confidentiality of research data in longitudinal studies." *American Council on Education Research Reports*, 1974, 2, 124–132.

17. Babbie, Earl R. *Survey Research Methods*. Belmont, Cal.: Wadsworth, 1973. 383p.

This book is a good textbook related to survey research.

18. Bachrack, Stanley, and Scoble, Harry. "Mail questionnaires efficiency: Controlled reduction of nonresponse." *Public Opinion Quarterly*, Summer 1967, 31 (2), 265–71.

A case study of a particular approach used to minimize nonresponse is described in this article.

This study is an example of tailoring study tactics to the particular population.

19.   Bailar, Barbara, and Lanphier, C. Michael. *Development of Survey Methods to Assess Survey Practices.* Washington, D.C.: American Statistical Association, 1978, 117p.
        This report describes the need for, background of, and procedures used to assess survey research practices throughout the United States.

20.   Ballweg, John A. "Husband/wife response similarities on evaluation and nonevaluative survey questions." *Public Opinion Quarterly,* Summer 1969, 33 (2), 249–254.
        Husband and wife responses are more likely to be similar when "hard" data (e.g., family income) rather than "soft" data (e.g., responsibility for discipline of children) is sought.

21.   Barath, Arpad, and Cannell, Charles F. "Effect of interviewer's voice intonation." *Public Opinion Quarterly,* Fall 1976, 40 (3), 370–373.
        Interviewer intonation may well have powerful effects on response behavior even in relatively easy tasks, such as recall of self-related episodic events.

22.   Bartholomew, Warren M. *Questionnaires in Recreation; Their Preparation and Use.* New York: National Recreation Association, 1963. 12p.
        This pamphlet contains a basic guide for using questionnaires. Issues such as question design and mailing are discussed in the context of questionnaire use in the area of recreation.

23.   Barton, Judith, et al. "Characteristics of respondents and non-respondents to a mail questionnaire." *Ameri-*

can Journal of Public Health, August 1980, 70 (8), 823–825.

A comparison of respondents and nonrespondents showed them to be quite similar with regard to age, education, employment status and other factors related to the nursing profession. The respondents comprised 70 percent of the sample.

24. Bauer, Rainald K., and Meissner, Frank. "Structures of mail questionnaires: test of alternatives." *Public Opinion Quarterly,* Summer 1963, 27 (2), 307–311.

A series of logically interdependent questions tend to generate more meaningful answers if put on one page of the questionnaire.

25. Bauer, E. Jackson. "Response bias in a mail survey." *Public Opinion Quarterly,* Winter 1947–48, 11 (4), 594–600.

In a survey of veterans, this author found that bias resulted from respondents having different degrees of interest in the subject of the questionnaire. Bias may also result from differences in educational level and marital status.

26. Begin, Guy; Boivin, Michel; and Bellerose, Jeannette. "Sensitive data collection through the random response technique: some improvements." *Journal of Psychology,* January 1979, 101 (1), 53–65.

Improvements in the use of the random response technique, such as utilizing a die as the random device, and interviewing in public places by both male and female interviewers are discussed.

27. Belkin, Marvin, and Lieverman, Seymour. "Effect of question wording on response distribution." *Journal of Marketing Research,* August 1967, 4 (3), 312–313.

A study is reported in which different question wordings were tested and different response distributions were found. A "which, if any" question yielded a higher level of purchase interest than a "would you" question. Reasons for this response are discussed.

28.   Belson, W. A. "Tape recording: its effect on accuracy of response in survey interviews." *Journal of Marketing Research,* August 1967, 4 (3), 253–260.
Matched samples were administered a questionnaire, but a tape recorder was used for one but not the other. After validating the replies with an independent source, it was discovered that there was no loss in accuracy for the sample in which the tape recorder was used. However, there were differences for subgroups within the taped sample.

29.   Benson, Lawrence E. "Mail surveys can be valuable." *Public Opinion Quarterly,* Summer 1946, 10 (2), 234–41.
Benson discusses some advantages and disadvantages of questionnaire use based on the experiences of the Gallup Poll.

30.   Benson, Sherwood; Booman, Wesley P.; and Clark, Kenneth E. "A study of interview refusals." *Journal of Applied Psychology,* April 1951, 35 (2), 116–119.
About 14 percent additional time was required to complete interviews originally refused. Significantly different answers were obtained from refusals as compared with nonrefusals.

31.   Berdie, Douglas R. "Questionnaire length and response rate." *Journal of Applied Psychology,* October 1973, 58 (2), 278–280.
This study investigated the effect of the length of questionnaires on response rate. One-, two-, and

four-page questionnaires were sent to 108 university professors at three levels (full, associate, or assistant) and to three colleges (College of Liberal Arts, Institute of Technology, and College of Agriculture). With the effect of question interest controlled, response rates were not found to be related to questionnaire length. No difference was found in response rates for professors at different levels or in different colleges.

32. Berdie, Douglas R., and Anderson, John F. "Mail questionnaire response rates: updating outmoded thinking." *Journal of Marketing*, January 1976, 40 (1), 71–73.

The authors look at the shortcomings of several commonly used response-rate ratios and suggest the "Item Response Rate Index" as an alternative approach to reporting response rates.

33. Berdie, Frances. "What test questions are likely to offend the general public?" *Journal of Educational Measurement*, Summer 1971, 8 (2), 87–93.

Certain types of questionnaire items may be seen as offensive by some people. This article examines which type of items are potentially offensive and suggests ways of overcoming this problem.

34. Berger, Philip K., and Sullivan, James E. "Instructional set, interview context, and the incidence of 'don't know' responses." *Journal of Applied Psychology*, October 28, 1970, 54 (5), 414–16.

Many writers have suggested stressing the importance of the subject's role as a means of inducing cooperation. Berger and Sullivan point out that overemphasizing the subject's importance may result in more "don't know" answers because stressing importance may lead to greater reluctance by the respondent to answer forthrightly.

35.   Bevis, J. C. "Economic incentive used for mail ques-
        tionnaires." *Public Opinion Quarterly,* Fall 1948, 12
        (3), 492–3.
        In this study of persons who had responded to
        advertisements in a national magazine, it was
        found that the inclusion of a 25-cent war stamp
        was more economically effective than inclusion of
        either a 10-cent or 50-cent war stamp.

36.   Bishop, George F.; Oldendick, Robert W.; and
        Tuchfarber, Alfred J. "Effects of presenting one ver-
        sus two sides of an issue in survey questions." *Public
        Opinion Quarterly,* Spring 1982, 46 (1), 69–85.
        Offering respondents an alternative position on
        an issue not only affects the nature of the re-
        sponse, it also influences whether an opinion is
        given at all. Less educated respondents are more
        likely to "acquiesce" to one-sided agree/disagree
        formats.

37.   Blair, Ed; Sudman, Seymour; Bradburn, Norman; and
        Stocking, Carol. "How to ask questions about drinking
        and sex: response effects in measuring consumer be-
        havior." *Journal of Marketing Research,* August 1977,
        14 (3), 316–321.
        A nationwide study based on a sample of 1,200
        adults examined responses to threatening behav-
        ioral questions presented in various formats. The
        findings indicated that threatening questions re-
        quiring quantified answers arc best asked in
        open-ended, long questions with respondent-
        familiar wording. Threatening questions requir-
        ing yes-or-no answers can be asked in any format.

38.   Blair, Ed. "More on the effects of interviewer's voice
        intonation." *Public Opinion Quarterly,* Winter 1977–
        78, 41 (4), 544–548.

Rising interviewer's voice intonations do not affect responses to "yes-no" question sequences.

39. Blair, Ed. "Using practice interviews to predict interviewer behaviors." *Public Opinion Quarterly*, Summer 1980, 44 (2), 257–260.
The results of this study showed that practice interviews afforded very good predictions of interviewers' field behaviors. Practice interviews may therefore be an effective screening device.

40. Blalock, Hubert. *Social Statistics*. New York: McGraw-Hill, 1960. 465p.
This excellent textbook on statistics contains a thorough discussion of techniques and problems involved in sampling procedures. The discussion of statistical techniques should be most helpful in deciding how to analyze different types of data obtained from questionnaires.

41. Blankenship, A. B. "Listed versus unlisted numbers in telephone survey samples." *Journal of Advertising Research*, February 1977, 17 (1), 39–42.
The authors indicate that if a telephone survey is to be done, the only dependable sample is that which can be selected through random digit dialing.

42. Blumberg, Herbert H.; Fuller, Carolyn; and Hare, A. Paul. "Response rates in postal surveys." *Public Opinion Quarterly*, Spring 1974, 28 (1), 113–123.
Higher response to postal surveys typically results from use of the following: a) more expensive mail services; b) a cover letter with a moderate level of ingratiation, the sender's title under the "signature," and some form of official sponsorship; c)

a questionnaire that is not overly long and that contains interesting items; d) a premium or incentive; e) a return envelope bearing an actual postage stamp; and f) a postcard "reminder/thank you."

43.   Blumenfeld, Warren S. "Effect of appearance of correspondence on response rate to a mail questionnaire survey." *Psychological Reports*, February 1973, 32 (1), 178.

The appearance of correspondence (personal appearance with director's signature vs. mimeographed with stylus-signed signature of director) had no effect on response rate in this study.

44.   Boek, Walter E., and Lade, James H. "A test of the usefulness of the post card technique in a mail questionnaire study." *Public Opinion Quarterly*, Summer 1963, 27 (2), 303–305.

An adaptation of the "postcard technique" used by both Cahalan and Bradt was tested in this study by the New York State Department of Health.

45.   Boyd, H. W., Jr. and Westfall, Ralph. "Interviewer bias revisited." *Journal of Marketing Research*, February 1965, 2 (1), 58–63.

Ten years ago the authors surveyed the problem of interviewer bias and concluded that it was one of the major sources of error in survey research. A recent survey of the subject confirms the continued existence of the problem with relatively little being done to solve it.

46.   Boyd, Harper W., Jr. and Westfall, Ralph. "Interviewer bias once more revisited." *Journal of Marketing Research*, May 1970, 7 (2), 249–253.

This article reviews the progress made since 1964 in providing answers to questions about reducing interviewer bias as a source of error.

47. Bradburn, N. M., and Mason, W. M. "The effect of question order on response." *Journal of Marketing Research,* November 1964, 1 (4), 57–61.
Significant sections of an interview schedule were systematically rotated to test the effects of question order. The major conclusion is that questions of self-report and self-evaluation are relatively unaffected by order of presentation.

48. Bradburn, Norman M.; Sudman, Seymour; Blair, Ed; and Stocking, Carol. "Question threat and response bias." *Public Opinion Quarterly,* Summer 1978, 42 (2), 221–234.
Respondents who report that questions about an activity would make most people very uneasy are less likely to report ever engaging in that activity than are persons who report less uneasiness.

49. Bradburn, Norman M., and Miles, Carrie. "Vague quantifiers." *Public Opinion Quarterly,* Spring 1979, 43 (1), 92–101.
The responses to many survey questions are often constructed in terms of vague quantifiers, such as "very," "pretty," or "not too." This study reports data that tries to make more precise quantitative estimates for these common vague quantifiers.

50. Bradburn, Norman, and Sudman, Seymour. *Improving Interview Method and Questionnaire Design.* San Francisco: Jossey-Bass, 1979. 214p.
As the title indicates, this book contains precriptions for improving the methods by which survey research is conducted.

51.   Bradt, Kenneth. "The usefulness of postcard technique in a mail questionnaire study." *Public Opinion Quarterly,* Summer 1955, 19 (2), 218–222.

This author used the "postcard technique" recommended by Cahalan and concludes that the technique also may be effective with groups whose members are not accustomed to complying with requests from supervisors.

52.   Brandt, Lewis. "A neglected issue concerning nonrespondents to mail questionnaires." *International Mental Health Research Newsletter,* 1965, 8 (2), 12–16.

When considering possible bias due to low response rates, it is important to determine whether the nonrespondents have even received the questionnaire. Brandt suggests use of certified mail with return receipt as a means of ascertaining this.

53.   Brechner, Kevin; Shippee, Glenn; and Obitz, Frederick W. "Compliance techniques to increase mailed questionnaire return rates from alcoholics." *Journal of Studies on Alcohol,* 1976, 37 (7), 995–996.

The effects of three compliance techniques were examined. None elicited more returns than did a conventional, mailed questionnaire.

54.   Brennan, Robert D. "Trading stamps as an incentive in mail surveys." *Journal of Marketing,* January 1958, 12 (3), 306–307.

Small incentives do not increase the percent of mail returns significantly. The additional cost therefore does not warrant them.

55.   Bridge, R. Gary; Reeder, Leo J.; Kanouse, David; Kinder, Donald R.; Tong Nagy, Vivian; and Judd,

Charles M. "Interviewing changes attitudes—sometimes." *Public Opinion Quarterly,* Spring 1977, 41 (1), 56–64.

Asking questions changed respondents' attitudes toward cancer, but interviewing about burglary prevention did not change attitudes toward crime. The evidence suggests that interview effects will occur when the respondent's attitudes and information are unfocused or ambiguous *and* the topic is important.

56. Brown, Morton. "Use of a postcard query in mail surveys." *Public Opinion Quarterly,* Winter 1965–66, 29 (4), 635–37.

Brown reports the use of a two-question postcard resulted in a higher return than a two-page questionnaire. In follow-ups to the original mailing, however, there was no difference between these two techniques.

57. Brown, Stephen W., and Coney, Kenneth A. "Comments on 'Mail survey premiums and response bias'." *Journal of Marketing Research,* August 1977, 14 (3), 385–387.

Whitmore's article (see *Journal of Marketing Research,* 13 [February 1976], 46–50) suggests that "no systematic bias is produced in mail surveys" as a result of including a premium. The author believes this conclusion is unwarranted on several grounds. For example, an unreasonably small incentive premium was used in the Whitmore study, possibly accounting for the negligible differences in response rates of the premium recipients and nonrecipients. (For Whitmore's reply, see *Journal of Marketing Research,* 14 [August 1977], 388–390.)

58.   Brown, Tommy L., and Wilkins, Bruce T. "Clues to
        reasons for nonresponse, and its effect upon variable
        estimates." *Journal of Leisure Research*, 1978, 10 (3),
        226–231.
              Seventeen mail questionnaire studies of leisure
              activities were examined. Studies of more specific
              audiences who are particularly interested and in-
              volved in the subject of the study, studies involv-
              ing specific resource areas, and studies that ad-
              dress an issue are shown to evoke higher response
              rates than those which are more descriptive in
              nature.

59.   Brunner, G. Allen, and Carroll, Stephen J., Jr. "The
        effect of prior telephone appointments on completion
        rates and response content." *Public Opinion Quarterly*,
        Winter 1967–68, 31 (4), 652–654.
              A prior telephone call, while not affecting re-
              sponse pattern, may have a marked detrimental
              effect upon the overall completion rate. Inter-
              viewers receive a much greater refusal rate over
              the telephone when they request an appointment
              as compared to that which they receive at the door
              when they request an immediate interview. Not-
              at-homes are not reduced appreciably by the
              phone call. A call may also substantially increase
              survey costs.

60.   Brunner, G. Allen, and Carroll, Stephen J., Jr. "The
        effect of prior notification on the refusal rate in fixed
        address surveys." *Journal of Advertising Research*,
        March 1969, 9 (1), 42–44.
              Letters forewarning of a survey do not necessarily
              increase response rates. It may be that the desired
              positive effect can only occur if the sponsoring

organization is known, respected, and trusted by
the respondents.

61.   Brunner, G. Allen, and Carroll, Stephen J., Jr.
        "Weekday evening interviews of employed persons are
        better." *Public Opinion Quarterly,* Summer 1969, 33
        (2), 265–267.
              A larger proportion of not-at-homes occurred dur-
        ing the daytime hours of Saturday than during the
        evening hours on weekdays. The proportion of
        refusals was higher for weekday evening hours
        than for Saturdays, since tiredness and irritability
        might occur more often after a day's work.

62.   Brunner, James A., and Brunner, G. Allen. "Are vol-
        untarily unlisted telephone subscribers really differ-
        ent?" *Journal of Marketing Research,* February 1971, 8
        (1), 121–124.
              This article explores differences among some se-
        lected dimensions between listed and voluntarily
        unlisted telephone subscribers. Several signifi-
        cant differences are pointed out and cautions in
        the use of telephone directory sampling are
        suggested.

63.   Buchman, Thomas A., and Tracy, John A. "Obtain-
        ing responses to sensitive questions: conventional
        questionnaire versus randomized response tech-
        niques." *Journal of Accounting Research,* Spring 1982,
        20 (1), 263–271.
              A comparison of responses to conventional ques-
        tionnaires with RRT (randomized response tech-
        nique) questionnaires shows a tendency toward
        more honest answers to sensitive questions
        through use of the RRT among a group of accoun-
        tants. The RRT approach lowered the response

rate since respondent anonymity made follow-up difficult.

64.   Butler, Richard P. "Effects of signed and unsigned questionnaires for both sensitive and nonsensitive items." *Journal of Applied Psychology,* June 1973, 57 (3), 348–349.

This study assessed the effects of signing and not signing questionnaires on items that were rated as sensitive. Tests showed that there were no significant differences for any of the items between the respondents (college seniors) who signed and those who did not sign their questionnaires.

65.   Cahalan, Don. "Effectiveness of a mail quesionnaire technique in the army." *Public Opinion Quarterly,* Fall 1951, 15 (3), 575–580.

The author describes a technique for determining who returns completed questionnaires while assuring anonymity. This technique consists of having respondents return a separate postcard indicating they have returned a questionnaire. Cahalan suggests this technique might be used most effectively with groups whose members are accustomed to complying with requests from superiors.

66.   Cannell, Charles F., and Fowler, Floyd J. "Comparison of a self-enumerative procedure and a personal interview: a validity study." *Public Opinion Quarterly,* Summer 1963, 27 (2), 250–264.

The clearest and most significant finding of this study is that the motivational level of the respondent has more effect on response error in the self-enumerative procedure than in the interview procedure, since filling out a written form demands more work on the part of the respondent.

Other comparisons between these two procedures are made.

67. Cannell, Charles F.; Oksenberg, Lois; and Converse, Jean M. "Striving for response accuracy: experiments in new interviewing techniques." *Journal of Marketing Research,* August 1977, 14 (3), 306–315.

68. Carp, Frances M. "Position effects on interview responses." *Journal of Gerontology,* September 1974, 29 (5), 581–587.
    The results of this study suggest that it may be necessary to present general questions prior to specific ones in order to avoid response contamination.

69. Carpenter, Edwin H. "Personalizing mail surveys: a replication and reassessment." *Public Opinion Quarterly,* Winter 1974–75, 38 (4), 614–620.
    Reduced personalization of a mail survey may hurt response. The *impression* of personalization may be as effective as actual personalization in achieving a higher rate of response.

70. Carpenter, Edwin H. "Evaluation of mail questionnaires for obtaining data from more than one respondent in a household." *Rural Sociology,* Summer 1977, 42 (2), 250–259.
    A comparison of households in which both adults responded to separate questionnaires to households in which only one adult completed a questionnaire indicates that a) the former had a lower response rate; b) item nonresponse was similar; c) characteristics of responding households were similar; d) data-gathering costs are increased somewhat but remain minuscule compared to in-person interviews; e) in 26 percent of the house-

holds receiving two questionnaires one writer
completed both forms.

71.   Cartwright, Ann, and Tucker, Wyn. "An attempt to
reduce the number of calls on an interview inquiry."
Public Opinion Quarterly, Summer 1967, 31 (2), 299–
302.
Letters were sent to half the people in a sample in
an attempt to reduce the number of calls on an
interview inquiry. The results showed that response rate was negatively affected by the letter.
The work and frustration involved in unsuc-
cessful, repeated calls may be unavoidable.

72.   Case, Peter B. "How to catch interviewer errors."
Journal of Advertising Research, April 1971, 11 (2), 39–
43.
Studies to date indicate that as many as one out of
four interviews in market surveys may contain
serious errors. A disproportionately large share of
interviewing errors is concentrated in a relatively
small group of interviewers.

73.   Cataldo, Everett F.; Johnson, Richard M.; Kellstedt,
Lyman A.; and Milvrah, Lester. "Card sorting as a
technique for survey interviewing." *Public Opinion
Quarterly,* Summer 1970, 34 (2), 202–215.
The authors conclude that card sorting is a fast
and interesting method of obtaining valid and reliable interview data, and one which appears to be
capable of counteracting at least some of the biasing effects of response set.

74.   Champion, Dean, and Sear, Alan. "Questionnaire response rate: A methodological analysis." *Social Forces,*
March 1969, 47 (3), 335–39.

The effects of various factors on response rate are tested in this study. The authors conclude that postage stamps elicit a higher response rate than metered postage, that the effect of questionnaire length on response rate needs further study, and that cover letters should be tailored to the study population to be of maximum benefit.

75. Childers, Terry L., and Ferrell, O. C. "Response rates and perceived questionnaire length in mail surveys." *Journal of Marketing Research*, August 1979, 16 (3), 429–431.
   The findings of this study suggest that 8½" x 11" paper trim size produces a better response rate than an 8½" × 14" paper trim size. Use of a one-sheet (front and back) versus a two-sheet (front only) questionnaire did not cause a significant difference in response rate.

76. Childers, Terry L., and Skinner, Steven J. "Gaining respondent cooperation in mail surveys through prior commitment." *Public Opinion Quarterly*, Winter 1979, 43 (4), 558–561.
   In this study the use of a prior commitment postcard did not increase mail survey response or speed of response beyond the results obtained for a control group. The salient nature of the questionnaire content to the survey recipients may have overpowered the effect of the postcard.

77. Childers, Terry L.; Pride, William M.; and Ferrell, O. C. "A reassessment of the effects of appeals on response to mail surveys." *Journal of Marketing Research*, August 1980, 17 (3), 365–370.
   The results of this study indicate that use of appeals presented as postscripts does not improve

survey response. Response bias was unaffected and the completeness of survey response was not improved.

78.   Chromy, James R., and Horvitz, Daniel G. "The use of monetary incentives in national assessment household surveys." *Journal of the American Statistical Association*, September 1978, 73 (363), 473–478.

This article describes a variable incentive procedure which provides respondents the opportunity to receive a larger incentive for providing more data. It is also demonstrated that when the costs of screening for eligible respondents are high (rare populations), the use of incentives to increase response rates may actually reduce the cost per unit of data collected.

79.   Clancey, Kevin J., and Wachsler, Robert A. "Positional effects in shared cost surveys." *Public Opinion Quarterly*, Summer 1971, 35 (2), 258–265.

A shared-cost survey is one in which space in a questionnaire and the costs of a survey are shared by a number of participants. The results of this investigation showed that responses to questions were similar whether they were asked early or late in the interview. The authors conclude that positional effects can safely be ignored.

80.   Clausen, J. A., and Ford, Robert N. "Controlling bias in mail questionnaires." *Journal of the American Statistical Association*, December 1947, 42 (240), 497–511.

Results of a study of veterans indicate that personalized salutation and handwritten signature on correspondence did not significantly increase response rate. The use of special delivery letters did, however, have a significant effect on response rate. Clausen and Ford also discuss, in some detail, the potential problem of nonresponse bias in studies using questionnaires.

81. Cochran, William G. *Sampling Techniques.* New York: John Wiley & Sons, 1963. 399p.
This book is the definitive source for sampling techniques useful when conducting surveys. Formulas for sample size are derived and discussed. The book requires a strong mathematical background on the part of readers.

82. Collins, W. Andrew. "Interviewers' verbal idiosyncracies as a source of bias." *Public Opinion Quarterly,* Fall, 1970, 34 (3), 416–422.
Interviewers' verbal habits (vocabulary and verbosity) pose a serious threat to the validity of much survey data.

83. Colombotos, John. "Personal versus telephone interviews: effect on responses." *Public Health Reports,* September 1969, 84 (9), 773–782.
In this study there were essentially no differences between the responses of physicians interviewed in person and those interviewed by telephone.

84. Coombs, Clyde H., and Coombs, Lolagene C. "'Don't know': item ambiguity or respondent uncertainty?" *Public Opinion Quarterly,* Winter 1976–77, 40 (4), 497–514.
The authors suggest ways in which to analyze "don't know" responses.

85. Cooper, S. L. "Random sampling by telephone: an improved method." *Journal of Marketing Research,* November 1964, 1 (4), 45–48.
A technique is described for obtaining sample telephone numbers, whether listed or not. The

inclusion of new but unlisted telephones can eliminate a major source of sampling error.

86.   Cotter, Patrick R.; Cohen, Jeffrey; and Coulter, Philip B. "Race-of-interviewer effects in telephone interviews." *Public Opinion Quarterly*, Summer 1982, 46 (2), 278–284.
Previous studies have found a race-of-interviewer effect in both personal interviews and on questionnaires filled out in the presence of an interviewer. This study shows the presence of the effect in telephone interviews on racial questions.

87.   Cox, Eli P., III; Anderson, Thomas, Jr.; and Fulcher, David G. "Reappraising mail survey response rates." *Journal of Marketing Research*, November 1974, 11 (4), 413–417.
Numerous studies have evaluated various techniques for increasing response rates in mail questionnaire surveys. This study examines two such techniques (personalized cover letters and follow-up postal reminders), but goes beyond response reliability to consider budget and time constraints as well as minimum sample size requirements for analysis purposes.

88.   Cox, Eli P., III. "A cost/benefit view of prepaid monetary incentives in mail questionnaires." *Public Opinion Quarterly*, Spring 1976, 40 (1), 101–104.
There was no relationship between the incremental cost per respondent of monetary incentives and the percentage of reduction in nonresponse.

89.   Cox, Eli P., III. "The optimal number of response alternatives for a scale: a review." *Journal of Marketing Research*, November 1980, 17 (4), 407–422.
Eighty years of literature on the optimal number

of response alternatives for a scale are reviewed. The author examines the major factors influencing the quality of scaled information, points out areas in particular need of additional research, and makes some recommendations for the applied researcher.

90. Cox, W. E. "Response patterns to mail surveys." *Journal of Marketing Research,* November 1966, 3 (4), 392–397.

The author shows by reviewing fifteen mail surveys that the intervals between mailings in a multi-wave survey can be reduced to seven days.

91. Craig, C. Samuel, and McCann, John M. "Item nonresponse in mail surveys: extent and correlates." *Journal of Marketing Research,* May 1978, 15 (2), 285–289.

Results of examining six marketing research surveys indicate that the extent of item nonresponse appears to be independent of questionnaire length and varies systematically with age and education. Activity-interest-opinion items are less likely to contain item nonresponse bias than other types of questions.

92. Crowley, Francis. "Compensation of subjects for participation in research." *School and Society,* October 1959, 87 (2160), 430–31.

The results of this study of New York City public high school teachers indicate that paying subjects may have a positive effect in motivating them to cooperate in completing a questionnaire.

93. Cummings, K. Michael. "Random digit dialing: a sampling technique for telephone surveys." *Public Opinion Quarterly,* Summer 1979, 43 (2), 233–244.

The findings of this study suggest that random

digit dialing is an efficient survey method, in terms of both cost in implementation and sampling precision.

94.   Daniel, Wayne W. "Nonresponse in sociological surveys: a review of some methods for handling the problem." *Sociological Methods and Research,* February 1975, 3 (2), 291–307.
        The seriousness of bias due to nonresponse in survey research is demonstrated. Sources and consequences of nonresponse are discussed and eight specific methods for dealing with the problem are presented in detail.

95.   Davis, Robert, and Barrow, Edward. "A critical study of the questionnaire in education." *Educational Administration and Supervision,* 1935, 21 (2), 137–144.
        A review of 500 questionnaire studies prior to 1932 is presented. The authors investigated the response rates obtained, types of response options, and type of appeal used to solicit response, the reporting of reliability and validity, and the nature of the information asked. This article is somewhat dated.

96.   Davis, Todd M. "Detecting subgroups in survey research." American Educational Research Association Annual Meeting, 1983.
        A procedure for analyzing survey data by the use of cluster analysis is presented. The application of cluster analysis in survey research is discussed.

97.   DeMaio, Theresa J. "Refusals: who, where and why." *Public Opinion Quarterly,* Summer 1980, 44 (2), 223–233.
        Refusals in households at which interviews had not been previously attempted were more likely to

occur among the older and more predominantly middle-class portions of this sample. Geographically, urban dwellers and westerners are most likely to refuse.

98. Deutcher, Irwin. "Physicians' reactions to a mailed questionnaire: A study in 'resistantialism'." *Public Opinion Quarterly,* Fall 1956, 20 (3), 599–604.
Comments from completed questionnaires returned by male physicians and dealing with "Public Images of Female Occupations" were used to infer reasons why others may not have responded. Some of these reasons suggested are resistance to the restrictions imposed by multiple-choice questions, specific concepts of the inquiry, and questions that "don't make sense."

99. Dickson, John P.; Casey, Michael; Wyckoff, Daniel; and Wynd, William. "Invisible coding of survey questionnaires." *Public Opinion Quarterly,* Spring 1977, 41 (1), 100–106.
This article considers the ethics as well as the benefits and costs of invisible coding in survey questionnaires.

100. Dillman, Don. "Increasing mail questionnaire response in large samples of the general public." *Public Opinion Quarterly,* Summer 1972, 36 (2), 254–257.
This article reports a study in which several methods for stimulating response rate were employed. The author concludes that manipulating many aspects of the mail questionnaire process rather than concentrating on specific techniques will be more productive. He also notes that persistence during the follow-up phase of a study is crucial.

101.   Dillman, Don A., and Frey, James H. "Contribution of personalization to mail questionnaire response as an element of a previously tested method." *Journal of Applied Psychology,* June 1974, 59 (3), 297–301.

The return rate for a mail questionnaire was higher among respondents receiving personalized cover letters than among those who did not. Prior contact by telephone did not increase response rates but did stimulate earlier return of questionnaires.

102.   Dillman, Don A.; Christenson, James A.; Carpenter, Edwin H.; and Brooks, Ralph M. "Increasing mail questionnaire response: a four state comparison." *American Sociological Review,* October 1974, 39 (5), 744–756.

The following procedures were used to elicit response to lengthy questionnaires tested on statewide samples of the general public in Arizona, Indiana, North Carolina, and Washington: photo-reduction and multilithing into booklet form; eye-catching cover page; straightforward and carefully ordered questions presented in a visually attractive manner; first class mail; cover letter emphasizing social usefulness and importance of individual respondents; personalization; and intensive follow-up efforts. The authors conclude that poor mail-questionnaire return rates are inexcusable.

103.   Dillman, Don A.; Gallegos, Jean Gorton; and Frey, James H. "Reducing refusal rates for telephone interviews." *Public Opinion Quarterly,* Spring 1976, 40 (1), 66–78.

Refusal rates for telephone interviews were not affected by substantial changes in the introductory remarks of the interviewer. A prior letter significantly lowered refusal rates. Sex of the interviewer had no effect.

104.   Dillman, Don A. *Mail and Telephone Surveys: The Total Design Method.* New York: John Wiley & Sons, 1978. 325p.
This book presents a unified approach for conducting survey research.

105.   Dohrenwend, Barbara Snell. "Some effects of open and closed questions on respondents' answers." *Human Organization,* Summer 1965, 24 (2), 175–184.
The author reports that there is no evidence that open questions possess the advantage of being more productive of depth since respondents often deviate from the topic of the questions. Neither is there any direct evidence that open questions produce more valid answers. The subject matter seems to be much more important than the form of the question in this regard. In the face of resistance, objective questions yield more valid responses on subjective topics than do direct subjective questions.

106.   Dohrenwend, Barbara Snell; Colombotos, John; and Dohrenwend, Bruce P. "Social distance and interviewer effects." *Public Opinion Quarterly,* Fall, 1968, 332 (3), 410–422.
The authors develop a model to answer the question, What kind of relationship between interviewer and respondent produces the best interview data? In terms of social distance between interviewer and respondent, they conclude that both too much and too little social distance will produce biasing effects.

107.   Dohrenwend, Barbara Snell. "An experimental study
         of payments to respondents." *Public Opinion Quarterly,*
         Winter 1970–1971, 34 (4), 621–624.
         In this experiment the offer of an honorarium
         made no difference in completion rates regardless
         of whether the interviewer was a student or a
         professional, a male or female, and regardless of
         whether the respondent was black or white, high
         or low income.

108.   Dohrenwend, Barbara Snell, and Dohrenwend, Bruce
         P. "Sources of refusals in surveys." *Public Opinion
         Quarterly,* Spring 1978, 32 (1), 74–83.
         A comparison of interviewer versus respondent
         responsibility for refusals indicates that it is pos-
         sible to identify cases for which each is respon-
         sible.

109.   Donald, Marjorie. "Implications of nonresponse for
         the interpretation of mail questionnaire data." *Public
         Opinion Quarterly,* Spring 1960, 24 (1), 99–114.
         This study, as many others, attempted to deter-
         mine in what predictable ways nonrespondents
         differ from respondents. The results of surveying
         members of the League of Women Voters suggest
         that the more actively involved in the organization
         a subject was, the more likely she was to respond
         to the mail questionnaire.

110.   Doob, Anthony N.; Freedman, Jonathan L.; and Carl-
         smith, Merrill Jr. "Effects of sponsor and prepayment
         on compliance with a mailed request." *Journal of Ap-
         plied Psychology,* June 1973, 57 (3), 346–347.
         A request to answer two questions on a stamped,
         addressed postcard was sent to 804 people se-
         lected from a telephone directory. The sponsor of
         this request was either a university or a commer-

cial firm. One-third of the subjects received 20¢ with the request, one-third received 5¢, and one-third received no money. People were more likely to comply with the request from the university than the commercial firm, and compliance varied directly with the amount of money enclosed with the request. The difference between sponsors disappeared with increasing amounts of money.

111. Duker, Sam. "The questionnaire is questionable." *Phi Delta Kappan,* May 1948, 29 (9), 386, 392.
This author discusses many of the problems that have discredited early studies using questionnaires.

112. Duncan, W. Jack. "Mail questionnaires in survey research: a review of response inducement techniques." *Journal of Management,* Spring 1979, 5 (1), 39–55.
This study examines twelve of the most frequently researched techniques for increasing response rates. Five techniques consistently produced higher responses: pre-notification, personalization, the inclusion of monetary incentives, follow-up, and higher class return postage. Two others, source of sponsorship and the type of appeal in the cover letter, increased response rates but in a situation-specific manner. Four factors had no effect on response rates: the address location or social setting in which the questionnaire was received; specification of deadlines; the color, length, form, or precoding of the instrument; and the interaction of multiple factors.

113. Dunkelberg, William C., and Day, George S. "Nonresponse bias and callbacks in sample surveys." *Journal of Marketing Research,* May 1973, 10 (2), 160–168.
Additional callbacks may result in a more repre-

sentative final sample, but such a result will cost more. This study provides evidence on the rate at which sample values converge on their estimated population distribution as the number of callbacks increases.

114.   Dunning, Bruce, and Cahalan, Don. "By-mail vs. field self-administered questionnaires: an armed forces survey." *Public Opinion Quarterly*, Winter 1973–74, 37 (4), 618–624.

A by-mail method is likely to be superior to the on-site, supervised method for military surveys on sensitive issues. It is superior in terms of response rate, economy, sampling flexibility, and ease of management when sampling from centralized personnel lists. The method may be useful for populations that are subject to considerable control: employees of large companies, government employees, and school teachers.

115.   Eastlock, J. O., Jr. and Assael, Henry. "Better telephone surveys through centralized interviewing." *Journal of Advertising Research*, March 1966, 6 (1), 2–7.

Working from a single location through Wide Area Telephone Service (WATS) brings three major benefits to survey research: stimulus equivalence, sampling precision, and quality control. A WATS System is more feasible for continuing rather than one-shot studies and for studies that demand extreme precision and control.

116.   Eckland, Bruce. "Effects of prodding to increase mailback returns." *Journal of Applied Psychology*, June 1965, 49 (3), 165–169.

Telephone calls and certified mail were used in this study of college dropouts to help achieve a 94 percent response rate. The author determined that responses before these follow-up techniques were not representative of the final responses. He also suggests that prodding subjects to respond does not affect the veracity of their response.

117. Eckland, Bruce. "Retrieving mobile cases in longitudinal surveys." *Public Opinion Quarterly*, 1968, 32 (1), 51–64.

Locating and maintaining current addresses of subjects is one of the essential tasks of a successful study using mail questionnaires. Eckland reviews the various techniques that have been successfully used by a number of other investigators. Some of these resources for locating addresses are certified mail, telephone companies, high schools and reunion committees, Retail Credit Company, and Social Security Administration.

118. Edgerton, Harold A.; Britt, Stewart; and Norman, Ralph D. "Objective differences among various types of respondents to a mailed questionnaire." *American Sociological Review*, August 1947, 12 (4), 435–444.

In their study of male contestants in a science talent search, these authors found that a higher percentage of contest winners returned questionnaires than did nonwinners. The authors also concluded that individuals who faithfully continue to reply to questionnaires year after year scored high on the Science Aptitude Examination.

119. Edsall, Richard L. "Getting 'not-at-homes' to interview themselves." *Journal of Marketing*, October 1958, 23 (2), 184–185.

A method for obtaining answers to survey questions from "not-at-homes" without expensive call-backs is described. The method consists of designing a self-explanatory and easy-to-answer questionnaire printed on a reply card and including a covering card to be signed by the interviewer.

120.   Eisinger, Richard A.; Janicki, W. Peter; Stevenson, Robert L.; and Thompson, Wendel L. "Increasing returns in international mail surveys." *Public Opinion Quarterly*, Spring 1974, 38 (1), 124–130.

Use of such techniques as registration, personalization, and mailing an advance postcard may effectively increase response rates in international mail surveys, but using more than one of these techniques in a single survey is not likely to produce more returns than if only one is used. Registration of letters produced significantly greater returns more consistently than other techniques. A second mailing conducted about four weeks after the first mailing should increase total return by 15–25 percent.

121.   Ellis, Robert; Endo, Calvin; and Armer, J. Michael. "The use of potential nonrespondents for studying nonresponse bias." *Pacific Sociological Review*, Spring 1970, 13 (2), 103–109.

The authors of this study conclude that "although survey researchers long have been beguiled by the possibility of viewing nonresponse as a continuum of resistance, the present data indicate that late respondents do not provide a suitable basis for estimating the characteristics of nonrespondents." This conclusion was based on a study of the social and academic demands of college life on students of the University of Oregon.

122. Ellison, Peter C. "Phone directory samples just as balanced as samples from computer random digit dialing." *Marketing News,* Jan. 11, 1980, 8.

Comparisons between the demographics of directory samples and random digit dialing samples showed no meaningful differences.

123. Epperson, William V., and Peck, Raymond C. "Questionnaire response bias as a function of respondent anonymity." *Accident Analysis and Prevention,* December 1977, 9 (4), 249–256.

California drivers who were considered negligent were compared on four primary criteria to test whether anonymous responses to questionnaires differed significantly from nonanonymous responses. Subjects in the anonymous condition gave significantly more positive comments on forced choice questions.

124. Erdos, Paul L. "How to get higher returns from your mail surveys." *Printer's Ink,* February 22, 1957, 258 (8), 30–31.

This author gives a list of considerations that he calls the "12-point law of high return mailing." These considerations include the prestige of the surveying organization, respondent interest, questionnaire legibility, questionnaire length, postage, and cover letters.

125. Erdos, Paul L. "Successful mail surveys: High returns and how to get them." *Printer's Ink,* March 1, 1957, 258 (9), 56–60.

This author suggests that the use of a pre-letter will significantly increase response rates.

126. Erdos, Paul L. *Professional Mail Surveys.* New York: McGraw-Hill, 1970. 289p.

This book details the process by which a mail survey is conducted. The discussion starts with "The Development of Mail Surveys" and continues through to "Ethical Standards in Mail Research."

127.   Erdos, Paul L., and Regier, James. "Visible vs. disguised keying on questionnaires." *Journal of Advertising Research*, February 1977, 17 (1), 13–18.
        Visible identification keys and codes may be used if their purpose is explained to people being surveyed without measurably affecting the response rate.

128.   Etzel, Michael J., and Walker, Bruce I. "Effects of alternative follow-up procedures on mail survey response rates." *Journal of Applied Psychology*, April 1974, 59 (2), 219–221.
        Three procedures were compared: 1) not sending a follow-up letter; 2) sending a follow-up letter with a duplicate questionnaire and return envelope; and 3) sending a follow-up letter without a duplicate questionnaire. Both groups receiving a follow-up letter had significantly higher response rates than the group receiving no follow-up letter. The difference in response rates between the two groups receiving follow-up letters was not significant.

129.   Falthzik, Alfred M. "When to make a telephone interview." *Journal of Marketing Research*, November 1972, 9 (4), 451–452.
        This study attempts to determine the most fruitful part of the week and time of day to interview housewives and female heads of households on the telephone. The mornings on Monday, Tues-

day, Wednesday, and Thursday were found to be the best times.

130. Fantasia, Saverio C., et al. "Effects of personalized sponsorship of an additional covering letter on return rate and nature of evaluative response." *Psychological Reports,* August 1977, 41 (1), 151–154.

A significantly greater number of questionnaires were returned from respondents who received both a personalized covering letter and a "highly personalized" covering letter than from those who received only a personalized covering letter. The high degree of personalization did not favorably bias the nature of the evaluative response.

131. Fasick, Frank A. "Some uses of untranscribed tape recordings in survey research." *Public Opinion Quarterly,* Winter 1977–78, 41 (4), 549–552.

The author presents a list of ways in which tape recordings can contribute to improved survey research.

132. Faulkenberry, G. David, and Mason, Robert. "Characteristics of non-opinion and no opinion response groups." *Public Opinion Quarterly,* Winter 1978, 42 (4), 533–543.

Respondents whose responses were classified as nonexistent opinions ("don't know") were less educated, had lower mass media use, and lower knowledge scores than respondents classed as holding ambivalent opinions ("no opinion").

133. Feild, Hubert S. "Effects of sex of investigator on mail survey response rates and response bias." *Journal of Applied Psychology,* December 1975, 60 (6), 772–773.

The results of this investigation indicated that

the investigator's sex does not necessarily introduce bias in mail surveys involving attitudes toward women. No significant differences were
found due to the investigator's sex for questionnaire return rates or for expressed attitudes toward women.

134.   Ferber, Robert. "The problem of bias in mail returns:
A solution." *Public Opinion Quarterly*, Winter 1948–
49, 12 (4), 669–676.
The author presents a discussion of the problem
of possible nonresponse bias in studies using
questionnaires. The author presents a statistical
technique for examining this bias. Although the
author claims the "ideal solution is . . . to interview all, or a randomly selected subsample of the
nonrespondents and compare their replies with
those of the respondents," the truly ideal situation would be to have no nonrespondents.

135.   Ferber, Robert. "Item nonresponse in a consumer survey." *Public Opinion Quarterly*, Fall 1966, 30 (3), 399–
415.
Item nonresponse increased for questions requiring some thought on the part of the respondent.
No relationship was found between frequency of
item nonresponse and the position of the question
on the questionnaire.

136.   Ferber, Robert, and Sudman, Seymour. "Effects of
compensation in consumer expenditure studies." *An-
nals of Economic and Social Measurement*, April 1974, 3
(2), 319–331.
Compensation may contribute to a higher rate of
response as well to more complete and accurate
information in panel studies (whether by personal

interview or by written record keeping) in comparison to one-time interviews.

137. Ferber, Robert, ed. *Handbook of Marketing Research.* New York: McGraw-Hill, 1974. 1417p.
This very valuable source contains many articles related to all aspects of survey research. A "must" for anyone serious about doing high quality surveys.

138. Fern, Edward F. "The use of focus groups for idea generation: the effects of group size, acquaintanceship, and moderator on response quantity and quality." *Journal of Marketing Research,* February 1982, 19 (1), 1–13.
Individual interviews generated more ideas than focus groups. Eight-member groups generated significantly more ideas than four-member groups. No differences were found between focus groups and unmoderated discussion groups and the effect of acquaintanceship was not clearly determined.

139. Ferriss, Abbott. "A note on stimulating response to questionnaires." *American Sociological Review,* April 1951, 16 (2), 247–249.
The results of this study, limited by lack of control groups, suggest that the use of a deadline for response stimulated immediate response and that including stamped, self-addressed return envelopes with questionnaires also stimulated response. The author states that the use of postcards for prodding did not seem effective in his study.

140. Fidler, Dorothy S., and Kleinknecht, Richard E. "Randomized response versus direct questioning: two

data-collection methods for sensitive information."
Psychological Bulletin, September 1977, 84 (5), 1045–
1049.

Two nonoverlapping random samples of 200 so-
rority women reported stigmatizing behaviors differently, depending upon whether direct questioning or a randomized response technique was
utilized. More sensitive questions showed a greater proportion of women reporting stigmatizing behaviors when guaranteed privacy of information
with the randomized response technique. Less
sensitive questions showed no difference between
the two data-collection methods.

141.   Finsterbusch, Kurt. "Demonstrating the value of mini
surveys in social research." *Sociological Methods & Research,* August 1976, 5 (1), 117–136.

Mini surveys (surveys of samples of 20 to 80 respondents) are advocated for descriptive and applied studies with limited survey funds and as a
probing instrument in tandem with full-scale surveys for analytical and basic research. Their informative value, which is greater than is commonly
recognized, is discussed. Five uses of mini-surveys
are presented: descriptions of populations, collab-
orations for experts, checks on previous findings,
probes for larger studies, or waves in a dynamic
survey study.

142.   Ford, Neil. "The advance letter in mail surveys."
Journal of Marketing Research, May 1967, 4 (2), 202–
204.

This article suggests that the use of pre-letters
significantly increases response rates.

143.   Ford, Neil. "Questionnaire appearance and response
rates in mail surveys." *Journal of Advertising Research,*
1968, 8 (3), 43–45.

Ford stresses the importance of designing a neat appearing and easy-to-complete questionnaire. The use of a printed folder type questionnaire, however, did not bring significantly higher response rates than questionnaires mimeographed on legal-size paper when used in a consumer shopping survey.

144. Forsythe, John B. "Obtaining cooperation in a survey of business executives." *Journal of Marketing Research,* August 1977, 14 (3), 370–373.

An attempt was made to obtain from 314 chief executives of business firms the names of certain of their subordinates and approval to survey them. Addressing initial letters to them by name, and the use of personal telephone follow-up calls, have a detrimental effect on response rate. Possible explanations are offered for these unexpected findings.

145. Francel, E. G. "Mail-administered questionnaires—A success story." *Journal of Marketing Research,* February 1966, 3 (1), 89–91.

The writer's experience over a two-year period with 14 industrial and consumer mail surveys is reported. Several suggestions are offered for increasing the rate of return on mail questionnaires, including a friendly cover letter and a short questionnaire.

146. Francis, Joe D., and Busch, Lawrence. "What we now know about 'I don't knows'." *Public Opinion Quarterly,* Summer 1975, 39 (2), 207–218.

Females, nonwhites, low-educated, low-income and noninvolved respondents with feelings of low political efficacy give a high number of "don't know" responses. These responses should not be treated as random. Survey researchers should be careful not to exclude these respondents from analysis or combine them with other response categories lest bias be introduced.

147.   Franzen, R. "The construction of a questionnaire". *Market Research*, May 1936, 17–19.

148.   Franzen, R., and Lazersfeld, Paul. "Mail questionnaire as a research problem." *Journal of Psychology*, July/October 1945, 20, 293–320.

The question of who returns mail questionnaires is the focus of this article. The authors conclude that mail questionnaires are more successful than interviews in obtaining "freer admission of unusual activities or interests." An appendix is included which discusses sources of bias in interviews.

149.   Frazier, George, and Bird, Kermit. "Increasing the response of a mail questionnaire." *Journal of Marketing*, 1958, 23 (2), 186–187.

These investigators found that the inclusion of a personal, handwritten postscript—"P.S. We need your help in this report. Could you please send it in promptly?"—had a significant effect in increasing response rate.

150.   Freed, Melvin N. "In quest of better questionnaires." *Personnel and Guidance Journal*, October 1964, 43 (2), 187–188.

This article gives ten "cardinal principles" for construction and use of questionnaires. These include specificity of goals, consideration of the use to be made of collected data, and avoidance of troublesome terms.

151.   Friedman, Hershey H., and Goldstein, Larry. "Effect of ethnicity of signature on the rate of return and

content of a mail questionnaire." *Journal of Applied Psychology*, December 1975, 60 (6), 770–771.

Travel agents were sent a questionnaire dealing with topics of current interest to them and signed by either a Jewish, Hispanic, or ethnically unidentifiable name. Analysis of the survey data suggested that the ethnicity of the signature has no significant effect either on the respondents' returning of the questionnaire or on the content of their responses.

152.   Friedman, Monroe, and Wasserman, Ira M. "Characteristics of respondents and non-respondents in a telephone survey study of elderly consumers." *Psychological Reports*, June 1978, 42 (3), 714.

In a study of persons 60 years of age and over, there was no variation in response by sex or by socioeconomic status. However, nonrespondents were approximately two years older than respondents. Poor health tended to be the primary reason for nonresponse.

153.   Frisbie, David A., and Brandenburg, Dale C. "Equivalence of questionnaire items with varying response formats." *Journal of Educational Measurement*, Spring 1979, 16 (1), 43–48.

Questionnaire items are not equivalent if only the endpoints of the response scale are defined rather than all scale points. Items are equivalent, however, when the same response choices are either lettered or numbered.

154.   Fuller, Carol. "Effect of anonymity on return rate and response bias in a mail survey." *Journal of Applied Psychology*, June 1974, 59 (3), 292–296.

Survey answer sheets were returned more frequently by those who were asked to identify these sheets in comparison to those respondents who

remained anonymous. Negative attitudinal statements were endorsed by a higher proportion of
anonymous respondents and positive attitudinal
statements were endorsed by a higher proportion
of identified respondents. Differences between
the two groups were not large, however.

155.   Furse, David H.; Stewart, David W.; and Rados,
David L. "Effects of foot-in-the-door, cash incentives,
and follow-ups on survey response." *Journal of Marketing Research,* November 1981, 18 (4), 473–478.
Researchers have been encouraged by findings
that compliance with a smaller request (a foot-in-
the-door) increases the probability of subsequent
compliance with a larger request and have sought
to exploit the technique to increase survey responses. In this study the "foot" had no effect on
initial responses to a survey, but did affect responses to a follow-up request. A cash incentive
worked significantly better than the "foot."

156.   Furst, Lyndon G., and Blitchington, W. Peter. "The
use of a descriptive cover letter and secretary pre-letter
to increase response rate in a mailed survey." *Personnel
Psychology,* Spring 1979, 32 (1), 155–159.
No significant difference was found in the rate of
response between those school administrators
who received a descriptive cover letter and those
who received no descriptive cover letter. However, those administrators whose secretaries had
been sent a pre-letter responded at a higher rate
than those whose secretaries received no pre-
letter.

157.   Futrell, Charles M., and Swan, John E. "Anonymity
and response by salespeople to a mail questionnaire."
Journal of Marketing Research, November 1977, 14 (4),
611–616.

Response rates, item omissions, response patterns, personality characteristics, and job performance were tested for relationships to anonymity on questionnaires mailed to 201 salespeople in a national hospital supply company. No significant differences were found between the identified group and the anonymous group.

158. Futrell, Charles M., and Lamb, Charles W. "Effect on mail survey return rates of including questionnaires with follow-up letters." *Perceptual and Motor Skills,* February 1981, 52 (1), 11–15.

Respondents were allocated to one of seven conditions. One group received only an initial mailing (questionnaire and cover letter). The remaining six were defined by two cross-factors—the number (1–3) of follow-up mailings and whether the follow-up mailings included only a reminder letter or a letter and another copy of a questionnaire. Only the follow-up questionnaires increased the response rate.

159. Gannon, Martin; Northern, Joseph; and Carrol, Stephen, Jr. "Characteristics of nonrespondents among workers." *Journal of Applied Psychology,* 1971, 55 (6), 586–588.

Checkers in food stores were surveyed in this study. Nonrespondents were found to be more often male, single, less educated, and with lower supervisory ratings than respondents.

160. Gannon, Martin J. "The proper use of the questionnaire survey." *Business Horizons,* October 1973, 16 (5), 89–94.

The use of the questionnaire survey in the assessment of organizational problems is discussed. A training session to increase the acceptance of the questionnaire results by managers is also de-

scribed. Major methods of presenting questionnaire data in organizations are summarized.

161.   Gelb, Betsy D. "Incentives to increase survey returns:
        social class considerations." *Journal of Marketing Re-
        search*, February 1975, 12 (1) 107–109.
        This study tests the relative effect on two social-
        class groups of two incentive techniques to in-
        crease survey returns: a monetary incentive dis-
        tributed unconditionally versus one distributed
        only after questionnaire return. The results
        showed the unconditional incentive more effec-
        tive among middle-class whites, but the condi-
        tional incentive more effective among lower-class
        blacks.

162.   Gibson, Frank, and Hawkins, Brett. "Interviews ver-
        sus questionnaires." *American Behavioral Scientist*,
        September–October 1968, 12 (1), NS-9—NS-11.
        In this study of Georgia legislators, which com-
        pared responses to mail questionnaires and inter-
        views asking the same question, it was concluded
        that "when surveying a relatively homogenous
        group, asking questions about which the group
        can be assumed to be familiar and promising ano-
        nymity of response, a questionnaire may produce
        substantially the same results as interviews at a
        much smaller cost."

163.   Giles, William F., and Feild, Hubert S. "Effects of
        amount, format, and location of demographic informa-
        tion on questionnaire return rate and response bias of
        sensitive and nonsensitive items." *Personnel Psychol-
        ogy*, Autumn 1978, 31 (3), 549–559.
        Three characteristics of demographic question-
        naire items were manipulated on a job satisfaction

survey administered to 888 faculty members in order to assess effects on survey return rate and response bias. Demographic factors analyzed were number of demographic items, format of items, and location of items. Significant results were obtained for the format manipulation: responses indicating higher satisfaction were obtained when the survey instrument contained questions which required both categorical and specific number answers rather than only questions requiring categorical responses. This bias occurred more frequently among sensitive than nonsensitive job satisfaction items.

164. Glasser, Gerald J., and Metzger, Gale D. "Random-digit dialing as a method of telephone sampling." *Journal of Marketing Research,* February 1972, 9 (1), 59–64.

This article reports on a study of the incidence of telephone ownership and telephone directory listings that was based on random-digit dialing (RDD). Various considerations important in the design and selection of RDD samples and in the execution of surveys based on such samples are presented.

165. Glasser, Gerald J., and Metzger, Gale D. "National estimates of nonlisted telephone households and their characteristics." *Journal of Marketing Research,* August 1975, 12 (3), 359–361.

This study of bias that arises from the use of telephone directories in sampling indicates that one in five telephone households are excluded from telephone directories either because numbers are unlisted by choice or because persons have moved too recently to be included in a directory.

166.   Godwin, R. Kenneth. "The consequences of large
        monetary incentives in mail surveys of elites." *Public
        Opinion Quarterly*, Fall 1979, 43 (3), 378–387.
        This report of an international mail survey of elite
        respondents using incentives up to 50 dollars
        found that larger incentives have a slight positive
        effect on the response rate and a substantial ef-
        fect on response quality.

167.   Goldstein, Hyman, and Kroll, Bernard H. "Methods
        of increasing mail responses." *Journal of Marketing*,
        July 1957, 22 (1), 55–57.
        The following techniques were used to increase
        the response to a mail survey: use of simple ques-
        tionnaire; inclusion of copy of original question-
        naire with each follow-up; use of a specific
        deadline date; inclusion of a return addressed,
        postage-paid envelope; and the use of extra-rate
        mail.

168.   Goldstein, Larry, and Friedman, Hershey H. "A case
        for double postcards in surveys." *Journal of Advertising
        Research*, April 1975, 15 (2), 43–47.
        No significant differences were found between
        double postcards and one-page questionnaires in
        validity, content, length, and depth of response.

169.   Goode, William, and Hatt, Paul. *Methods in Social
        Research*. New York: McGraw-Hill, 1962, 386p.
        Discussions of several topics pertinent to ques-
        tionnaire use are included in this general so-
        ciology research text. Topics covered include de-
        sign of questionnaires, reliability, and validity.

170.   Goodstadt, Michael S.; Chung, Linda; Kronitz, Ree-
        na; and Cook, Gaynoll. "Mail survey response rates:

their manipulation and impact." *Journal of Marketing Research*, August 1977, 14 (3), 391–395.

Response rates to mail questionnaires were significantly increased by the use of 25¢ premiums, but not by the use of a free-book reward for responding in this study of 2,416 randomly selected magazine readers. Because speed of response and favorability of expressed opinions are correlated, the broadest spectrum of opinions is best obtained by maximizing response rates.

171. Goudy, Willis J. "Interim response to a mail questionnaire: impacts on variable relationships." *Sociological Quarterly*, Spring 1978, 19 (2), 253–265.

Return bias, differences caused by the impact of interim response on variable relationships, in the examination of substantive conclusions did not subside until the first three response waves were accumulated.

172. Gough, Harrison G., and Hall, Wallace B. "A comparison of physicians who did not respond to a postal questionnaire." *Journal of Applied Psychology*, December 1977, 62 (6), 777–780.

The authors conclude that responders to mail surveys will apparently constitute an unbiased sample of a professional group if their number is large and if they represent 75 percent or more of those asked to reply.

173. Goulet, Waldemar M. "Efficacy of a third request letter in mail surveys of professionals." *Journal of Marketing Research*, February 1977, 14 (1), 112–114.

A third letter requesting the return of a questionnaire from business executives increased the response rate for the total survey by 5.6 percent.

174.   Greeley, Andrew; Pinto, Leonard; and Sudman, Sey-
        mour. "Effectiveness of self-administered question-
        naires." *Journal of Marketing Research*, August 1965, 2
        (3), 293–297.
             This article describes the costs, cooperation
             rates, and responses for both the self-adminis-
             tered questionnaire and the personal interview
             based upon an experiment by the National Opin-
             ion Research Center. A comparison of the two
             methods does not reveal large differences, sug-
             gesting that it may be generally possible to com-
             bine answers from personal and self-administered
             forms.

175.   Green, Paul E., and Rao, Vithala R. "Rating scales
        and information recovery—how many scales and re-
        sponse categories to use?" *Journal of Marketing*, July
        1970, 34 (3), 33–39.
             The authors demonstrate the desirability of using
             six-point response scales.

176.   Greenburg, Allen, and Manfield, Manuel. "On the
        reliability of mailed questionnaires in product tests."
        Journal of Marketing, January 1957, 21(3), 342–345.
             This study of opinions toward a certain lipstick
             used both a mail questionnaire and subsequent
             interviews asking the same questions. Com-
             parison of the questionnaire and interview data
             show very similar results indicating, for this
             study, that the questionnaire was reliable.

177.   Groves, Robert M. "On the mode of administering a
        questionnaire and responses to open-end items." *Social
        Science Research*, September 1978, 7 (3), 257–271.
             Telephone interviews tend to produce short an-
             swers to open-ended items, especially by younger,

affluent respondents. These respondents tend to provide detailed responses in personal interviews.

178. Groves, Robert. "An empirical comparison of two telephone sample designs." *Journal of Marketing Research,* November 1978, 15, 622–631.
This study found that from 35 to 80 percent of random digit dialed numbers are not working household numbers.

179. Groves, Robert M. "Actors and questions in telephone and personal interview surveys." *Public Opinion Quarterly,* Summer 1979, 43 (2), 190–205.
Achieved response rates demonstrated lower cooperation on the telephone than in person. Few telephone respondents preferred the telephone as a means of answering questions, but the vast majority of personal interview respondents preferred face-to-face interviews. There was greater uneasiness about discussing sensitive topics on the telephone, more refusals to answer questions about financial status, and more inquiries about how much longer the interview would last.

180. Groves, Robert M. *Surveys by Telephone: A National Comparison with Personal Interviews.* New York: Academic Press, 1979. 358p.
This book presents data from a study that shows the general comparability of telephone surveys to personal interviewing as a method of collecting survey data.

181. Groves, Robert M., and Magilavy, Lou J. "Increasing response rates to telephone surveys: a door in the face or a foot in-the-door?" *Public Opinion Quarterly,* Fall 1981, 45 (3), 346–358.

Those respondents who granted the first request (answers to a two-question interview schedule) did grant a longer interview without need for persuasion more often than those who did not receive any initial request.

182.   Gullahorn, John, and Gullahorn, Jeanne. "Increasing returns from nonrespondents." *Public Opinion Quarterly*, Spring 1959, 23 (1), 119–121.

Former Fulbright and Smith-Mundt grantees who received a special delivery questionnaire follow-up responded at a significantly higher rate than grantees who received the follow-up via regular mail.

183.   Gullahorn, Jeanne, and Gullahorn, John. "An investigation of the effects of three factors on response to mail questionnaires." *Public Opinion Quarterly*, Summer 1963, 27 (2), 294–296.

These authors found, in this study of former Fulbright and Smith-Mundt grantees, that questionnaires sent by first-class mail were completed and returned at a higher rate than questionnaires sent by third-class mail. Similarly, the use of a postage stamp on return envelopes was more effective in eliciting returns than business reply envelopes. The use of different colored questionnaires was not found to have a significant effect on response rate.

184.   Gunn, Walter J., and Rhodes, Isabelle N. "Physician response rates to a telephone survey: effects of monetary incentive level." *Public Opinion Quarterly*, Spring 1981, 45 (1), 109–115.

Increases in monetary incentive level are effective in increasing the response rate to a 25-minute telephone interview among private practice physicians.

185. Hack, Schuyler W., and Gleason, Edwin M. "Using monetary inducements to increase response rates to mailed surveys: a replication and extension of previous research." *Journal of Applied Psychology*, April 1974, 59 (2), 222–225.

Previous research has shown that response rates to mailed questionnaires could be significantly increased by including a monetary incentive of 25¢. Using a sample of college students, the present study (15 years later) indicates that 25¢ is still an effective incentive. The authors recommend using this incentive only with those individuals who do not respond to the initial mailout.

186. Hackler, James C., and Bourgette, Patricia. "Dollars, dissonance, and survey returns." *Public Opinion Quarterly*, Summer 1973, 37 (2), 276–281.

When two subsamples were compared eight days after distribution of a questionnaire, 71 percent of the group which had received a dollar incentive had returned questionnaires, compared with 39 percent of the group who received no incentive.

187. Hammond, E. C. "Inhalation in relation to type and amount of smoking." *Journal of the American Statistical Association*, 1959, 54 (285), 35–51.

In this survey to obtain information on smoking habits, the author found that mentioning different topics in different cover letters had an effect on response rate. The use of postage stamps on return envelopes stimulated higher response rates than did the use of business reply envelopes not requiring a stamp.

188.   Hansen, Robert A. "A self-perception interpretation
        of the effect of monetary and nonmonetary incentives
        on mail survey respondent behavior." *Journal of Mar-
        keting Research*, February 1980, 17 (1), 77–83.
            The results of this study support the hypothesis
        that when incentives are used the level of com-
        pliance, as measured by response quality, is re-
        duced. However, monetary rather than nonmone-
        tary incentives yield a significantly higher
        response rate and faster response.

189.   Hansen, Robert A., and Robinson, Larry M. "Testing
        the effectiveness of alternative foot-in-the-door manip-
        ulations." *Journal of Marketing Reserch*, August 1980,
        17 (3), 359–364.
            High and low involvement "foot-in-the-door" ma-
        nipulations generate significantly higher response
        rates and faster response times than a noncontact
        control situation. In addition, short-form ques-
        tionnaires generate a higher return rate. High
        involvement "foot" treatments generate higher
        response rates than low involvement "foot"
        treatments.

190.   Hanson, Robert H., and Marks, Eli S. "Influence of
        the interviewer on the accuracy of survey results."
        Journal of the American Statistical Association, Sep-
        tember 1958, 53 (282), 635–655.
            Important factors in interviewer influence on the
        accuracy of survey results include: a tendency to
        omit or alter a question, complexity in the con-
        cept or wording of an inquiry, and the degree to
        which probing tends to alter initial respondent
        replies.

191.   Harris, James R., and Guffey, Hugh J., Jr. "Question-
        naire returns: stamps versus business reply envelopes

revisited." *Journal of Marketing Research*, May 1978, 15 (2), 290–293.

The use of stamps produces a significantly higher response rate in comparison to the use of business reply permits, but the differential between the two options appears to be diminishing. Because of increases in the cost associated with postal permits, stamps tend to be more cost effective than permits except for large mailings with relatively low expected return rates.

192.   Hartley, James; Davies, Lindsey, and Burnhill, Peter. "Alternatives in the typographic design of questionnaires," *Journal of Occupational Psychology*, December 1977, 50 (4), 299–304.

Four questionnaire layouts are examined to determine which were quickest to type, cheapest to produce, easiest to fill in, and easiest to code. Different layouts appear to serve different purposes, but one layout appears to be best when all evaluation factors are considered.

193.   Hartmann, Elizabeth L.; Isaacson, H. Lawrence; and Jurgell, Cynthia M. "Public reaction to public opinion surveying." *Public Opinion Quarterly*, Summer 1968, 32 (2), 295–298.

Most people who have been interviewed do not feel that they have been asked objectionable questions or that their privacy has been invaded.

194.   Hatchett, Shirley, and Schuman, Howard. "White respondents and race-of-interviewer effects." *Public Opinion Quarterly*, Winter 1975–76, 39 (4), 523–528.

White respondents are at least as susceptible to race-of-interviewer effects as black respondents. For blacks, the least educated seem to be the most vulnerable. For whites, the most educated seem most vulnerable.

195.   Hauck, Matthew. "Is survey postcard verification effective?" *Public Opinion Quarterly*, Spring 1969, 33 (1), 116–120.

Based upon this experiment, it is suggested that the postcard method of interview verification should not be used as a primary form of quality control on surveys.

196.   Hauck, Matthew, and Cox, Michael. "Locating a sample by random digit dialing." *Public Opinion Quarterly*, Summer 1974, 38, 253–260.

This article describes a study in which random digit dialing was used as a technique to locate a special population via household screening questions.

197.   Hawkins, Del I. "The impact of sponsor identification and direct disclosure of respondents rights on the quantity and quality of mail survey data." *The Journal of Business*, October 1979, 52 (4), 577–590.

The identification of a department store as the sponsor of a survey reduced the response rate significantly from that obtained from a research firm or university sponsor. In addition, a definite statement of the respondent's right to refuse to participate has a significant negative impact on the response rate when the department store is identified as the sponsor. Neither treatment appears to have a major effect on the nature of the obtained responses.

198.   Hawkins, Del I., and Coney, Kenneth A. "Uninformed response error in survey research." *Journal of Marketing Research*, August 1981, 18 (3), 370–374.

Uninformed response error refers to the tendency

on the part of respondents to express an opinion about issues of which they have no knowledge. The presence of a "don't know" option appears to reduce uninformed responses without reducing the response rate for the questionnaire itself or the response to questions about which the respondents have information.

199. Heaton, Eugene E., Jr. "Increasing mail questionnaire returns with a preliminary letter." *Journal of Advertising Research,* December 1965, 5 (4), 36–39.
This study of automobile purchasers found that the use of pre-letters significantly increased the response rate of a mail questionnaire. Results presented are based on returns received within two weeks of the questionnaire mailings.

200. Heberlein, Thomas A., and Baumgartner, R. "Factors affecting response rates to mailed questionnaires: a quantitative analysis of the published literature." *American Sociological Review,* August 1978, 43 (4), 447–462.
A study of 98 mailed questionnaire response rate experiments revealed that number of contacts and the judged salience to the respondent were found to explain slightly over half of the variance in the final response. Government organization sponsorship, the type of population, the length of the questionnaire, questions concerning other individuals, the use of a special class of mail or telephone on the third contact, and the use of metered or franked mail on the outer envelope affected final response independent of contacts and salience.

201. Heberlein, Thomas A., and Baumgartner, Robert. "Is a questionnaire necessary in a second mailing?" *Public Opinion Quarterly,* Spring 1981, 45 (1), 102–108.

The authors conclude that, in general, adding a questionnaire in a second mailing has little influence on the overall response to a mailed questionnaire study.

202.   Heller, Frank A. "Group feedback analysis: A method of field research." *Psychological Bulletin,* August 1969, 72 (2), 108–117.
        Heller describes a research method that is an alternative to questionnaire use. He calls this three-stage method "group feedback analysis."

203.   Hendrick, Clyde; Borden, Richard; Giesen, Martin; Murray, Edward J.; and Seyfried, B. A. "Effectiveness of ingratiation tactics in a cover letter on mail questionnaire response." *Psychonomic Science,* March 25, 1972, 26 (6), 349–351.
        There were no differences in return rate due to ingratiation tactics (adjectives in cover letter flattering the respondent vs. no adjectives; adjectives in cover letter flattering the solicitor vs. no adjectives) for a one-page questionnaire. For a seven-page questionnaire, return rates were lower when either both tactics (double ingratiation) or neither (standard polite letter) were used.

204.   Henley, James R., Jr. "Response rate to mail questionnaires with a return deadline." *Public Opinion Quarterly,* Fall 1976, 40 (3), 374–375.
        A higher response rate resulted from including a deadline. After the deadline, there was a tendency toward convergence in response rates as control group returns continued while experimental returns virtually ceased.

205.   Hensley, Wayne E. "Increasing response rate by choice of postage stamps." *Public Opinion Quarterly,* Summer 1974, 38 (2), 280–284.

Dissimilar stamps on the outer and inner envelopes are more effective in eliciting responses
than are the same stamps. The pairing of a commemorative stamp and meter postage, in either
combination on the inner and outer envelope, is
superior to all other pairings.

206.   Henson, Ramon; Cannell, Charles F.; and Lawson,
         Sally. "Effects of interviewer style on quality of re-
         porting in a survey interview." *Journal of Psychology,*
         July 1976, 13 (2), 221–227.
         "Professional" and "interpersonal" (rapport) in-
         terview styles are compared. In spite of re-
         spondents' more favorable attitudes towards the
         interpersonal interviews, accuracy was not signif-
         icantly greater in these rapport interviews. Re-
         spondents, however, reported more completely
         under rapport conditions.

207.   Herman, Jeanne Brett. "Mixed-mode data collection:
         telephone and personal interviewing." *Journal of Ap-
         plied Psychology,* August 1977, 62 (4), 399–404.
         A mixed-mode telephone interview/personal in-
         terview method of data collection was examined
         in a study of voting. The strategy involved inter-
         viewing in person those individuals who could not
         be contacted by telephone or who refused to par-
         ticipate in a telephone interview. The response
         rate for the mixed-mode was 92 percent. Quality
         of data collected by the two modes was similar.
         The cost was less than if all interviews had been
         personal. Respondents interviewed by telephone
         were more likely than those interviewed in person
         to disclose their vote.

208.   Herriot, Roger A. "Collecting income data on sample
         surveys: evidence from split-panel studies." *Journal of
         Marketing Research,* August 1977, 14 (3), 322–329.

Different census questionnaire formats administered to large samples (60,000 and 19,700) yielded very similar estimates of personal income.

209.   Herzog, A. Regula, and Bachman, Jerald G. "Effects of questionnaire length on response quality." *Public Opinion Quarterly*, Winter 1981, 45 (4), 549–559.

Respondents answering items included in large sets toward the later parts of a long questionnaire were more likely to give identical answers to most or all of the items, compared with those responding to items in smaller sets or in shorter questionnaires.

210.   Herzog, A. Regula; Rodgers, Willard L.; and Kulka, Richard A. "Interviewing older adults: a comparison of telephone and face-to-face modalities." *Public Opinion Quarterly*, Fall 1983, 47 (3), 405–418.

Telephone surveys tend to underrepresent older persons, and older persons who do participate in a telephone survey are disproportionately well educated. Implications of the lower response rate among older persons are softened by the fact that response distributions across a range of questions show little difference by interview mode between older persons and persons of other age groups.

211.   Hesseldenz, Jon S., and Smith, Barbara G. "Computer prepared questionnaires and grouping theories: considerations for mail surveys in academic settings." *Research in Higher Education*, 1977, 6 (1), 85–94.

Possible respondents in a survey of doctoral graduates were sent either computer-prepared or offset-printed questionnaires, personalized and identical in content. No difference was found in the overall response rates to the two types of instruments. But when the responses were categorized by the academic major of each recipient according to the theories of Halland and Biglan, differential response rates appeared. Interactions of questionnaire type and grouping category were also evident.

212. Hinrichs, John, and Gatewood, Robert. "Differences in opinion-survey response patterns as a function of different methods of survey administration." *Journal of Applied Psychology,* December 1967, 51 (6), 497–502.
The location where respondents completed a questionnaire was found to influence the responses given in this study of male technical employees in a large organization. More favorable responses were given to opinion questions dealing with the "company in general" when respondents completed the questionnaire at their place of work under supervision than when they completed it in a non-office location.

213. Hinrichs, J. R. "Effects of sampling, follow-up letters, and commitment to participation on mail attitude survey response." *Journal of Applied Psychology,* April 1975, 60 (2), 249–251.
Three studies examined differences in response rates to mail surveys. One study suggested that higher response rates may be due to the feeling of the individual that he/she was singled out and had a special role in a study. In the second study, a follow-up letter increased response rates significantly. In the third study a postcard request to indicate intentions to complete the survey was sent with a questionnaire to half of the respondents. This half had a higher response rate than the non-postcard group.

214. Hochstim, Joseph R. "A critical comparison of three strategies of collecting data from households." *Journal*

of the American Statistical Assocation, September 1967, 62 (319), 976–989.

Returns and findings from three strategies of data collection are compared. Each strategy contains personal interviews, telephone interviews, and mail questionnaires in different combinations— one mainly personal, one mainly telephone, and one mainly mail. The responses from the three strategies were found to be highly comparable. The only important difference was cost per interview, with personal interviewing being the most costly method.

215.   Hochstim, Joseph, and Athanasopoulos, Demetrios. "Personal follow-up in a mail survey: Its contribution and its cost." *Public Opinion Quarterly,* Spring 1970, 34 (1), 69–81.

This study attempts to assess the effect of nonrespondent bias. The authors recommend a combination of mail inquiries, telephone calls, and household visits as a possible way to help overcome nonresponse bias.

216.   Hodgkinson, Harold L., and Edelstein, Stewart. "Questionnaires: In fact there is error." *Educational Researcher,* August 1972, 1 (8), 9–10.

The authors of this article "were able to investigate the internal consistency between two questionnaires dealing with exactly the same information coming from the same institution, responded to by two different people." They found that responses to their questions asking for factual responses varied depending on which administrator completed the questionnaire.

217.   Holdaway, Edward. "Different response categories and questionnaire response patterns." *Journal of Experimental Education,* Winter 1971, 40 (2), 57–60.

The results of this study of undergraduate students reveal differences in response patterns when there were differences in the naming and placement of response categories. Different results were obtained depending on whether "undecided" was placed at the midpoint of an agreement-disagreement scale, or separated from that scale. Naming of the midpoint as "undecided" or "neutral" also produced different response patterns.

218.   Honomichl, Jack. "CRT interview systems spring into action." *Advertising Age,* July 16, 1979, 28–30.
Experience of various companies (AT&T, Chilton) with the use of CRT (cathode ray tube) systems for survey research is presented.

219.   Honomichl, Jack. "No end to growth of CATI systems." *Advertising Age,* April 13, 1981, 86–88.
CATI (Computer Assisted Telephone Interviewing) systems in various installations throughout the U.S. are described.

220.   Hornik, Jacob. "Time cue and time perception effect on response to mail surveys." *Journal of Marketing Research,* May 1981, 18 (2), 243–248.
Perceived short completion time stimulates a heavier, more immediate response but does not produce noticeable changes in response quality and bias. It is more advantageous to use a short cue rather than a no time cue approach because without a time cue the questionnaire completion time is perceived to be much longer.

221.   Hornik, Jacob. "Impact of pre-call request form and gender interaction on response to a mail survey." *Journal of Marketing Research,* February 1982, 19 (1), 144–151.
Various grammatical forms (earnestly ask for gen-

erous help, "please, won't you," etc.) have neither consistent nor large effects on the quality of
response. The ingratiation appeal and the polite
imperative forms were the most effective in gen-
erating responses, particularly when used by
females who made the pre-call. These forms produced the highest response rate and response
speed.

222.   Horowitz, Joseph L., and Sedlacek, William E. "Initial returns on mail questionnaires: a literature review
and research note." *Research in Higher Education*,
1974, 2 (4), 361–367.
Differences in method of reproduction (typed,
photocopied, mimeographed), status of researcher
(professor, graduate student), and personalization
of signature (hand signed in ink, mimeographed
facsimile) did not significantly influence the initial rate of return of mail questionnaires among a
group of college professors. It is concluded that
the initial return rate will not be significantly
affected by using the most efficient, least expensive method available.

223.   House, James S.; Gerber, Wayne; and McMichael,
Anthony J. "Increasing mail questionnaire response: a
controlled replication and extension." *Public Opinion
Quarterly*, Spring 1977, 41 (1), 95–99.
Certified mail follow-up procedures produce substantially higher response rates than first-class
mail among both closed and general populations.
The improvement in response is less expensive
per returned questionnaire.

224.   Houston, Michael J., and Jefferson, Robert W. "The
negative effects of personalization on response patterns in mail surveys." *Journal of Marketing Research*,
February 1975, 12 (1), 114–117.

A personalized approach to a mail survey had a
negative effect on the response pattern of subjects
who felt they may be subsequently contacted by a
sales agent.

225.   Houston, Michael J., and Jefferson, Robert W. "On
the personalization-anonymity relationship in mail
surveys—reply." *Journal of Marketing Research*, February 1976, 13 (1), 112–113.
As the level of personal attention conveyed to a
respondent in a mail survey increases, the loss of
anonymity becomes more salient to the respondent who is sensitive to individual attention. It is
this loss of anonymity associated with personalization rather than the loss of confidentiality
that may cause response rates to decline.

226.   Houston, Michael J., and Ford, Neil M. "Broadening
the scope of methodological research on mail surveys."
Journal of Marketing Research, November 1976, 13 (4),
397–403.
Response speed and quality have been neglected
in methodological studies on mail surveys. This
report includes a discussion of these factors and a
review of the findings of studies that have included them as dependent variables. With respect
to response speed, the most promising device
seems to be prior notification by telephone of a
forthcoming questionnaire.

227.   Houston, Michael J., and Nevin, John R. "The effects
of source and appeal on mail survey response patterns." *Journal of Marketing Research*, August 1977, 14
(3), 374–378.
A mail survey involving 2,000 households assessed the effect of various cover-letter "appeals"
on response rate, speed, and completeness. It was
concluded that the sponsor of a survey (univer-

sity, commercial firm, etc.) determines the most
effective "appeal" strategy.

228.   Hoyt, John S., Jr. "Do quantifying adjectives mean
        the same thing to all people?" Minneapolis: University
        of Minnesota, Agricultural Extension Service, 1972.
        12p.
        A questionnaire was sent to 2,900 people request-
        ing opinions regarding the meaning of some com-
        monly used quantifying adjectives. Results
        showed that the numerical meaning of some of
        the adjectives varied considerably among respon-
        dents.

229.   Hubbard, Frank. "Questionnaires." *Review of Educa-
        tional Research,* December 1939, 9 (5), 502–509.
        Some past studies dating from before 1939 that
        deal with reliability and validity are discussed in
        this article. Also discussed are tactics which peo-
        ple have used to increase response rates in their
        studies.

230.   Hubbard, Frank. "Questionnaires, interviews, per-
        sonality schedules." *Review of Educational Research,*
        December 1942, 12 (5), 534–541.
        The author reviews some articles prior to 1942
        that deal with questionnaires, interviews, and
        personality schedules. The brief discussion of
        questionnaires includes question wording and
        pre-testing, sampling, follow-ups, reliability, and
        special uses of questionnaires.

231.   Huffman, Harry. "Improving the questionnaire as a
        tool of research." *The National Business Education
        Quarterly,* October 1948, 17 (1), 15–18 & 55–61.
        Huffman discusses some of the frequently cited
        limitations to which studies using questionnaires

can be susceptible. He also presents some general suggestions for developing a questionnaire.

232. Hunt, Shelby D.; Sparkinan, Richard D., Jr.; and Wilcox, James B. "The pretest in survey research: issues and preliminary findings." *Journal of Marketing Research*, May 1982, 19 (2), 269–273.

Respondent verbalizations in pretesting are not uniformly effective in identifying all types of faulty survey questions.

233. Huxley, Stephen J. "Predicting response speed in mail surveys." *Journal of Marketing Research*, February 1980, 17 (1), 63–68.

The pattern of relatively rapid returns in the early stages followed by a gradual tapering off is described by a simple mathematical function. This article indicates how the parameters of this function can be estimated and how it can be used to predict response speed, forecast the time needed to achieve a desired number of responses or estimate the number of questionnaires that ought to be mailed out initially.

234. Jacoby, Jacob, and Matell, Michael S. "Three-point Likert scales are good enough." *Journal of Marketing Research*, November 1971, 8 (4), 495–500.

The authors conclude that both reliability and validity are independent of the number of scale points used for Likert-type items.

235. Jahoda, Marie; Deutsch, Morton; and Cook, Stuart W. *Research Methods in Social Relations*. Published for the Society for the Psychological Study of Social Issues; New York: Holt, Rinehart and Winston, March 1962. 622p.

This general research text contains useful discussions of sampling techniques and some issues specifically related to questionnaires.

236.   Johnson, Weldon T., and Delamater, John D. "Response effects in sex surveys." *Public Opinion Quarterly,* Summer 1976, 40 (2), 165–181.
        Respondent refusals and invalid reporting is neither more nor less problematic in sex research than surveys on other topics. Respondent reports of sexual matters are not systematically related to interviewer characteristics, such as gender, sexual experiences, or technical competence.

237.   Jolson, Marvin A. "How to double or triple mail-survey response rates." *Journal of Marketing,* October 1977, 41 (4), 78–81.
        The use of a well-administered initial phone contact in advance of a mail survey may offer the potential for doubling or tripling return rates. The effectiveness of the method is highly dependent on the design of the phone message and the skills of the personnel who deliver it.

238.   Jones, Wesley H., and Linda, Gerald. "Multiple criteria effects in a mail survey experiment." *Journal of Marketing Research,* May 1978, 15 (2), 280–284.
        This study investigated the effect of cover-letter message, survey sponsorship and type of return postage on response rate, quality of response, and response bias.

239.   Jones, Wesley H. "Generalizing mail survey inducement methods: population interactions with anonymity and sponsorship." *Public Opinion Quarterly,* Spring 1979, 43 (1), 102–111.

The results of this mail response experiment show the presence of significant interactive effects between population characteristics and manipulations of sponsorship and anonymity assurance. Assurance of anonymity appears to have a more positive effect on response rates in higher income, more highly educated populations. In populations experiencing higher rates of membership change, assurance of anonymity was found to depress response rates substantially.

240.   Jones, Wesley H., and Lang, James R. "Sample composition bias and response bias in a mail survey: a comparison of inducement methods." *Journal of Marketing Research,* February 1980, 17 (1), 69–76.
        Inducement techniques (sponsorship, cover letter message, notification method, and questionnaire format) that increase mail questionnaire response rates do not necessarily improve the precision of survey results.

241.   Jordan, Lawrence A.; Marcus, Alfred C.; and Reeder, Leo G. "Response styles in telephone and household interviewing: a field experiment." *Public Opinion Quarterly,* Summer 1980, 44 (2), 210–222.
        Two independent groups were sampled and interviewed in this study, one by a form of random digit dialing and interviewed by telephone and the other on an area probability basis and interviewed face-to-face. Few sociodemographic differences were found between the telephone and household samples. However, the telephone sample had more missing data for family income, more acquiescence, evasiveness, extremeness of response bias on attitude questions, and more responses to checklists.

242.   Kahle, Lynn R., and Sales, Bruce Dennis. "Person-
        alization of the outside envelope in mail surveys." *Pub-
        lic Opinion Quarterly*, Winter 1978, 42 (4), 547–550.
        The results of two experiments imply that indi-
        vidually addressing envelopes is an important fac-
        tor in personalization but that postage expense is
        not.

243.   Kalton, Graham; Collins, Martin; and Brook, Lindsay.
        "Experiments in wording opinion questions." *Applied
        Statistics*, 1978, 27 (2), 149–161.
        Experiments are reported which assess the ef-
        fects of offering different response options and
        the effects of response order and context. It is
        demonstrated that the association between the
        answers to questionnaire items may well be sub-
        ject to question effects.

244.   Kanuk, Leslie, and Berenson, Conrad. "Mail surveys
        and response rates: a literature review." *Journal of
        Marketing Research*, November 1975, 12 (4), 440–453.
        Widely accepted techniques to increase response
        rates to mail questionnaires are based on limited
        evidence. The only techniques which seem to be
        consistently effective in increasing response rates
        are follow-up letters and monetary incentives en-
        closed with the mail questionnaires.

245.   Kassarjian, Harold H., and Nakanishi, Masao. "A
        study of selected opinion measurement techniques."
        Journal of Marketing Research, May 1967, 4, 148–153.
        Various methods used in marketing research for
        measuring attitudes, opinions, preferences, or be-
        liefs were compared (Likert rating, open-choice
        preference, open-choice objection, equal weight,
        weighted ranks, single choice, order-of-merit,

paired comparison). Most of the methods produce nearly identical results.

246. Kawash, Mary B., and Aleamoni, Lawrence M. "Effect of personal signature on the initial rate of return of a mailed questionnaire." *Journal of Applied Psychology,* December 1971, 55 (6), 589–592.

In a study of University of Illinois faculty, a personal signature on the cover letter accompanying a questionnaire concerning audiovisual materials was no greater an inducement to respond than a cover letter bearing a mimeographed facsimile.

247. Keane, John G. "Low cost, high return mail surveys." *Journal of Advertising Research,* September 1963, 3 (3), 28–30.

Keane reports that postcard follow-ups are an effective yet inexpensive means of increasing questionnaire returns.

248. Kegeles, S. Stephen; Fink, Clinton F.; and Kirscht, John P. "Interviewing a national sample by long-distance telephone." *Public Opinion Quarterly,* Fall 1969, 33 (3), 412–419.

Response rates and information validity are as high when obtained from a telephone interview as from a face-to-face interview. The costs of telephone interviews are substantially lower.

249. Kephart, William, and Bressler, Marvin. "Increasing the responses to mail questionnaires: A research study." *Public Opinion Quarterly,* Summer 1958, 22 (2), 123–132.

The use of special delivery mail was found effective in this study as a response-rate stimulator. The effect of cash inducement was also tested

and the inclusion of a quarter with the questionnaire increased response rates; a similar effect
was not observed when pennies, nickels, or dimes
were used.

250.   Kerin, Roger A. "Personalization strategies, response
rate and response quality in a mail survey." *Social
Science Quarterly*, June 1974, 55 (1), 175–181.

One or more personal contacts in the introductory
strategy of a survey tends to produce higher returns, a greater item response to personal questions, and a higher incidence of distorted replies
than impersonal contacts in the introductory
strategy. The nature of the follow-up has no differential impact on response rate and item response to personal questions.

251.   Kerin, Roger A., and Peterson, Robert A. "Personalization, respondent anonymity, and response distortion in mail surveys." *Journal of Applied Psychology*,
February 1977, 62 (1), 86–89.

A comparison of mail-survey and credit-
application responses revealed that distortion in
reporting family income and occupation of wife
was related to the use of personalized cover
letters.

252.   Kernan, Jerome B. "Are 'bulk-rate' occupants really
unresponsive?" *Public Opinion Quarterly*, Fall 1971, 35
(3), 420–422.

In this study neither personalized addressing nor
first-class postage significantly affected response
rates to a mail questionnaire.

253.   Kimball, Andrew E. "Increasing the rate of return in
mail surveys." *Journal of Marketing*, October 1961, 25
(6), 63–64.

The desirability of using simple, inexpensive incentives, such as air-mail stamps and attached coins, in a mail survey is illustrated.

254. Kincaid, Harry V., and Bright, Margaret. "The tandem interview: a trial of the two-interviewer team." *Public Opinion Quarterly*, Summer 1957, 21 (2), 304–312.
The tandem interview involves the use of two interviewers per respondent. The authors outline some of the advantages of the tandem technique, describe some of its potential applications, and discuss problems it is likely to produce.

255. Kincaid, Harry V., and Bright, Margaret. "Interviewing the business elite." *American Journal of Sociology*, November 1957, LXIII (3), 304–311.
Procedural problems associated with interviewing top-ranking business executives are described. Decisive conditions include the sponsorship and affiliation of the researchers, the practical emphasis given to the subject, and the competence of the interviewers.

256. Kish, Leslie. *Survey Sampling*. New York: John Wiley & Sons, 1965. 643p.
This detailed text covers just about all aspects of sampling related to survey research. Issues related to obtaining sample frames and nonresponse bias are discussed, as well as the details of sample design themselves.

257. Klecka, William R., and Tuchfarber, Alfred J. "Random digit dialing: a comparison to personal surveys." *Public Opinion Quarterly*, Spring 1978, 42 (1), 105–114.
The accuracy and efficiency of random digit dial-

ing telephone surveys was compared to a personal interview survey based on a complex probability sample. The results were very similar, indicating that random digit dialing is an accurate and cost-effective alternative to traditional personal interviewing surveys for most research applications.

258.   Klein, Stuart; Maher, John; and Dunnington, Richard. "Differences between identified and anonymous subjects in responding to an industrial opinion survey." *Journal of Applied Psychology*, April 1967, 51 (2), 152–160.

This survey of manufacturing employees found that responses were most distorted when the subjects were placed in "high threat" situations where their identities would be known. Items dealing with salary and ratings of top management produced distorted responses under these conditions.

259.   Knox, John. "Maximizing responses to mail questionnaires: A new technique." *Public Opinion Quarterly*, Summer 1951, 15 (2), 366–367.

In a study of unemployed railroad firemen, a chance to win a prize was offered as an incentive for people to respond. The author cautions that persons who consider using such incentives should check the legality of such procedures with postal authorities.

260.   Knudsen, Dean D.; Pope, Hallowell; and Irish, Donald P. "Response differences to questions on sexual standards: an interview-questionnaire comparison." *Public Opinion Quarterly*, Summer 1967, 31 (2), 290–297.

A larger proportion of respondents who received a

personal interview claimed restrictive norms toward premarital sex relations than did questionnaire respondents.

261.   Komorita, S. S., and Graham, William K. "Number of
scale points and the reliability of scales." *Educational
and Psychological Measurement,* Winter 1965, 25 (4),
987–995.
The results of this study indicate that with a relatively homogeneous set of items the reliability of a
scale is independent of the number of item scale
points. If the items are relatively heterogeneous,
however, the results suggest that the reliability of
the scale can be increased not only by increasing
the number of items but also by increasing the
number of item scale points. Just how heterogeneous the scale must be before one can expect a
reasonable increase in reliability is a matter for
further research.

262.   Koos, Leonard V. *The Questionnaire in Education.* New
York: Macmillan, 1928. 178p.
This small, early book summarizes the uses to
which questionnaires had been put in educational
research prior to 1928.

263.   Kraut, Allen I.; Wolfson, Alan D.; and Rothenberg,
Alan. "Some effects of position on opinion survey
items." *Journal of Applied Psychology,* December 1975,
60 (6), 774–776.
This study tested the effect of putting opinion
survey items in different positions in a questionnaire. Respondents answered with less extreme
responses and were slightly more likely to omit
replies when items were placed later in the questionnaire. The findings suggest that comparisons

of responses to identical items used in different
surveys may be misleading if they appeared in a
different position or context.

264.   Krohn, Marvin; Waldo, Gordon P.; and Chiricos,
         Theodore G. "Self-reported delinquency: a com-
         parison of structured interviews and self-administered
         checklists." *Journal of Criminal Law and Criminology,*
         1975, 65 (3), 545–553.
         There were no significant differences in re-
         sponses between the use of structured interviews
         and self-administered checklists.

265.   Labrecque, David P. "A response rate experiment
         using mail questionnaires." *Journal of Marketing,* Oc-
         tober 1978, 42 (4), 82–83.
         Cover letters with the owner's signature rather
         than letters signed by the service manager (of a
         marina in northern New England) produced a
         higher response rate. Personalization and the use
         of commemorative stamps were not significantly
         related to response rate.

266.   Lamb, Charles W., Jr. and Stem, Donald E., Jr. "An
         empirical validation of the randomized response tech-
         nique." *Journal of Marketing Research,* November
         1978, 15 (4), 616–621.
         A convenience sample of 312 upper-division stu-
         dents was used to examine whether randomized
         response models significantly reduce measure-
         ment error in marketing studies on sensitive is-
         sues. Results show that these models minimize
         measurement error and provide more accurate es-
         timates of sensitive behavior than conventional
         interview techniques.

267.   Landy, Frank I., and Bates, Frederick. "The non-effect of three variables on mail survey response rate. *Journal of Applied Psychology*, August 1973, 58 (1), 147–148.
         Type of postage, degree of personalization, and nonmonetary inducement were varied in an attempt to modify return rates for a mail survey. None of these nor their interactions had any effect on rate of return.

268.   Lansdowne, Jerry. "The mailed questionnaire in panel research: Some empirical observations." *Social Forces*, September 1970, 49 (1), 136–140.
         Of particular interest in this study were the findings that 30 percent of nonrespondents had not even received a questionnaire because they had moved or were deceased and that nearly half of the nonrespondents based their decision not to respond on the political nature of certain questions.

269.   Lansing, John B., and Eapen, A. T. "Dealing with missing information in surveys." *Journal of Marketing*, October 1959, 24 (2), 21–27.
         Techniques that can be employed to deal with various types of missing information (refusals, not-at-homes, missed dwellings, incomplete interviews) are explained.

270.   Laurent, Andre. "Effects of question length on reporting behavior in the survey interview." *Journal of the American Statistical Association*, June 1972, 67 (338), 298–305.
         Longer questions were found to elicit more information than shorter ones. The data from the longer questions were also more accurate.

271.   Lawson, Faith. "Varying group responses to postal
         questionnaires." *Public Opinion Quarterly*, Spring
         1949, 13 (1), 114–116.
         In a British survey on gambling, response rates
         varied for people in different occupations. Psy-
         chologists had a higher response rate than other
         groups. The author suggests that people who feel
         strongly about the subject of the questionnaire
         are more likely to respond.

272.   Layne, Ben H., and Thompson, Dennis N. "Ques-
         tionnaire page length and return rate." *Journal of So-
         cial Psychology*, April 1981, 113 (2), 291–292.
         Four hundred graduate students completed a one-
         or three-page questionnaire consisting of 30
         items, all of which required a Likert-type re-
         sponse. Results indicate that neither question-
         naire page length nor a follow-up letter related to
         response rate.

273.   Lehmann, Donald R., and Hulbert, James. "Are three-
         point scales always good enough?" *Journal of Marketing
         Research*, November 1972, 9 (4), 444–446.
         It is suggested in this study that if the goal of
         research is to focus on group or average behavior,
         two or three scale points are enough. If the focus
         is on individual behavior, five- to seven-point
         scales should be used.

274.   Leslie, Larry. "Increasing response rates to long ques-
         tionnaires." *The Journal of Educational Research*, April
         1970, 63 (8), 347–350.
         The author is concerned with techniques for
         achieving high response rates, particularly in
         studies using questionnaires of extreme length.
         Among the techniques discussed are printing,
         study sponsorship, use of telephone follow-ups,

and limitation of questions to those essential to the study.

275. Levine, Sol and Gordon, Gerald. "Maximizing returns on mail questionnaires." *Public Opinion Quarterly,* Winter 1958–1959, 22 (4), 568–575.

In this study, which obtained a 100 percent return, techniques used to stimulate response rate included pre-letters, careful questionnaire design, careful question construction, and pretesting.

276. Lindsay, E. E. "Questionnaires and follow-up letters." *Pedagogical Seminary,* September 1921, 28 (3), 303–307.

One of the earlier studies investigating response rates and follow-up letters is reported in this article.

277. Linsky, A. S. "A factorial experiment in inducing responses to a mail questionnaire." *Sociology and Social Research,* 1965, 49 (2), 183–189.

All combinations of four factors were examined for their effect on survey response rates: 1) personalization of the cover letter; 2) an argument in the cover letter stressing the importance of the research; 3) an explanation of the place and importance of the respondent in the study; and 4) an appeal to help those conducting the study. Personalization and the place and importance of the respondent were the only two factors to have a significant effect on response rate.

278. Linsky, Arnold S. "Stimulating responses to mailed questionnaires: a review." *Public Opinion Quarterly,* Spring 1975, 39 (1), 82–101.

Pre-contact, postcard enclosure, follow-up, type

of envelope, length of questionnaire, printed vs. mimeographed questionnaire, precoded vs. open-ended questionnaire, color of questionnaire, anonymity, cover letters, argument for social utility, appeals to help, sponsoring organizations and titles, use of deadlines, cash rewards, size of rewards, meaning of rewards, noncash rewards are factors that affect response rates. The importance of these factors is examined based on a review of the literature.

279.   Locander, William B., and Burton, John P. "The effect of question forms on gathering income data by telephone." *Journal of Marketing Research*, May 1976, 13 (2), 189–192.
        Questions regarding income using the "less than" or "split point" format produced median income figures which compared more favorably with an adjusted census median income figure in comparison to a "more than" format.

280.   Locander, William; Sudman, Seymour; and Bradburn, Norman. "An investigation of interview method, threat and response distortion." *Journal of the American Statistical Association*, June 1976, 71 (354), 269–275.
        Response distortion is shown to increase sharply as the "threat" inherent in a question increases. Not one of the four interviewing techniques described (face-to-face, random response, telephone, self-administered) was clearly superior for all types of threatening questions.

281.   Longworth, Donald S. "Use of a mail questionnaire." *American Sociological Review*, June 1953, 18 (3), 310–313.
        Longworth describes a procedure that used six pre-tests to determine a method of questionnaire

distribution which would yield the highest response rate from his subjects.

282. Lovelock, Christopher H.; Stiff, Ronald; Cullwick, David; and Kaufman, Ira M. "An evaluation of the effectiveness of drop-off questionnaire delivery." *Journal of Marketing Research*, November 1976, 13 (4), 358–364.

This report describes and evaluates the effectiveness of an approach in which questionnaires designed for self-administration are delivered and collected personally rather than by mail. For lengthy questionnaires, personal delivery by lightly trained survey takers appears to yield higher response rates than mail surveys at competitive costs. The delivery approach also provides for more precisely controlled samples and clearer identification of the nature of the nonresponse bias.

283. Lundberg, George A. *Social Research*. New York: Greenwood Press, 1942. 380p.

Generally covered in this early text are basic issues relevant to social research.

284. Lyons, William, and Durant, Robert F. "Interviewer costs associated with the use of random digit dialing in large area samples." *Journal of Marketing*, Summer 1980, 44 (3), 65–69.

This study focuses upon the amount of extra interviewer expense incurred by using a random digit dialing as opposed to a directory-based sample selection method in large area residential surveys. A formula is developed for estimating this extra cost given the expected parameters of a future survey.

285.   Macek, Albert J., and Miles, Guy H. "IQ score and
        mailed questionnaire response." *Journal of Applied Psy-
        chology,* April 1975, 60 (2), 258–259.
            Respondents with higher I.Q. scores are easier to
        trace and respond more readily to a mail question-
        naire than respondents with lower I.Q. scores.

286.   MacLachlan, James; Czepiel, John; and La Barbera,
        Priscilla. "Implementation of response latency mea-
        sures." *Journal of Marketing Research,* November 1979,
        16 (4), 573–577.
            Response latency refers to the amount of time a
        respondent deliberates before answering a ques-
        tion. There is an inverse relationship between
        latency and probability that a question is an-
        swered correctly.

287.   Mager, Robert. *Developing Attitude Toward Learning.*
        Palo Alto, Cal.: Fearon Publishers, 1968. 104p.

288.   Magid, Frank N.; Fotion, Nicholas G.; and Gold,
        David. "A mail-questionnaire adjunct to the inter-
        view." *Public Opinion Quarterly,* Spring 1962, 26 (1),
        111–114.
            Appropriate uses of a mail-questionnaire to sup-
        plement an interview are presented. Advantages
        are that mail questionnaires might be shorter and
        that more reliable data might be obtained than in
        the face-to-face situation.

289.   Maloney, Paul W. "Comparability of personal attitude
        scale administration with mail administration with
        and without incentive." *Journal of Applied Psychology,*
        August 1954, 38 (4), 238–239.
            Residential customers of a public utility were ad-
        ministered an attitude scale. Three methods of

administration were used: personal interview, mail with financial incentive, and mail without financial incentive. The methods were found to be reasonably comparable.

290. Mandell, Lewis, and Lundsten, Lorman L. "Some insight into the underreporting of financial data by sample survey respondents." *Journal of Marketing Research,* May 1978, 15 (2), 294–299.

This study demonstrates that the reporting of financial assets can be somewhat improved by asking more detailed questions and also by motivating respondents to search their financial records. The modest gains, however, raise the question of whether these approaches are cost effective.

291. Manfield, Manuel. "A pattern of response to mail surveys." *Public Opinion Quarterly,* Fall 1948, 12 (3), 493–499.

Based on the experience of the Veterans Administration with mail surveys, the author describes when respondents tend to return questionnaires. These findings have been used to establish cut-off dates and in spacing mail follow-ups. He cautions that his findings are based on surveys of specialized groups and may or may not be generalizable to other groups.

292. Martin, David J., and McConnell, Jon P. "Mail questionnaire response induction: The effect of four variables on the response of a random sample to a difficult questionnaire." *Social Science Quarterly,* September 1970, 51 (2), 409–414.

This study tested the effects of four techniques for increasing response rates. Neither personalization of the correspondence nor appealing to the importance of the subject was found effective as a response-rate stimulator. However, the use of commemorative stamps was more effective than business-reply franked envelopes.

293.   Mason, Ward S.; Dressel, Robert J.; and Bain, Robert K. "An experimental study of factors affecting response to a mail survey of beginning teachers." *Public Opinion Quarterly,* Summer 1961, 25 (2), 296–299.
Length of questionnaire and mode of addressing (name and address or code number) generally appeared to be nonrelated to rate of response or various respondent characteristics.

294.   Matteson, Michael T. "Type of transmittal letter and questionnaire color as two variables influencing response rates in a mail survey." *Journal of Applied Psychology,* August 1974, 59 (4), 535–536.
Among members of a national professional organization, a greater number of returns were received from those receiving a semipersonal rather than a form letter. There were no significant differences in rate of return among the groups receiving the semipersonal letter in relationship to the color of the questionnaire. A greater number of colored questionnaires were returned among the groups receiving the form letter.

295.   Mayer, C. S. "The interviewer and his environment." *Journal of Marketing Research,* November 1964, 1 (4), 24–31.
Many environmental factors influence the performance and effectiveness of an interviewer. This article attempts to establish the significance of some of them (e.g., day and time of call, sex of respondent, result obtained on previous call, etc.).

296.   Mayer, Charles, and Pratt, Robert. "A note on non-response in a mail survey." *Public Opinion Quarterly,* Winter 1966–67, 30 (4), 637–646.
        In this survey of persons involved in automobile accidents, the authors separated nonrespondents into two categories: those who refuse to respond and those who never receive a questionnaire. They found that each category produced a "different, and sometimes offsetting bias."

297.   Mayer, Charles S., and Piper, Cindy. "A note on the importance of layout in self-administered questionnaires." *Journal of Marketing Research,* August 1982, 19 (3), 390–391.
        The importance of questionnaire layout for self-administered questionnaires is illustrated by an empirical example.

298.   Mayer, E. N. "Postage stamps do affect results of your mailing." *Printer's Ink,* October 4, 1946, 217 (1), 91.
        Mayer recommends using colored and varied types of postage as ways of increasing response to business mailings. Although Mayer's article is geared to increasing orders from mail advertising campaigns, its relevance to mailing questionnaires and receiving by return mail completed questionnaires is obvious. He suggests that commemorative stamps may increase return mail, but usually only if used immediately after their original issuance.

299.   McCall, Chester H. *Sampling and Statistics Handbook for Research.* Ames: Iowa University Press, 1982.
        This survey text provides the needed statistical information and sampling formulas necessary to conduct and analyze sample surveys. An excellent reference source.

300.   McCrohan, Kevin F., and Lowe, Larry S. "A cost/benefit approach to postage used on mail questionnaires." *Journal of Marketing*, Winter 1981, 45 (1), 130–133.

No significant differences were found in response rates, responses, or demographic characteristics among groups responding to different mail strategies in a mail questionnaire. The authors conclude that the optimal mailing strategy uses third-class postage on the sending envelopes and a business-reply permit on the return envelope.

301.   McDaniel, Stephen W., and Rao, C. P. "The effect of monetary inducement on mailed questionnaire response quality." *Journal of Marketing Research*, May 1980, 17 (2), 265–268.

A monetary inducement of 25¢ was found to decrease item omission and response error significantly. Some support was also shown for improving completeness of answers.

302.   McDonagh, Edward C., and Rosenblum, A. Leon. "A comparison of mailed questionnaires and subsequent structured interviews." *Public Opinion Quarterly*, Spring 1965, 29 (1), 131–136.

This study designed an empirical test of the differences between responses obtained from returned questionnaires and from interviews with a sample of the nonrespondents. For this population, in this study, the responses of those completing questionnaires were not significantly different from those obtained from interviewed respondents.

303.   McFarland, Sam G. "Effects of question order on survey responses." *Public Opinion Quarterly*, Summer 1981, 45 (2), 208–215.

The results of this study demonstrate the importance of question order in survey design. Specific questions which precede general questions on an issue may influence respondents to express greater interest in the general questions.

304.　McGinnis, Michael A., and Hollon, Charles J. "Mail survey response rate and bias: the effect of home versus work address." *Journal of Marketing Research,* August 1977, 14 (3), 383–384.

A 60-item closed questionnaire was mailed to 238 packaging engineers. Response rates did not differ between those who received the questionnaire at work and those who received it at home. It would, therefore, appear that the use of mailing lists that mix work and home addresses does not seem likely to bias mail questionnaire results.

305.　Menezes, Dennis, and Elbert, Norbert F. "Alternative semantic scaling formats for measuring store image: an evaluation." *Journal of Marketing Research,* February 1979, 16 (1), 80–87.

There were no marked differences between the Stapel, Likert, and semantic differential scales in measuring store image.

306.　Messmer, Donald J., and Seymour, Daniel T. "The effects of branching on item nonresponse." *Public Opinion Quarterly,* Summer 1982, 46 (2), 270–277.

Branching instructions significantly increase the rate of item nonresponse for items immediately following the branch.

307.　Mikhailov, Stoyan. "The indirect questionnaire as a tool for sociological research." *Mens en Maatschappy,* November–December 1966, 41, (6), 455–459.

This author advocates using the "indirect questionnaire" as a research tool. In this method, an observer completes a questionnaire after observing the subject or gathering relevant information from other people.

308.   Miller, Peter V., and Cannell, Charles F. "A study of experimental techniques for telephone interviewing." *Public Opinion Quarterly*, Summer 1982, 46 (2), 250–269.
Different combinations of three interviewing techniques (commitment, instructions, and feedback) were studied to determine whether respondent reporting in the telephone interview could be improved. Such techniques did improve reporting but the results were not as strong as expected.

309.   Mitchell, Ann. "A comparison between a written and a doorstep approach in research interviewing." *Sociological Review*, August 1980, 28 (3), 635–639.
The best method of seeking interviews with a divorced population would seem to be a doorstep rather than a written request.

310.   Moore, Clarence C. "Increasing the returns from questionnaires." *Journal of Educational Research*, October 1941, 35 (2), 138–141.
Results from a questionnaire survey of school superintendents indicate that a typewritten letter of transmittal sent with a questionnaire was more effective in getting returns than a duplicated letter.

311.   Mooren, Robert, and Rothney, John. "Sampling problems in follow-up research." *Occupations*, May 1952, 30 (8), 573–578.
A response rate of 100 percent was achieved in this study of high school graduates. Responses

from those who required two, three, or four follow-ups were significantly different from responses of early respondents.

312. Mooren, Robert, and Rothney, John. "Personalizing the follow-up study." *Personnel and Guidance Journal,* March 1956, 34 (7), 409–412.

This study of high school graduates compared the effects on response rate of "personalized" versus mimeographed questionnaires and follow-ups. No significant difference was found between these two approaches.

313. Morrisey, Elizabeth R. "Sources of error in the coding of questionnaire data." *Sociological Methods and Research,* November 1974, 3 (2), 209–232.

The number of errors associated with coding decisions was found to vary directly with the level of complexity of the task.

314. Moser, C. A., and Kalton, G. *Survey Methods in Social Investigation.* London: Heinemann Educational Books Limited, 1971. 549p.

The contents of this text cover many aspects of survey research and design. The chapters on questionnaires are extremely insightful and well-written.

315. Mullner, Ross M.; Levy, Paul S.; Byre, Calvin S.; and Matthews, Dale. "Effects of characteristics of the survey instrument on response rates to a mail survey of community hospitals." *Public Health Reports,* September–October 1982, 97 (5), 465–469.

Four characteristics of a survey instrument were varied to investigate their effect on response rates of community hospitals to a survey conducted by the American Hospital Association: a) the perceived length of the questionnaire; b) the order of the questions; c) the orientation of the appeal made in the cover letter; and d) the presence or absence of a promise to share the results of the study with respondents. The perceived length of the questionnaire and the order of questions were found to have a significant effect on response rates, but the orientation of the cover letter and a promise to share the results of the study with the respondents were found to be insignificant.

316.   Myers, James H., and Haug, Arne F. "How a preliminary letter affects mail survey returns and costs." *Journal of Advertising Research*, September 1969, (3), 37–39.

A preliminary letter increased survey returns but at a higher cost per return than when no preliminary letter was used.

317.   Myers, Vincent. "Toward a synthesis of ethnographic and survey methods." *Human Organization*, Fall 1977, 36 (3), 244–251.

Aspects of conventional and unconventional survey theory and practice are compared in terms of use among young, minority men and women from lower socioeconomic backgrounds.

318.   Narayana, Chem L. "Graphic positioning scale: an economical instrument for surveys." *Journal of Marketing Research*, February 1977, 14 (1), 118–122.

Graphic positioning scales allow the rating of several stimuli (brands) on one scale. In a sample of 60 marketing students, this type of scale saved 43 percent in average response time compared to traditional attitude scales.

319.   Nederhof, Anton J. "Effects of preliminary contacts on volunteering in mail surveys." *Perceptual and Motor Skills*, June 1982, 54 (3), 1333–1334.

Advance telephone and mail contacts did not lead to significantly different response rates. The advance telephone contact, however, did give rise to volunteer bias (the tendency to respond). Females volunteered less often than male subjects. Preliminary mail contacts were not related to volunteer bias. Follow-up contacts are preferable instead of advance telephone calls.

320.   Nederhof, Anton J. "The effects of material incentives in mail surveys: two studies." *Public Opinion Quarterly*, Spring 1983, 47 (1), 103–111.
Using samples of the general public in the Netherlands, two studies examined the effects of including a material nonmonetary incentive in mail surveys. Such incentives produced a higher initial response rate, but follow-ups reduced the effect of the incentives. They appeared to produce no response bias. When methods that produce high response rates are used, the effect of nonmonetary incentives on response rate disappears.

321.   Nemanich, Dorothy. "Is keypunch verification really necessary?" *Public Opinion Quarterly*, Summer 1972, 36 (2), 260–262.
The author of this study comparing verified and nonverified keypunch cards suggests that verification of keypunch data is often not justified because of its cost, particularly when the cards are "cleaned" by the computer.

322.   Neter, John, and Waksberg, Joseph. "Conditioning effects from repeated household interviews." *Journal of Marketing*, April 1964, 28 (2), 51–56.
The effects of repeated interviewing on respondent reports and behavior is examined along a number of different dimensions.

323.   Nevin, John R., and Ford, Neil M. "Effects of a dead-
         line and a veiled threat on mail survey responses."
         Journal of Applied Psychology, February 1976, 61 (1),
         116–118.
         Using a systematic sample of 1,040 students, this
         study found that a) deadline dates did not stimu-
         late a heavier, more immediate response but did
         seem to decrease the rate of returns following the
         deadline data; and b) sending a veiled threat
         follow-up letter greatly increased the response
         rate over the more casual follow-up letter.

324.   Newman, Wheldon. "Differences between early and
         late respondents to a mailed survey." *Journal of Adver-
         tising Research,* June 1962, 2 (2), 37–39.
         This article reports that a dollar premium in-
         cluded with the questionnaire produced higher
         response rates than a 25-cent incentive, which in
         turn was more effective than no incentive.

325.   Nichols, Robert, and Meyers, Mary. "Timing
         postcard follow-ups in mail questionnaire surveys."
         Public Opinion Quarterly, Summer 1966, 30 (2), 306–
         307.
         A postcard follow-up mailed three days after the
         original questionnaire was found to be the single
         most effective follow-up device in this study of
         college students. The highest response rate for
         any group in this study was achieved with a com-
         bination of follow-up reminders.

326.   Nixon, John. "The mechanics of questionnaire con-
         struction." *Journal of Educational Research,* March
         1954, 47 (7), 481–487.
         This excellent article gives a concise outline of
         the fundamentals of questionnaire construction.
         Nixon covers such issues as questionnaire ap-

pearance, kinds of paper and ink, questionnaire instructions, cover letters, mailing, and follow-ups.

327.   Noelle-Newmann, Elizabeth. "Wanted: rules for wording structured questionnaires." *Public Opinion Quarterly,* Summer 1970, 24 (2), 191–201.

The author presents evidence from split-ballot field experiments to show how precodes can influence results, how questionnaire monotony lames respondents' good will, how follow-up questions reduce replies to a first question, how the position of questions in context anchors association, and why alternatives must be expressly stated.

328.   Norman, Ralph. "A review of some problems related to the mail questionnaire technique." *Educational and Psychological Measurement,* 1948, 8 (2), 235–245.

Studies related to the use of questionnaires in research, written prior to 1948, are reviewed in this article. Topics covered include the use of follow-ups, the form of the questionnaire, time of issuance of the questionnaire, length of the questionnaire, and the issue of the representativeness of respondents.

329.   Norton, John. "The questionnaire." *National Education Association Research Bulletin,* 1930, vol. 8, no. 1.

This bulletin prepared by the Research Division of the National Education Association in 1930 comprehensively examines the uses and abuses of questionnaires in education, the advantages and disadvantages of questionnaires, questionnaire study design, and criteria for judging the quality of questionnaires.

330.   Nuckols, R. C. "The validity and comparability of mail and personal interview surveys." *Journal of Marketing Research,* February 1964, 1 (1), 11–16.

The author compares the validity of life insurance ownership data obtained by personal interview with that obtained by mail-panel surveys by checking response against company records. The comparison showed that the response distributions were sufficiently similar for an analysis of either set of data to have led to the same conclusions about the public's reaction to life insurance.

331.   O'Dell, William F. "Personal interviews or mail panels?" *Journal of Marketing,* October 1962, 26 (4), 34–49.

Criteria are presented for making a choice between a mail panel and personal interviewing for the single survey.

332.   Ognibene, Peter. "Traits affecting questionnaire response." *Journal of Advertising Research,* June 1970, 10 (3), 18–20.

Respondents to a mail questionnaire showed stronger leadership traits, were more gregarious, and had more ambitious reading habits than nonrespondents.

333.   Olivia, Peter F. "Survey research: nuisance or help?" *Western Carolina University Journal of Education,* Winter 1976, 7 (3), 14–17.

This article discusses the various weaknesses of survey-type research, especially the questionnaire. The length of the questionnaire, the nature of some of the items, and the wording of the follow-up letter are critiqued. Eleven precautionary measures are suggested for ensuring a higher percentage of returns and more accurate information from the respondents.

334. Olmsted, Donald W. "The accuracy of the impressions of survey interviewers." *Public Opinion Quarterly*, Winter 1962, 26 (4), 635–647.

The main finding of this study is that interviewer impressions of what the overall survey results would be were remarkably similar to the actual results. Whether they formed accurate perceptions during the interviewing or whether the perceptions influenced the results is discussed.

335. Oppenheim, Abraham Naffali. *Questionnaire Design and Attitude Measurement.* New York: Basic Books, 1966. 298p.

A general discussion of survey design, questionnaire design, question wording, and other areas related to survey technique is the basis of this textbook. Considerable attention is given to the measurement of attitudes and the use of various attitude scales.

336. Orr, David, and Neyman, Clinton A., Jr. "Considerations, costs and returns in a large-scale follow-up study." *The Journal of Educational Research,* April 1965, 58 (8), 373–378.

The cost and efficiency of questionnaire followups are the subject of this article based on data from Project Talent.

337. Pace, C. Robert. "Factors influencing questionnaire returns from former university students." *Journal of Applied Psychology,* June 1939, 23 (3), 388–397.

This 1939 study was designed to discover the activities, problems, and attitudes of University of

Minnesota alumni who had been out of school from about 5 to 13 years. For this study, the following factors influenced the promptness of questionnaire return: employment at the professional level, jobs in the same field as university specialization, economic status for men, cultural status for women, job satisfaction, and morale. From this the author makes the often-questioned assumption that "the method of comparing early and late returns . . . does provide a simple and valuable tool for determining the probable direction of response bias."

338.   Parasuraman, A. "More on the prediction of mail survey response rates." *Journal of Marketing Research,* May 1982, 19 (2), 261–268.

The author discusses some omissions in, and limitations of, recent efforts to model mail survey returns over time. Additional data are analyzed to develop a generalized model of response rate over time. Also, a practical approach is proposed for estimating mailing requirements for surveys that have specific time deadlines and response requirements.

339.   Parsons, Robert, and Medford, Thomas. "The effect of advance notice in mail surveys of homogenous groups." *Public Opinion Quarterly,* Summer 1972, 36 (2), 258–259.

In surveys both of alumni from a certain university and of leaders of religious sects, the authors claim that money spent for pre-letters could have been better used to increase sample size or construct more elaborate follow-ups. They suggest that pre-letters may not be necessary for surveys of homogeneous groups.

340. Parten, Mildred. *Surveys, Polls and Samples.* New York: Harper & Bros., 1950. 624p.
A general discussion of many aspects of surveys is found in this textbook. Chapters on the "Construction of the Schedule or Questionnaire" and "Mail Questionnaire Procedures" are of some relevance.

341. Paterson, Donald G., and Tinker, Miles A. *How to Make Type Readable.* New York: Harper & Bros., 1940. 209p.
Results of extensive studies dealing with the effects on reading rate and legibility of typographical variables are reported in this book. These variables include kinds and sizes of type in relation to width of line, color of print and paper, printing surfaces, and other considerations.

342. Patton, Michael Q. *Qualitative Evaluation Methods.* Beverly Hills, Cal.: Sage, 1980. 379p.
This text presents alternatives to large sample, quantitative research methods.

343. Pavalko, Ronald M., and Lutterman, Kenneth G. "Characteristics of willing and reluctant respondents." *Pacific Sociological Review,* October 1973, 16 (4), 463–476.
The higher the measured intelligence, high school rank, educational plans, educational attainment, and occupational attainment of a child, the more likely the parent is to respond on the first wave of a mail questionnaire. In addition, early response is directly related to the socioeconomic status of the respondent.

344. Payne, Stanley L. "Thoughts about meaningless questions." *Public Opinion Quarterly,* 1951, 14, 687–696.

Examples of "meaningless" questions are cited, and guidelines for asking meaningful questions are presented.

345.   Payne, Stanley L. *The Art of Asking Questions.* Princeton, N.J.: Princeton University Press, 1951. 249p.
         This excellent and humorous little book presents basic issues of question wording in a delightfully easy-to-read manner. Practically all the pitfalls into which people commonly fall with poorly worded questions are exposed by Payne.

346.   Payne, Stanley L. "Some advantages of telephone surveys." *Journal of Marketing,* January 1956, 20 (3), 278–281.
         The author cites examples from his own experience which illustrate the statistical and economic advantages of telephone surveys.

347.   Payne, Stanley L. "Combination of survey methods." *Journal of Marketing Research,* May 1964, 1 (2), 61–62.
         Personal interviews, telephone interviews, and mail questionnaires are often viewed as alternative methods. A home-use product test is reported in this article, which utilizes all three methods in obtaining information from the same households.

348.   Payne, Stanley L. "Are open-ended questions worth the effort?" *Journal of Marketing Research,* November 1965, 2 (4), 417–418.
         An experiment with open-ended questions finds them inefficient and no more productive of depth or of valid answers than check-box questions. Their use may be confined to the development and pretesting phases of surveys.

349.   Pearlin, Leonard I. "The appeals of anonymity in
         questionnaire response." *Public Opinion Quarterly,*
         Winter 1961, 25 (4), 640–647.
         This study demonstrates that appeals of ano-
         nymity can derive from social and personal char-
         acteristics of respondents (feelings of incompe-
         tence, a cautious approach to people and things,
         and lack of enthusiasm for the work), as well as
         from the character of the questions that are
         asked. Anonymity is a useful feature of question-
         naire administration for reasons that go beyond
         avoiding threat or the arousal of fear.

350.   Perreault, William D., Jr. "Controlling order-effect
         bias." *Public Opinion Quarterly,* Winter 1975–76, 39
         (4), 544–551.
         Computer text processing is described as a tech-
         nique for randomizing the sequence of question-
         naire material in which order effect may be a
         problem.

351.   Petry, Glenn H., and Quackenbush, Stanley F. "The
         conservation of the questionnaire as a research re-
         source." *Business Horizons,* August 1974, 17 (4), 43–
         47.
         The sources and quality of questionnaires re-
         ceived by corporations are analyzed. Given the
         large number of poor quality questionnaires re-
         ceived by corporations, the authors warn that
         without improvements, the researcher and the
         business executive may lose an important re-
         search tool.

352.   Phillips, Derek L., and Clancy, Kevin J. "Modeling
         effects in survey research." *Public Opinion Quarterly,*
         Summer 1972, 36 (2), 246–253.
         This study examines the bias produced by model-

ing effects (investigators consciously or uncon-
sciously project their own views on those whom
they are studying). The authors conclude that
although modeling effects are minor, they call
into question the assumption that interviewer
opinions are not a source of bias in respondents'
answers.

353.   Phillips, Marjorie. "Problems of questionnaire investigation." *Research Quarterly,* October 1941, 12 (3),
528–537.
This article reviews some of the standard limitations and conveniences of questionnaires and contains some general suggestions for conducting a
questionnaire study.

354.   Plog, Stanley. "Explanations for a high return rate on
a mail questionnaire." *Public Opinion Quarterly,* Summer 1963, 27 (2), 297–298.
This brief article attempts to account for factors
that resulted in a high response rate. These factors were specifically related to the particular
study, but may be generalized to other groups.

355.   Pomeroy, Wardell B. "The reluctant respondent."
Public Opinion Quarterly, Summer 1963, 27 (2), 287–
293.
The author proposes that poorly trained interviewers and faulty interviewing create more reluctance on the part of respondents than any
other factor.

356.   Powers, Edward A.; Morrow, Paula; Gordy, Willis J.;
and Keith, Patricia M. "Serial order preference in
survey research." *Public Opinion Quarterly,* Spring
1977, 41 (1), 80–85.
Serial order preference—the tendency to select a
particular response category because of the rank

order position of response options—was not present in this study. The authors conclude that continued attention to serial order preference in survey research does not seem warranted.

357. Presser, Stanley, and Schuman, Howard. "The measurement of a middle position in attitude surveys." *Public Opinion Quarterly*, Spring 1980, 44 (1), 70–85.
    Offering a middle alternative in forced-choice attitude questions significantly increases the size of that category, but tends not to otherwise affect univariate distributions. Less intense respondents are more affected by question form than those who feel more strongly.

358. Pressley, Milton M., and Tullar, William L. "A factor interactive investigation of mail survey response rates from a commercial population." *Journal of Marketing Research*, February 1977, 14 (1), 108–111.
    Within a sample of 280 commercial, industrial, administrative, or other business respondents, the use of a 10¢ coin increased the response rate. Questionnaire color and cartoon illustrations did not make a difference.

359. Pressley, Milton M. "Improving mail survey responses from industrial organizations." *Industrial Marketing Management*, July 1980, 9 (3), 231–235.
    A number of suggestions are offered for obtaining, on a consistent basis, a 50–70 percent response within two to five weeks in mail surveys of industrial respondents. The article is structured into lists of dos and don'ts.

360. Price, D. O. "On the use of stamped return envelopes with mail questionnaires." *American Sociological Review*, October 1950, 15 (5), 672–673.
    In this study, the inclusion of a stamp on the

return envelope was more effective than an un-
stamped envelope in stimulating replies and payment of a membership fee.

361.   Pucel, David; Nelson, Howard; and Wheeler, David.
         "Questionnaire follow-up returns as a function of in-
         centives and responder characteristics." *Vocational
         Guidance Quarterly,* March 1971, 19 (3), 188–193.
         A variety of incentives were used by these investi-
         gators to stimulate response rate. These incen-
         tives included mailing subjects a pencil or packet
         of coffee, the use of colored paper, the use of pre-
         letters, and combinations of the above. Differen-
         tial response rates were noted, with highest re-
         sponse rates from subjects who received coffee, a
         colored questionnaire, and a pre-letter.

362.   Reeder, Leo G. "Mailed questionnaires in longitudinal
         health studies: the problem of maintaining and max-
         imizing response." *Journal of Health and Human Behav-
         ior,* Summer 1960, 1 (2), 123–129.
         An explanatory letter, the use of careful follow-
         up procedures, brevity of the questionnaire, use
         of university letterhead and personal signatures
         were some of the factors contributing to the suc-
         cess of a longitudinal study of heart disease.

363.   Reid, Seerley. "Respondents and non-respondents to
         mail questionnaires." *Educational Research Bulletin,*
         April 15, 1942, 21 (4), 87–96.
         This article reports results which found dif-
         ferences in responses from respondents who re-
         plied to the first mailing of a questionnaire, those
         who responded to a follow-up, and a sample of
         nonrespondents. The article suggests these dif-
         ferences may be due to different levels of interest
         in the subject matter of the questionnaire.

364. Reingen, Peter H., and Kernan, Jerome B. "Compliance with an interview request: a foot-in-the-door, self-perception interpretation." *Journal of Marketing Research*, August 1977, 14 (3), 365–369.

The foot-in-the-door technique suggests that compliance with a relatively large request is more likely to occur if preceded by compliance with a small request of a similar nature. In a study of 133 New York residents, this technique was implemented by initially asking fewer rather than more questions of a respondent. The results show that the technique works as well as a money incentive. A telephone solicitation in contemplation of a mail questionnaire presents a natural setting for this procedure.

365. Reuss, C. F. "Differences between persons responding and not responding to a mailed questionnaire." *American Sociological Review*, August 1943, 8 (4), 433–438.

A study of college students suggests that intelligence, rural background, and loyalty to the sponsoring institution were characteristics of subjects who were most likely to respond.

366. Reynolds, Fred D., and Johnson, Deborah K. "Validity of focus-group findings." *Journal of Advertising Research*, June 1978, 18 (3), 21–24.

A comparison of qualitative (focus-group) and quantitative (mail survey) data showed similar findings. In particular, if interest is in detecting the direction of changes in the behavior of consumers—the focus groups have a viable position as a research tool for decision-making as well as for hypothesis generation.

367. Rich, Clyde L. "Is random digit dialing really neces-

sary?" *Journal of Marketing Research,* August 1977, 14 (3), 300–305.

This article suggests that for some surveys the exclusion of nonpublished telephone households may not be a serious problem. Random digit dialing, which attempts to deal with this problem, may therefore be most appropriate in geographic areas where the proportion of "nonpubs" is high. The decision on whether random digit dialing is really necessary (worth the extra cost) should be based on the purpose and objectives of each survey.

368.   Roberts, Robert E.; McGory, Owen F.; and Forthofer, Ronald N. "Further evidence on using a deadline to stimulate responses to a mail survey." *Public Opinion Quarterly,* Fall 1978, 42 (3), 407–410.

Specifying a return deadline (in three weeks) appears to speed up returns. An appeal to social utility does not seem to be an effective stimulator of mail survey returns.

369.   Robertson, Dan H., and Bellenger, Danny. "A new method of increasing mail survey responses: contributions to charity." *Journal of Marketing Research,* November 1978, 15 (4), 632–633.

The authors investigated the effectiveness of two types of incentives in producing responses to a mail survey: a personal cash payment versus an identical (one dollar) contribution to a charity of the respondent's choice. The charity incentive resulted in an increased response rate.

370.   Robin, Donald P., and Walter, C. Glenn. "The effect on return rate of messages explaining monetary incentives in mail questionnaire studies." *The Journal of*

Business Communication, Spring 1976, 13 (3), 49–54. The results of this study indicate that a monetary incentive does affect the return rate for mailed questionnaires, but different messages accompanying a monetary reward have little or no effect.

371. Robin, Stanley. "A procedure for securing returns to mail questionnnaires." *Sociology and Social Research,* 1965, 50 (1), 24–35.
This often cited article describes a procedure for achieving high response rates. The procedure advocated is based on techniques used in a number of studies which achieved response rates of 66 to 95 percent.

372. Robins, Lee N. "The reluctant respondent." *Public Opinion Quarterly,* Summer 1963, 27 (2), 276–286.
Refusals to be interviewed were more often found among those with routine white-collar occupations, low education, and foreign-born parents, and among those located in the same town as the study headquarters. The amount of sensitive information to be elicited was unrelated to willingness to be interviewed. Apparently subjects with a history of antisocial behavior present no special problems in interrupted interviews, high refusal rates, or stalling.

373. Robinson, R. A., and Agisim, Philip. "Making mail surveys more reliable." *Journal of Marketing,* April 1951, 15 (4), 415–424.
Suggestions are made for producing good mail survey samples. A study of the day-by-day replies to mail surveys showed that about half of all questionnaires that will come in will have been re-

turned after a week. In two weeks approximately 90 percent of the responses will be returned. At the end of three weeks almost all who will answer the questionnaire will have sent their replies.

374.   Robinson, R. A. "How to boost returns from mail surveys." *Printer's Ink,* June 6, 1952, 239 (10), 35–37.
        Several aspects which help achieve high response rates in studies using questionnaires are discussed in this article. These include questionnaire construction, use of premiums, cover letters, and follow-ups.

375.   Roeher, G. Allen. "Effective techniques in increasing response to mailed questionnaires." *Public Opinion Quarterly,* Summer 1963, 27 (2), 299–302.
        Achieving a high response rate is stressed as essential by this author, who lists some "response rate stimulators." The factor he feels was most effective was establishing an atmosphere of personalization in all contacts with people who were asked to complete a questionnaire.

376.   Rogers, Theresa F. "Interviews by telephone and in person: quality of responses and field performance." *Public Opinion Quarterly,* Spring 1976, 40 (1), 51–65.
        The results of this experiment show that the quality of data obtained by telephone on complex attitudinal and knowledge items as well as on personal items is comparable to that collected in person.

377.   Roscoe, A. Marvin; Lang, Dorothy; and Sheth, Jagdish N. "Follow-up methods, questionnaire length, and market differences in mail surveys." *Journal of Marketing,* April 1975, 39 (2), 20–27.
        A telephone reminder was more effective in in-

creasing response rate in comparison to a postcard reminder, regardless of questionnaire length.

378. Rosenau, James. "Meticulousness as a factor in the response to mail questionnaires." *Public Opinion Quarterly,* Summer 1964, 28 (2), 312–314.

Rosenau reports results that suggest people who respond to questionnaires may be more "meticulous" about such matters than nonrespondents, which indicates that "responses to surveys are in no small part a function of habits and attitudes that are highly personal and deeply ingrained." People who filled out an address card at a conference were found more likely to complete the mail questionnaires than were people who did not fill out the card.

379. Rosenberg, Morris. *The Logic of Survey Analysis.* New York: Basic Books, 1968. 283p.

This text presents a conceptual framework and specific details related to the analysis of survey data.

380. Ross, H. Laurence. "The inaccessible respondent: a note on privacy in city and country." *Public Opinion Quarterly,* Summer 1963, 27 (2), 269–275.

This study shows that in terms of respondent accessibility rural interviewing may be easier than urban interviewing.

381. Rucker, M. H., and Arbaugh, J. E. "A comparison of matrix questionnaires with standard questionnaires." *Educational and Psychological Measurement,* Fall 1979, 39 (3), 637–643.

Two studies, each with 158 married women, were conducted to compare responses to matrix questionnaires with those to standard questionnaires. In the first study, the matrix format was used to reduce questionnaire size and therefore mailing costs. However, this format also produced significantly fewer returns. A second study comparing matrix and standard questionnaires of equal size found similar response rates but more incomplete returns for the matrix form.

382.   Ruckmick, Christian A. "The uses and abuses of the questionnaire procedure." *Journal of Applied Psychology,* 1930, 14 (1), 32–41.
       This 1930 article discusses some of the advantages of using questionnaires and also some problems and sources of error which can be a danger in questionnaire use.

383.   Schmiedeskamp, Jay W. "Reinterviews by telephone." *Journal of Marketing,* January 1962, 26 (1), 28–34.
       The effectiveness of telephone surveys for gathering information about consumer attitudes, financial optimism, and plans to buy are evaluated. Such surveys are particularly suitable when the respondents have been previously interviewed by personal contact.

384.   Schuman, Howard. "The random probe: a technique for evaluating the validity of closed questions." *American Sociological Review,* April 1966, 31 (2), 218–222.
       "Random probing" involves the use of follow-up probes for a set of *closed* questionnaire items *randomly* selected from the interview schedule for each respondent. Recorded comments are used by the investigator to compare the intended purpose of the question and chosen alternative with its meaning as perceived and acted upon by the respondent. This technique may be especially useful in doing research in other cultures.

385. Schuman, H., and Presser, S. "Question wording as an independent variable in survey analysis." *Sociological Methods & Research,* November 1977, 6 (2), 151–176.

Hypotheses are tested which relate to the effect on responses of different wordings of questions designed to obtain the same information. Middle options, no opinions, open/closed questions, agree-disagree, forced choice, and two-way questions are all tested and results reported.

386. Schwartz, Alvin. "Interviewing and the public." *Public Opinion Quarterly,* Spring 1964, 28 (1), 135–142.

Factors affecting the participation and nonparticipation of people in interviews are presented. The results of two exploratory studies regarding public relations aspects of interviewing are described.

387. Schwartz, David A. "Coping with field problems of large surveys among the urban poor." *Public Opinion Quarterly,* Summer 1970, 34 (2), 267–272.

Community relations; local field offices; full-time supervision; interviewer recruitment, training, payment; and home office field coordination are discussed in relationship to large surveys among the urban poor.

388. Schwirian, Kent P., and Blain, Harry R. "Questionnaire-return bias in the study of blue-collar workers." *Public Opinion Quarterly,* Winter 1966–1967, 30 (4), 656–663.

Questionnaire-return bias is present among a sample of blue-collar workers and has a serious effect upon the estimation of population parameters and the nature of the association among variables.

389.   Schyberger, A. B. "Study of interviewer behavior."
         Journal of Marketing Research, February 1967, 4 (1),
         32–35.
         Only small differences were detected between the
         behavior of experienced and inexperienced inter-
         viewers. Interviewers paid by the interview ap-
         pear to do as reliable a job as interviewers paid by
         the hour. Interviewers deviated from instructions
         surprisingly often, regardless of their experience,
         training or method of payment.

390.   Scott, Christopher. "Research on mail surveys." *Jour-
         nal of the Royal Statistical Society*, Series A (General),
         1961, 124 (2), 143–205.
         The article summary states that "[f]ive recent mail
         surveys carried out by the [British] Government
         Social Survey are examined for their bearing on
         mail survey technique. Experimental features in-
         troduced into these studies allow measurement of
         non-response bias, of early/late response bias, of
         response by non-addressees, of the influence of a
         variety of factors on the response rate, and of
         response reliability and validity. An attempt is also
         made to evaluate all published research on each
         topic, and thus to present a definitive summary of
         the present state of knowledge about mail survey
         technique." This article is geared toward those
         who already have a substantial background in the
         area of questionnaires.

391.   Seitz, R. M. "How mail surveys may be made to pay."
         Printer's Ink, December 1, 1944, 209 (9), 17–19.
         Some general suggestions for conducting a mail
         survey are presented in this article. Topics dis-
         cussed include reasons for using a mail survey,
         when to use a mail survey, whom to survey, the
         form of the questionnaire, and questionnaire
         items.

392.   Sessions, Frank R.; Epley, Robert J.; and Moe, Edward O. "The development, reliability and validity of an all-purpose optical scanner questionnaire form." *Public Opinion Quarterly,* Fall 1966, 30 (3), 423–428.
         The authors report a study to test reliability and validity of different types of optical scanner questionnaire forms.

393.   Shackleton, V. J., and Wild, J. M. "Effect of incentives and personal contact on response rate to a mailed questionnaire." *Psychological Reports,* April 1982, 50 (2), 365–366.
         For 89 partially sighted school leavers, seventeen to twenty years old, the combination of a financial incentive and personal contact significantly increased the speed of return of questionnaires but did not affect the eventual response rate.

394.   Shannon, J. R. "Percentages of returns in reputable educational research." *Journal of Educational Research,* October 1948, 42 (2), 138–141.
         Three groups of research reports prior to 1947 were examined to determine the mean percentages of response rate. The mean response rate varied from 63 to 87 percent.

395.   Sharma, Sureshwar, and Singh, Y. P. "Does the colour pull responses?" *Manas: A Journal of Scientific Psychology,* 1967, 14 (2), 77–79.
         Three different colored questionnaires (yellow, pink, and white) were mailed to subjects in this study. Response rates did not significantly differ among groups whose members received a different colored questionnaire.

396.   Sharp, Laurie M., and Frankel, Joanne. "Respondent burden: a test of some common assumptions." *Public Opinion Quarterly,* Spring 1983, 47 (1), 36–53.

The length of a survey instrument is shown to be significantly related to a respondents' sense of being burdened. The more a respondent believes in the usefulness of a survey and denies the privacy-invading character of survey questions, the less burdened a respondent feels.

397.   Sheets, Thomas; Radlinski, Allen; Kohne, James; and Brunner, G. Allen. "Deceived respondents: once bitten, twice shy." *Public Opinion Quarterly,* Summer 1974, 38 (2), 261–263.

False market surveys have a deleterious effect upon respondent willingness to cooperate in subsequent market research studies. The implication for field researchers is either to stay away from areas that have had recent, heavy, direct, sales efforts or to plan for higher refusal rates in such areas.

398.   Sheth, Jagdish N., and Roscoe, A. Marvin. "Impact of questionnaire length, follow-up methods, and geographical location on response rate to a mail survey." *Journal of Applied Psychology,* April 1975, 60 (2), 252–254.

Questionnaire length was found to have no significant effect on the rate of return (4 pages vs. 6 pages). The telephone reminder was the best follow-up method in comparison to a) a postcard reminder and a second mailing of the questionnaire; b) a letter alert followed by a telephone interview; and c) a telephone interview without a letter alert. Response rates differed by geographical region and some follow-up methods worked better in some areas than in others.

399.   Sheth, Jagdish N.; LeClaire, Arthur; and Wachspress, David. "Impact of asking race information in

mail surveys." *Journal of Marketing,* Winter 1980, 44 (1), 67–70.

The results of this study clearly indicate that there was virtually no impact of asking race information on the response rate. Those respondents who did refuse to provide race information had a more general refusal syndrome.

400. Shosteck, Herschel, and Fairweather, William R. "Physician response rates to mail and personal interview surveys." *Public Opinion Quarterly,* Summer 1979, 43 (2), 206–217.

Mail and personal administration of a questionnaire dealing with physician antibiotic prescription practices are compared. The mail survey required less time, was less costly, and generated higher response rates than equivalent personal contacts.

401. Shuttleworth, F. K. "A study of questionnaire technique." *Journal of Educational Psychology,* December 1931, 22 (9), 652–658.

A 25-cent incentive enclosed with the mail questionnaire was found to increase the response rate in this study.

402. Shuttleworth, F. K. "Sampling errors involved in incomplete returns to mail questionnaires." *Journal of Applied Psychology,* August 1941, 25 (4), 588–591.

The question of bias resulting from an incomplete response is discussed in this article. Results reported indicate that there is a difference between early (incomplete) responses and later (complete) responses.

403. Siemiatycki, Jack. "A comparison of mail, telephone, and home interview strategies for household health

surveys." *American Journal of Public Health,* March 1979, 69 (3), 238–245.

Strategies which began with mail or telephone contact, followed by other methods (including home interview), provided response rates as high as a home interview strategy (all between 80 and 90 percent) for one-half the cost of home interviews when used as the sole method. The telephone response rate was higher than the mail response rate.

404.   Simon, Raymond. "Responses to personal and form letters in mail surveys." *Journal of Advertising Research,* March 1967, 7 (1), 28–30.

Results from three studies show mixed findings regarding the comparative effectiveness of cover letters that are either personally typed or mimeographed. Two of the studies found the personally typed letter to be a more effective response rate stimulator, but the other study found the mimeographed form letter more effective. The author stresses the importance of considering the characteristics of the particular group being studied before deciding which to use.

405.   Singer, Eleanor. "Agreement between 'inaccessible' respondents and informants." *Public Opinion Quarterly,* Winter 1972–73, 36 (4), 603–611.

Under the following conditions the use of informants as substitutes for respondents may yield comparable results: when questions are relatively objective, when informants have a high degree of observability with respect to respondents, when the population is fairly homogeneous, and when the setting of the interview provides no clear-cut motivation to distort responses. Studies of the aged or the chronically ill may satisfy these conditions.

406.   Singer, Eleanor. "Informed consent: consequences for response rate and response quality in social surveys." *American Sociological Review*, April 1978, 43 (2), 144–162.

The request for and timing of a signature to document consent had a significant effect on the probability of securing a response. The data also suggest that asking for a signature before an interview has a sensitization effect so that better data are obtained if the respondent is asked to sign a consent form afterwards.

407.   Singer, Eleanor, and Kohnke-Aquirre, Luane. "Interviewer expectation effects: a replication and extension." *Public Opinion Quarterly*, Summer 1979, 43 (2), 245–260.

Interviewers' evaluations of the general difficulty of a survey have no effect on the cooperation rate they obtain, but do affect responses to individual questions. Interviewers who expect more difficulty with a study, or who expect certain parts of it to be difficult to ask, tend to get higher nonresponse rates to sensitive questions and lower estimates of sensitive behavior.

408.   Singer, Eleanor, and Frankel, Martin R. "Informed consent procedures in telephone interviews." *American Sociological Review*, June 1982, 47 (3), 416–427.

Information about the content of the interview and information about its purpose were manipulated. Neither of these significantly affected the response rate to the survey as a whole, item nonresponse, or response quality.

409.   Singer, Eleanor; Frankel, Martin R.; and Glassman, Mare B. "The effect of interviewer characteristics and expectations on response." *Public Opinion Quarterly,* Spring 1983, 47 (1), 68–83.
        Interviewer age, the size of the interviewing assignment, and interviewer expectations strongly effect cooperation rates.

410.   Sivan, John E.; Epley, Donald E.; and Burns, William L. "Can follow-up response rates to a mail survey be increased by including another copy of the questionnaire?" *Psychological Reports,* August 1980, 47 (1), 103–106.
        In a first follow-up of a mail survey of 990 business respondents, a letter-only follow-up was as effective as a letter plus questionnaire follow-up. In the second follow-up, returns from the letter-plus-questionnaire were almost twice that of the letter-only group.

411.   Skelly, Florence R. "Interviewer-appearance stereotypes as a possible source of bias." *Journal of Marketing,* July 1954, 19 (1), 74–75.
        In surveys dealing with relatively controversial subjects or products, or with subjects or products around which stereotypes have arisen, field interviewers should be screened to eliminate those whose appearance resembles the stereotypes.

412.   Skinner, Steven J., and Childers, Terry L. "Respondent identification in mail surveys." *Journal of Advertising Research,* December 1980, 57–61.
        The use of return address for respondent identification purposes was not felt to affect adversely the quality of survey data. Ninety percent of the respondents elected to include their name and address on the return envelope.

413. Skipper, James K., Jr. and Ellison, Margaret D. "Personal contact as a technique for increasing questionnaire returns from hospitalized patients after discharge." *Journal of Health and Human Behavior*, 1966, 7 (3), 211–214.

Face-to-face pre-questionnaire contact with subjects was found to be an effective alternative to pre-letters in this study of discharged hospital patients.

414. Sletto, Raymond F. "Pretesting of questionnaires." *American Sociological Review*, April 1940, 5 (2), 193–200.

In this frequently cited article, Sletto includes a discussion of an elaborate process of the development of a questionnaire and stresses the importance of pretesting. Results of this study suggest that questionnaire length may not itself inhibit response rate. Postcard follow-ups were found as effective as and less costly than follow-up letters. For this study of college freshmen, an appeal to altruism in the cover letter was effective in stimulating response rate.

415. Slocum, W. L.; Empey, L. T.; and Swanson, H. S. "Increasing response to questionnaires and structured interviews." *American Sociological Review*, April 1956, 21 (2), 221–225.

These authors recommend two techniques for maximizing response rates: attempts to convince the subject of the social utility of the survey and attempts to impress upon subjects the importance of their role as a respondent.

416. Smead, Raymond J. "Ring policy in telephone surveys." *Public Opinion Quarterly*, Spring 1980, 44 (1), 115–116.

Only four rings are necessary to reach 97 percent of those respondents at home. Time should therefore not be wasted by allowing the phone to ring more than four times.

417.   Smith, Keith. "Signing off in the right color can boost mail survey response." *Industrial Marketing,* November 1977, 62, 59–62.

Using a green inked signature in a survey containing a signed letter may increase returns by 10 or 15 percent when other factors affecting response are controlled.

418.   Snelling, W. Rodman. "The impact of a personalized mail questionnaire." *The Journal of Educational Research,* November 1969, 63 (3), 126–129.

A personalized approach was found to help maximize response rates in this study of liberal arts college science graduates. Ways to achieve personalization included salutation by nickname, individually typed letters, and letters signed by a faculty member identified as having the most rapport with the subject.

419.   Snyder, Mark, and Cunningham, Michael R. "To comply or not comply; testing the self-perception explanation of the 'foot-in-the-door' phenomenon." *Journal of Personality and Social Psychology,* January 1975, 31 (1), 64–67.

An experiment was conducted to test the self-perception explanation of the "foot-in-the-door" phenomenon of increased compliance with a substantial request after prior compliance with a smaller demand. Subjects approached with a small request (eight telephone survey questions) were more likely to reply to a second request than subjects initially approached with a large request (answer 50 questions).

420.   Sobal, Jeff. "Disclosing information in interview introductions: methodological consequences of informed consent." *Sociology and Social Research,* April 1982, 66 (3), 348–361.

Two studies are reported. The first suggests that fuller introductions are not significantly different from more abbreviated ones in terms of rapport and cooperation and bias. The implication is that withholding information has no "methodological" benefits. The second study found no difference in refusals in relationship to the length of introduction, but it did find a significant difference in disclosing the time the interview would last. Telling potential respondents that the interview would last 20 minutes rather than "a few minutes" resulted in more refusals.

421.   Sorensen, Stefan, and Jonsson, Erland. "On the importance of the phrasing of questions in medichygienic social surveys." *Environmental Research,* October 1975, 10 (2), 190–195.

In a laboratory experiment it was possible to show that the choice of verbal expression for the reaction to noise stimulus can influence the incidence of annoyance reactions. The results from the laboratory study could not be verified in a field experiment, however.

422.   Sosdian, Carol P., and Sharp, Laure M. "Nonresponse in mail surveys: access failure or respondent resistance." *Public Opinion Quarterly,* Fall 1980, 44 (3), 396–402.

The authors conclude that survey professionals

have been too eager to accept and internalize the notion of growing resistance to surveys. They suggest that it may be more useful to examine the technical issue of respondent access rather than to emphasize reducing respondent burden.

423.   Speer, David C., and Zold, Anthony. "An example of self-selection bias in follow-up research." *Journal of Clinical Psychology*, January 27, 1971, 27 (1), 64–68.
        Data from people who responded before a telephone follow-up urging cooperation differed from responses of people who responded after the phone call.

424.   Stafford, J. E. "Influence of preliminary contact on mail returns." *Journal of Marketing Research*, November 1966, 3 (4), 410–411.
        The author evaluates the effects of two types of preliminary contacts—advance letters and phone calls—on questionnaire returns from a sample of 1,247 students. Phone calls were more effective than advance letters in increasing mail questionnaire returns.

425.   Stanton, Frank. "Notes on the validity of mail questionnaire returns." *Journal of Applied Psychology*, February 1939, 23 (1), 95–104.
        Stanton points out the necessity of using follow-up techniques as a means of increasing response rates and decreasing possible response rate bias.

426.   Stevens, Robert E. "Does precoding mail questionnaires affect response rates?" *Public Opinion Quarterly*, Winter 1974–75, 38 (4), 621–622.
        In this experiment precoding of a mail questionnaire did not influence the response rate.

427. Stoke, Stuart, and Lehman, Harvey. "The influence of self-interest upon questionnaire replies." *School and Society,* September 27, 1930, 32 (822), 435–438.

The contention of this article is that, "The questionnaire technique is peculiarly vulnerable when employed for the collection of personal information or when used with subjects who see (or who imagine they see) an opportunity to advance their personal interests by means of the returns made by them." Results of a study are reported that indicate those students doing poorly in a psychology class were most prone to overestimate the number of times they used reserve library books.

428. Stover, Robert V., and Stone, Walter J. "Hand delivery of self-administered questionnaires." *Public Opinion Quarterly,* Summer 1974, 38 (2), 284–287.

Leaving a questionnaire at a respondent's home to be filled out at the respondent's convenience compares favorably to other survey techniques in terms of cost, response rate, and response validity.

429. Suchman, Edward, and McCandless, Boyd. "Who answers questionnaires?" *Journal of Applied Psychology,* December 1940, 24 (6), 758–769.

This often cited article reports that two main factors influenced the questionnaire returns in the authors' studies: those more interested in the topic under investigation and those most highly educated responded at a higher rate.

430. Sudman, Seymour. "New uses of telephone methods." *Journal of Marketing Research,* May 1966, 3 (2), 163–167.

Survey interviewing costs can be reduced by mak-

ing advance appointments by telephone, with no
reduction in cooperation.

431.   Sudman, Seymour. "Quantifying interviewer quality." *Public Opinion Quarterly*, Winter 1966–1967, 30
(4), 664–667.
A method is described that will help field supervisors quantify interviewer quality.

432.   Sudman, Seymour. *Reducing the Cost of Surveys*. Chicago: Aldine Pub. Co., 1967. 246p.
The content of this book deals with ways to reduce the cost of survey research. Although the
majority of the book is devoted to interviews,
there is also a brief introduction to the topic of
optical scanning and its use in survey research.

433.   Sudman, Seymour. "Uses of telephone directories for
survey sampling." *Journal of Marketing Research*, May
1973, 10 (2), 204–207.
The use of directories in combination with random digit dialing is described by the author as a
more efficient procedure for phone interviews.
Telephone directories may also be used to estimate the percentage of households without
phones or listed numbers.

434.   Sudman, Seymour, and Bradburn, Norman. "Effects
of time and memory factors on response in surveys."
Journal of the American Statistical Association, December 1973, 68 (344), 805–815.
The use of records reduces telescoping effects (an
event is remembered as occurring more recently
than it really did) but not forgetting. Aided recall
reduces forgetting, but does not reduce and may
even increase telescoping.

435.   Sudman, Seymour, and Ferber, Robert. "A comparison of alternative procedures for collecting consumer expenditure data for frequently purchased products." *Journal of Marketing Research,* May 1974, 11 (2), 128–135.
        Compensating a household for supplying consumer expenditure data increased both the level of cooperation and expenditures reported. The auspices of the survey (government versus university) did not make much difference. Diaries yield more complete and accurate information than telephone techniques.

436.   Sudman, Seymour, and Bradburn, Norman. *Response Effects in Surveys.* Chicago: Aldine, 1974. 257p.
        This book reports the results of analyzing more than 900 research reports of survey research data. The authors computer analyzed these reports to determine what variables cause response effects (i.e., intruding barriers that prevent the attainment of accurate data) during surveys.

437.   Sudman, Seymour. *Applied Sampling.* New York: Academic Press, 1976. 249p.
        This text describes the basic sampling designs that are useful when conducting surveys. The style is nontechnical so that readers with a limited mathematical background will be able to follow the discussion.

438.   Sudman, Seymour, and Bradburn, N. "Modest expectations: the effects of interviewers' prior expectations on responses." *Sociological Methods & Research,* November 1977, 6 (2), 177–182.
        This article reports that whether or not interviewees believe an interview will be difficult does

not influence the response effects actually obtained very much.

439.   Sudman, Seymour. "Estimating response to follow-ups in mail surveys." *Public Opinion Quarterly,* Winter 1982, 46 (4), 582–584.
A simple method for estimating the effectiveness of successive follow-ups in mail surveys is presented.

440.   Sudman, Seymour, and Bradburn, Norman. *Asking Questions.* San Francisco: Jossey-Bass, 1982. 397p.
This book describes the effects of asking questions in differing styles.

441.   Tallent, Norman, and Reiss, William. "A note on an unusually high rate of return for a mail questionnaire." *Public Opinion Quarterly,* Winter 1960, 23, 579–581.
Techniques used in a study that achieved a high response rate are described in this report.

442.   Tedin, Kent L., and Hofstetter, Richard. "The effect of cost and importance factors on the return rate for single and multiple mailings." *Public Opinion Quarterly,* Spring 1982, 46 (1), 122–128.
Importance factors, notably certified mail, are shown to be of greatest consequence in comparison to cost factors for the return rate of mail questionnaires.

443.   Thomas, Charles C. "Questioning the questionnaire." *Pension World,* February 1978, 14 (2), 38–40.
A list of suggestions is presented in order to improve the use of questionnaires by pension plan sponsors and investment managers.

444. Thornberry, Owen, and Massey, James. "Correcting for undercoverage bias in random digit dialed national health surveys." *American Statistical Association, Proceedings of the Section on Survey Research Methods,* 1978, 224–230.

This survey of 40,000 people found that estimates of sociodemographic characteristics from households with telephones are very similar to estimates obtained from a combination of households with and without telephones.

445. Thorndike, Robert L., and Hagan, Elizabeth. *Measurement and Evaluation in Psychology and Education.* New York: John Wiley, 1955. 575p.

This basic text in psychological and educational measurement contains thorough and easily understandable discussions of reliability and validity.

446. Toops, Herbert A. "Validating the questionnaire method." *Journal of Personnel Research,* 1924, 2 (4–5), 153–169.

An attempt is made here to meet the objection that questionnaires are not valid because of unrepresentative response rates. An elaborate discussion is included describing creative procedures used as follow-ups to motivate former trade school students and to respond to a questionnaire. The author demonstrates the creativity and persistence necessary to a successful questionnaire study.

447. Toops, Herbert A. "The returns from follow-up letters to questionnaires." *Journal of Applied Psychology,* 1926, 10 (1), 92–101.

Results from a survey of colleges regarding their use of intelligence tests indicate that the results would not have been different if no follow-ups had been used to secure a high response rate. The possibility of obtaining completed questionnaires from all or nearly all respondents is discussed with a recommendation for the use of follow-up letters.

448.   Toops, Herbert A. "The factor of mechanical arrangement and typography in questionnaires." *Journal of Applied Psychology*, April 1937, 21 (2), 225–229.

Some suggestions regarding ways of arranging questionnaire format are discussed in this article.

449.   Tortora, Robert D. "A note on sample size estimation for multinomial populations." *The American Statistician*, August 1978, 32 (3), 100–102.

This article describes a procedure for determining sample sizes for survey questions that have more than two response options.

450.   Troldahl, V. C., and Carter, R. E. "Random selection of respondents within households in phone surveys." *Journal of Marketing Research*, May 1964, 1 (2), 71–76.

When interviewing by telephone it is relatively difficult to make a random selection of adult respondents from within the households reached. The authors propose a new technique for within household selection and present data concerning the effects of this procedure as used in surveys in Minneapolis-St. Paul, and Champaign-Urbana, Illinois.

451.   Tyebjee, Tyzoon T. "Telephone survey methods: the state of the art." *Journal of Marketing*, Summer 1979, 43 (3), 68–78.

The telephone survey is the dominant method of collecting marketing research and public opinion data. The advantages of the telephone survey are presented along with special situations in which a research manager may need to turn to other methods.

452. U.S. Department of H.E.W. "A summary of studies of interviewing methodology." *Vital and Health Statistics*, March 1977, Series 2—No. 69, 78p.

This entire volume is devoted to studies designed to test the effectiveness of certain questionnaire designs and interviewing techniques used in the collection of data on health events in household interviews and to investigate the role of behaviors, attitudes, perceptions, and information levels of both the respondent and the interviewer.

453. Veiga, John F. "Getting the mail questionnaire returned: some practical research considerations." *Journal of Applied Psychology*, April 1974, 59 (2), 217–218.

One hundred managers received a questionnaire that was to be returned by either a stamped envelope, a business reply envelope, or their firm's interplant mail system. Results suggest that the interplant mail system provided the greatest return rate, at lowest cost, without respondent bias. The business reply envelope produced a very poor response rate.

454. Vigderhous, Gideon. "Scheduling telephone interviews: a study of seasonal patterns." *Public Opinion Quarterly*, Summer 1981, 45 (2), 250–259.

Weekday evening hours during the spring and fall are optimal times for contacting households for personal interviews.

455. Vincent, Clark E. "Socioeconomic status and familial variables in mail questionnaire responses." *American Journal of Sociology*, May 1964, LXIX (6), 647–653.

Mail-questionnaire research may elicit a disproportionately high response from subjects whose background included "verbal discipline by mother" as opposed to "physical discipline by father."

456.   Vocino, Thomas. "Three variables in stimulating responses to mailed questionnaires." *Journal of Marketing*, October 1977, 41 (4), 76–77.
A deadline in the questionnaire cover letters had no positive effect on response rate. A cover letter on organizational letterhead, signed by a well-known individual, resulted in a slightly larger response than a cover letter on university stationery, signed by a less well-known individual. Use of commemorative postage stamps was less effective than the use of postage meters.

457.   Waisanen, F. B. "A note on the response to a mailed questionnaire." *Public Opinion Quarterly*, Summer 1954, 18 (2), 210–212.
The use of a phone call to inform subjects that they will be receiving a questionnaire is suggested as a means to increasing response rates.

458.   Walker, Bruce J., and Burdick, Richard K. "Advance correspondence and error in mail surveys." *Journal of Marketing Research*, August 1977, 14 (3), 379–382.
The results of this experimental study suggest that advance correspondence produces a higher response rate, but at a higher cost per usable return then using no advance correspondence.

459.   Wallace, David. "A case for—and against—mail questionnaires." *Public Opinion Quarterly*, Spring 1954, 18 (1), 40–52.
Wallace suggests that 50 percent or more of persons who respond to a mail questionnaire are "habitual questionnaire responders." He also sug-

gests that the use of questionnaires be limited to homogenous groups.

460.   Warren, Craig B.; Pearce, Jacqueline; and Korth, Bruce. "Magnitude estimation and category scaling." *Standardization News,* March 1982, 15–16.

This study compared the effects on responses of a nine-point rating scale with categories compared to a magnitude estimation format which instructed people to assign a number to indicate the extent of their satisfaction. The two procedures yielded the same results.

461.   Watkins, David. "Relationship between the desire for anonymity and responses to a questionnaire on satisfaction with university." *Psychological Reports,* February 1978, 42 (1), 259–261.

There was no significant difference between the responses of 363 students who supplied their names on a survey of attitudes toward the university and the responses of 61 students who chose to remain anonymous.

462.   Watson, John J. "Improving the response rate in mail research." *Journal of Advertising Research,* June 1965, 5 (2), 48–50.

A list of variables which may improve the response rate in mail surveys is presented.

463.   Watson, Richmond. "Investigations by mail." *Market Research,* 1937, 7, 11–17.

464.   Weaver, Charles N.; Holmes, Sandra L.; and Glenn, Norval D. "Some characteristics of inaccessible respondents in a telephone survey." *Journal of Applied Psychology,* April 1975, 60 (2), 260–262.

Characteristics of inaccessible respondents in a

telephone survey were investigated. The highest refusal rates occurred for the oldest age group. Black respondents had an unusually high inaccessibility rate (42 percent).

465.   Webb, Eugene J.; Campbell, Donald T.; Schwartz, Richard D.; and Sechrest, Lee. *Unobtrusive Measures: Nonreactive Research in the Social Sciences*. Chicago: Rand McNally, 1972. 225p.
         Interesting methods for collecting data, which can be used as possible alternatives to questionnaires, are discussed in this book.

466.   Weeks, M. F.; Jones, B. L.; Folsom, R. E., Jr.; and Benrud, C. H. "Optimal times to contact sample households." *Public Opinion Quarterly*, Spring 1980, 44 (1), 101–114.
         The chances of finding a person aged 14+ at home on a weekday generally improved later in the day and were best in the late afternoon and early evening. In inner-city areas, the afternoon hours were more productive for nonwhites than for whites. Saturday was the best day of the week for finding a household respondent at home.

467.   Weeks, Michael F., and Moore, R. Paul. "Ethnicity-of-interviewer effects on ethnic respondents." *Public Opinion Quarterly*, Summer 1981, 45 (2), 245–249.
         Findings regarding the effects of race-of-interviewer in white/black dichotomies may be generalized to other ethnic groups as well.

468.   Weilbacher, William M., and Walsh, H. R. "Mail questionnaires and the personalized letter of transmittal." *Journal of Marketing*, January 1952, 16 (3), 331–336.
         In this study of fraternity alumni, a personalized

letter of transmittal was not found to affect response rate significantly.

469. Weiss, Carol H. "Interviewing low-income respondents: a preliminary review." *Welfare in Review,* October 1966, 4 (8), 1–7.
Data that exist on the responses of the poor in the interview are not as bleak as some have supposed, although there is room for a good deal of improvement. The interview is still to be considered an appropriate research tool for use with this population.

470. Weiss, Carol. "Research organizations interview the poor." *Social Problems,* December 1974, 22 (2), 246–259.
A survey of researchers who conducted their own personal interview surveys of low-income populations revealed that interviewing poor people is not as difficult as expected; receptivity and completion rates are generally good. Indigenous interviewers (those matched to respondents by class and race/ethnicity) are rated least adequate on performance of most interviewing tasks. Their main strengths are contacting, locating, and establishing rapport with respondents.

471. Weiss, W. H. "Questionnaires." *Supervision,* November 1980, 42 (11), 7–8.
A brief overview of the advantages and disadvantages of questionnaires in comparison to other data collecting methods is presented for individuals who are unfamiliar with the use of questionnaires.

472. Westbrook, Robert A. "A rating scale for measuring product/service satisfaction." *Journal of Marketing,* Fall 1980, 44 (4), 68–72.

A promising new measure for the study of consumer satisfaction, the Delighted-Terrible (D-T) scale is described. The author examines the suitability of this measure for marketing studies of consumer satisfaction/dissatisfaction. Reliability, validity, and selected measurement properties are evaluated empirically.

473.   Wheatley, John J. "Self-administered written questionnaires or telephone interviews?" *Journal of Marketing Research,* February 1973, 10 (1), 94–96.
        This study showed essentially no difference in the nature of the response to the same set of questions, whether administered by telephone or self-administered in writing by the respondent. Either method may be used, depending on cost considerations and the need for speed.

474.   Whitmore, William J. "Mail survey premiums and response bias." *Journal of Marketing Research,* February 1976, 13 (1), 46–50.
        An analysis of 1,000 new car purchasers, half of whom were sent a premium in the mail survey and half of whom were not, revealed little to suggest that systematic bias results from inclusion of a premium (an inexpensive key ring) with a questionnaire.

475.   Wildman, Richard C. "Effects of anonymity and social setting on survey responses." *Public Opinion Quarterly,* Spring 1977, 41 (1), 74–79.
        Anonymity and social setting (home or business address) had no appreciable effect on quality of response or speed of return, although social setting did have an effect on return rate (higher return rate among those receiving a questionnaire at place of business).

476.   Wildt, Albert R., and Mazis, Michael B. "Determinants of scale response: label versus position." *Journal of Marketing Research*, May 1978, 15 (2), 261–267.
        In this article the meaning of the adjective labels used and the location of the labels in relation to scale endpoints were both found to have an impact on subject response.

477.   Williams, Alan, and Wechsler, Henry. "The mail survey: Methods to minimize bias due to incomplete responses." *Sociology and Social Research*, July 1970, 54 (4), 533–535.
        Williams recommends the addition of a telephone follow-up to the procedure suggested by Robin. A phone call permits communication between subject and investigator and can increase response rates.

478.   Williams, Bill. *A Sampler on Sampling*. New York: John Wiley & Sons, 1978. 254p.
        The purpose of this text is "to convey an understanding of the principles of statistical sampling to the nonmathematically inclined person." The objective is admirably met in the easy-to-read, instructive introduction to the concepts and practice of sampling.

479.   Williams, J. Allen, Jr. "Interviewer role performance: a further note on bias in the information interview." *Public Opinion Quarterly*, Summer 1968, 32 (2), 287–294.
        This study clearly demonstrates that the interviewer's role performance affects responses when status distance and the threat potential of interview questions are held constant.

480.   Williams, Lawrence K.; Seybolt, John W.; and Pinder, Craig C. "On administering questionnaires in or-

ganizational settings." *Personnel Psychology,* Spring 1975, 28 (1), 93–103.

Suggestions for administering questionnaires in organizational settings are offered: using a neutral, familiar room; fostering a relaxed environment; providing a nonthreatening excuse for nonreaders to volunteer information; and emphasizing that researchers are not tied to the management or the union.

481. Winett, Richard A.; Stewart, Gary; and Majors, James S. "Prompting techniques to increase the return rate of mailed questionnaires." *Journal of Applied Behavior Analysis,* Fall 1978, 11 (3), 437.

Four different prompts were studied to examine effects on the return rate of questionnaires mailed to clergy and physicians concerning their mental health practices: a) a single phone call, b) a memo, c) a personal letter and new questionnaire with or without a telephone call, and d) a double call. The single call and package alone about doubled the overall return rate; the package and the call increased the return rate about two-and-a-half fold; and the double call almost tripled the return rate. The memo was ineffective.

482. Wiseman, Frederick. "Methodological bias in public opinion surveys." *Public Opinion Quarterly,* Spring 1972, 36 (1), 105–108.

Responses given in a public opinion polling are not always independent of the method used to collect the data. Response bias is likely to be a problem in telephone and personal interviews whenever the question being asked is one for which there exists a socially undesirable response.

483.   Wiseman, Frederick. "Factor interaction effects in
        mail surveys." *Journal of Marketing Research*, August
        1973, 10 (3), 330–333.
        Four factors were examined to determine whe-
        ther there are interaction effects that improve re-
        sponse rates in mail surveys (small monetary in-
        centive, nature of return envelope, follow-up
        reminder, offer of survey results). The data sug-
        gest that the factors operate independently and
        that there are few interaction effects.

484.   Wiseman, Frederick. "A reassessment of the effects of
        personalization on response patterns in mail surveys."
        Journal of Marketing Research, February 1976, 13 (1),
        110–111.
        The author reviews some of the literature on the
        effects of personalization and calls for more inves-
        tigation of this topic. See reply by M. J. Houston
        and R. W. Jefferson (*Journal of Marketing Re-
        search*, February 1976, 112–113).

485.   Wiseman, Frederick, and McDonald, Philip. "Non-
        contact and refusal rates in consumer telephone sur-
        veys." *Journal of Marketing Research*, November 1979,
        16 (4), 478–484.
        Data supplied by major research firms and manu-
        facturers indicate that many studies have a high
        degree of nonresponse due, in large part, to con-
        trollable factors. Telephone surveys that made
        four attempts to reach people, with five telephone
        rings each time, were found to be optimally effi-
        cient. Also, interviews of ten minutes or less were
        found to reduce terminations.

486.   Wolfe, Arthur C., and Treiman, Beatrice R. "Postage
        types and response rates in mail surveys." *Journal of
        Advertising Research*, February 1979, 19 (1), 43–48.

This study suggests that it is worth the trouble of affixing a stamp to the return envelope rather than using a postal meter and that it is more effective to affix a commemorative stamp than a regular stamp to this envelope. In regard to the outer envelope, choice of postage stamps seems to make very little difference.

487. Wolfe, David F. "A new questionnaire design." *Journal of Marketing*, October 1956, 21 (12), 186–190.

A semimechanical questionnaire with several unique design characteristics is described. The questionnaire offers many advantages in increased accuracy of reporting, in improved field efficiency, in mechanical processing, and in reduced costs in printing, mailing, and handling. Ideal questions are those which can be precoded.

488. Wolfe, Lee M. "Characteristics of persons with and without home telephones." *Journal of Marketing Research*, August 1979, 16 (3), 421–425.

An analysis of NORC surveys shows that in most cases data based on households with telephones will vary by only about 2 percent from data based on all households.

489. Wotruba, Thomas R. "Monetary inducement and mail questionnaire response." *Journal of Marketing Research*, November 1966, 3 (4), 398–400.

The comparative effectiveness of a 25-cent inducement sent with the questionnaire, a promise of 50 cents for returning a completed questionnaire, and no monetary inducement was investigated in this study. The 25-cent incentive was found to be most effective and economically efficient.

490. Yu, Julie, and Cooper, Harris. "A quantitative review of research design effects on response rates to questionnaires." *Journal of Marketing Research*, February 1983, 20 (1), 36–44.

Response rates in 93 journal articles were examined and found to be increased by personal and telephone (versus mail) surveys, either prepaid or promised incentives, nonmonetary premiums and rewards, and increasing amounts of monetary reward. Other factors that increased responding were preliminary notification, foot-in-door techniques, personalization, and follow-up letters. Questionnaire length, the effects of a cover letter, assurances of anonymity, stating a deadline, providing postage, and the social utility or help-the-researcher types of appeal significantly affect response rates.

491. Zdep, S. M., and Rhodes, Isabelle N. "Making the randomized response technique work." *Public Opinion Quarterly*, Winter 1976–1977, 40 (4), 531–537.

The ability of the randomized response technique (RRT) to obtain sensitive information on surveys was compared to two other methods involving self-administered questionnaires. The RRT proved to be superior to the other methods.

492. Zdep, S. M.; Rhodes, Isabelle N.: Schwarz, R. M.; and Kilkenny, Mary J. "The validity of the randomized response technique." *Public Opinion Quarterly*, Winter 1979, 43 (4), 544–549.

The randomized response technique is a method designed to obtain reliable information when dealing with sensitive issues on surveys. The results of this study suggest that the RRT tends to become increasingly appropriate as the perceived sensitivity of a question increases.

493.   Zehner, Robert B., and McCalla, Mary Ellen. "Re-
        sponse rates and prior letters." *Journal of Advertising
        Research*, February 1977, 17 (1), 31–35.
            A preliminary letter, even one with an inter-
        viewer's note, did not lead to measurably higher
        overall rates of response in a nationwide study.
        Interviewer experience and training did not make
        a difference in the effect of the letter.

494.   Zelan, Joseph. "Interviewing the aged." *Public Opin-
        ion Quarterly*, Fall 1969, 33 (3), 420–424.
            Aged respondents, characterized by high involve-
        ment in a range of normal roles, presented no
        special problems to interviewers.

Appendix A:

SAMPLE QUESTIONNAIRES

On pages 206 through 233, following, are presented four sample questionnaires, three of them reduced photographs of the originals. Each new questionnaire begins on a left-hand page.

TASK FORCE ON GRADUATE ASSISTANTS

Please indicate your response by circling the appropriate alternative.

1. Do you believe most teaching assistants (T.A.'s) have a sincere interest in the undergraduate students in their classes?

Yes   No   (16)

2. Have teaching assistants in your classes been: (Circle one only)

Generally Satisfactory	Sometimes Satisfactory	Sometimes Unsatisfactory	Generally Unsatisfactory
1	2	3	4

(17)

3. When you have gone to teaching assistants for help about classwork, have they usually been helpful?

Yes   No   I have not gone   (18)

4. Do you feel free to take your academic problems to teaching assistants?

Yes   No   (19)

[At 75% of real size, the following eight pages, in pairs, show the four pages of the original questionnaire, on two 8½" x 11" sheets.]

5. Have you ever been asked to evaluate the teaching performance of your teaching assistants? Yes No (20)

6. Do you believe a teaching assistant should:

   A. Grade papers Yes No (21)

   B. Teach an entire course by himself Yes No (22)

   C. Assist the professor in teaching the course Yes No (23)

   D. Write course examinations Yes No (24)

   E. Talk with students who are having difficulties in the course Yes No (25)

   F. Determine final course grades Yes No (26)

7. How often have you experienced the following in regard to teaching assistants:

	Always	Often	Sometimes	Seldom	Never	
A. They were too busy to see me	1	2	3	4	5	(27)
B. They kept appointments	1	2	3	4	5	(28)
C. They had office hours	1	2	3	4	5	(29)
D. They kept their office hours	1	2	3	4	5	(30)

(over)

[The four original pages of this questionnaire were printed on split-pea soup color heavy stock paper.]

8. What suggestions do you have for improving the effectiveness of teaching assistants? (please discuss below)

[These two pages show page 2 of the original.]

9. In what ways have you found teaching assistants most helpful? (please discuss below)

TASK FORCE ON GRADUATE ASSISTANTS

OPINIONS

Please indicate your degree of agreement with each of the following statements by circling how you feel about graduate assistants at the University of Minnesota.

		Strongly Agree	Agree	Neutral	Disagree	Strongly Disagree	
1.	Most graduate assistants make a valuable contribution to the educational function of the University.	SA	A	N	D	SD	(40)
2.	In most cases, graduate assistant are more effective in working with undergraduate students than are professors.	SA	A	N	D	SD	(41)
3.	Graduate assistants should be paid more.	SA	A	N	D	SD	(42)
4.	Graduate assistantships should be eliminated.	SA	A	N	D	SD	(43)
5.	The majority of job grievances expressed by graduate assistants are justified.	SA	A	N	D	SD	(44)
6.	Undergraduate classes should not be taught by graduate assistants.	SA	A	N	D	SD	(45)
7.	The Association of Teaching and Research Assistants (ASTRA) is a worthwhile organization.	SA	A	N	D	SD	(46)

[These two pages show page 3 of the original.]

8. Graduate assistants are more concerned with their own course work than with their responsibilities as graduate assistants.   SA   A   N   D   SD (47)

9. Departmental graduate assistantships should be given only to students within that department.   SA   A   N   D   SD (48)

10. Graduate assistants should have an active role in determining their job assignments.   SA   A   N   D   SD (49)

11. Graduate assistants' salaries are adequate for their needs.   SA   A   N   D   SD (50)

12. The University should maintain a job placement office for all masters and doctoral graduates.   SA   A   N   D   SD (51)

13. Research projects should not be directed by graduate assistants.   SA   A   N   D   SD (52)

14. Most people overemphasize the importance of graduate assistants.   SA   A   N   D   SD (53)

15. The work graduate assistants do justifies their pay.   SA   A   N   D   SD (54)

16. If a graduate assistant, by reason of conscience, refused to work on a specific project, his appointment should be terminated.   SA   A   N   D   SD (55)

17. Graduate assistants should not be required to work at all during quarter breaks (last day of finals week until first day of classes).   SA   A   N   D   SD (56)

(over)

	Strongly Agree	Agree	Neutral	Disagree	Strongly Disagree	
18. There should be a university-wide system of recognition for superior graduate assistant performance.	SA	A	N	D	SD	(57)
19. Each department should have a system of recognition for superior graduate assistant performance.	SA	A	N	D	SD	(58)
20. The most important factor in determining job retention should be how the graduate assistant performs his duties.	SA	A	N	D	SD	(59)
21. Excellence in performance as a graduate assistant should be given special reward such as tuition waivers, honor awards, etc.	SA	A	N	D	SD	(60)
22. Graduate assistants are exploited by the University as a source of cheap labor.	SA	A	N	D	SD	(61)
23. Each department should have orientation or "pre-service" meetings specifically designed to assist graduate assistants in the performance of their duties.	SA	A	N	D	SD	(62)
24. Each department should have regular (at least once a month) in-service instruction on teaching and/or research techniques to aid graduate assistants.	SA	A	N	D	SD	(63)

[These two pages show page 4 of the original.]

25. Graduate assistants should play an active role in:

	Always	Often	Sometimes	Seldom	Never	
1. Selection of faculty	1	2	3	4	5	(64)
2. Selection of graduate assistants	1	2	3	4	5	(65)
3. Promotion of faculty	1	2	3	4	5	(66)
4. Promotion of graduate assistants	1	2	3	4	5	(67)
5. Development of curriculum	1	2	3	4	5	(68)
6. Development of instructional techniques	1	2	3	4	5	(69)
7. Development of research projects and/or techniques	1	2	3	4	5	(70)

[The End]

university measurement services center
9 clarence avenue s.e. minneapolis, minnesota 55414

COLLOQUIA QUESTIONNAIRE

I. INSTRUCTOR-RELATED ITEMS

1. Do the following characterize your instructor?

		Yes	No
a.	Well informed on subject matter of course	Y	N
b.	Stimulates interest in the subject	Y	N
c.	Explains difficult ideas clearly	Y	N
d.	Encourages criticism of his/her own ideas	Y	N
e.	Enthusiastic toward his/her teaching	Y	N
f.	Organizes class sessions well	Y	N

2. How does the fact that your instructor is an undergraduate affect your attitude toward him/her?

a. ____ it bothers me

b. ____ it makes no difference

c. ____ I like it

[At 75% real size, the following four pages, in pairs, show the two pages of the original questionnaire, on both sides of an 8½″ x 11″ sheet.]

II. *ATTITUDE TOWARD THE COURSE*

1. Have the expectations you had about this course been fulfilled?

    a. ____ Yes

    b. ____ No

2. If this course were offered again, would you recommend it to your friends?

    a. ____ Yes

    b. ____ No

3. Of how much value to you was this course?

    a. ____ Much value

    b. ____ Some value

    c. ____ No value

4. Would you like to see more courses taught by undergraduate students?

    a. ____ Yes

    b. ____ No

    c. ____ Uncertain

5. Has this course caused you to alter your career plans?

    a. ____ Yes

    b. ____ No

[The original sheet was a light canary yellow, medium-weight paper.]

6. Did this course cover the following areas to your satisfaction?

	Yes	No
a. historical development of sociology	Y	N
b. the career prospects of sociology majors	Y	N
c. the relationship of sociology to other academic areas	Y	N
d. current theories and methods of sociology	Y	N
e. information about the U of M sociology department	Y	N

7. Has this course helped you decide whether or not to major in sociology?

   a. ____ Yes

   b. ____ No

8. Has this course changed your opinion of what a person employed in sociology does?

   a. ____ Yes

   b. ____ No

9. Which aspects of the course did you like most?

10. What suggestions do you have for improving this course?

[The End]

University Measurement Services Center
University of Minnesota
9 Clarence Avenue S.E.
Minneapolis, Minnesota 55414

I.   Reactions to the Externship Program

1. Of how much value to you was the <u>seminar</u> portion of
    the externship program?

                        ____ a. Much value
                        ____ b. Some value
                        ____ c. Little value
                        ____ d. No value
2. Of how much value to you was the <u>field</u> portion of
    the externship program?
                        ____ a. Much value
                        ____ b. Some value
                        ____ c. Little value
                        ____ d. No value
3. Were you satisfied with the <u>seminar</u> portion of the
    externship program?
                        ____ a. Yes
                        ____ b. No
                        ____ c. Uncertain
4. Were you satisfied with the <u>field</u> portion of the
    externship program?
                        ____ a. Yes
                        ____ b. No
                        ____ c. Uncertain
5. Was the amount of time allowed for discussion during
    the <u>seminar</u> satisfactory?
                        ____ a. Yes
                        ____ b. No, too much time
                                  spent in discussion
                        ____ c. No, too little time
                                  allowed for discussion
6. What suggestions do you have for improving the
    <u>seminar</u> portion of the externship program?

7. What suggestions do you have for improving the <u>field</u>
    portion of the externship program?

[At approximately real size, the following two pages are a retyped
version page for page of the two sides of one original leaf on an
8½" x 11" sheet.]

8. During the <u>field</u> portion of the externship program, what diagnostic, therapeutic and/or surgical techniques did you carry out under supervision of the practitioner?

II. Attitude Changes Resulting from the Program

1. Have the <u>field</u> experiences of the externship program made your classroom experiences seem more relevant?

          ____ a. No
          ____ b. Yes (Describe below in what ways)

2. Do you believe the externship program has made you feel more confident about your competence as a veterinarian?

          ____ a. No
          ____ b. Yes (Describe below in which ways)

3. Have your externship experiences changed your opinion of what a practicing veterinarian does?

          ____ a. No
          ____ b. Yes (Describe below in what ways)

4. Have your externship experiences caused you to alter your career plans?

          ____ a. No
          ____ b. Yes (Describe below in what ways)

[The two original pages, one leaf, of this questionnaire were printed on a grainy medium salmon colored, medium-weight paper.]

GENERAL MOTORS CORPORATION

ORGANIZATIONAL DESCRIPTION QUESTIONNAIRE

This questionnaire is designed for you to describe how people are working together within your organization, and how effectively your organization is operating today.

It is important that you answer each question as thoughtfully and frankly as possible if this questionnaire is to be helpful and accurate in describing your organization.

[At 75% of real size, the following 14 pages, in pairs, show the first seven of the eight pages of the original questionnaire. The eighth, labelled "Do Not Write on This Page" was blank to allow no pencil-mark interference with the numerous spaces for answers on page 7.]

The completed questionnaire will be processed automatically by equipment which summarizes the answers in statistical form so that individuals cannot be identified. To maintain this complete confidentiality, please do not write your name anywhere on the questionnaire.

Form S
Organizational Research and Development Department
Personnel Administration and Development Staff
Revised 12/22/72

COPYRIGHT 1972, GENERAL MOTORS CORPORATION

NCS Trans-Optic S373C-3

[The original questionnaire was brown ink on white heavy-weight paper, which made up a double-stapled booklet of optical scanner-readable 8½″ by 11″ sheets.]

INSTRUCTIONS

1. Please answer all questions in order.

2. Most questions can be completed by filling in one of the answer spaces. If you do not find the exact answer that fits your case, use the one that is closest to it.

3. For most of these questions, you will have seven possible answers to choose from to indicate your thinking about each question. Although you are to pick only one answer for each question, in completing the entire questionnaire try to use the full range of answers.

4. Remember, the accuracy of your description depends on your being straightforward in answering this questionnaire. You will not be identified with your answers.

5. This questionnaire is designed for machine scanning of your answers. Questions are answered by marking the appropriate answer spaces (circles) as illustrated in this example:

Q. Which is the only marking instrument that will be read properly?

6. Please use a soft pencil and carefully observe these important requirements:

2

[These two pages show page 2 of the original.]

— Make heavy black marks that fill the circle.

— Erase cleanly any answer you wish to change.

— Where written numbers are called for, stay well within the area designated.

7. Definitions: To accurately complete this questionnaire you will need to know that when a question refers to:

a. Your ORGANIZATION, it means the largest unit where you work. Typically, this will mean your plant.

b. Your SUPERVISOR, it means the person to whom you report directly.

c. Your WORK GROUP, it means all those persons who report to the same supervisor that you do.

8. IDENTIFICATION OF SUPERVISOR: Questionnaire results can be summarized for each supervisor for later review with his people only when three or more people have identified the same supervisor. To determine this, take the separate sheet with the names of all the supervisors in your organization or unit. Find your supervisor's name on the list (he's the person you report to directly). Now, copy the number you find to the left of his name in these boxes. Below each box blacken the circle that is numbered the same as the number in the box. If your supervisor is not on the list, print his (or her) name in this space below:

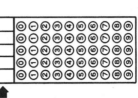

NAME_____

9. Now that you have completed the instructions, please begin with question 1 on the following page.

3.

About Your Organization

All the questions below are about what it is like to work for this organization in general. Remember, "organization" means the largest unit where you work. In most cases, this will mean your plant.

To What Extent:

	Not At All
	To A Very Little Extent
	To A Little Extent
	To Some Extent
	To A Great Extent
	To A Very Great Extent
	Completely

1. Do you have the information you need to do your job in the best possible way? . . . . ⑦⑥⑤④③②①

2. Do you know about this organization's goals and objectives? . . . . ⑦⑥⑤④③②①

12. How are disagreements between departments settled here?

⑤ Almost always recognized and resolved

④ Usually recognized and resolved

③ Sometimes disagreements are recognized and resolved

② Often avoided or denied

① Almost always avoided or denied

In general, how much say do each of the following have on what goes on in your department?

[These two pages show page 3 of the original.]

Scale headings: None / Very Little / Little / Some / Great Deal / Very Great Deal / Complete Say

13. First-level supervisors (foremen, office supervisors, etc.)

14. Top managers within the organization (plant manager, persons reporting directly to him)

15. Employes (people who have no subordinates)

16. Middle-managers (department heads, general supervisors)

17. Divisional level staff management

18. Local union leaders

19. GM corporate management

3. Are the equipment and resources you use to do your work efficient and well-maintained?

4. Does this organization have a promotion system that lets the best qualified person rise to the top?

5. Does this organization try to improve working conditions?

6. Does this organization suffer from a lack of planning?

7. Is there a great deal of criticism by employes about this organization?

8. Is this organization better run now than in the past?

9. Has this organization kept your way open to advancement?

10. Is information widely shared here so that those who make decisions have all the available know-how?

11. Do departments that need to pull together "on the same team" really help each other?

[It should be noted that the one leaf of pages 3 and 4, and the one leaf of pages 5 and 6, are arranged so that pencil marks (answers) on either side line up perfectly with and do not intrude upon the pencilled-in circles of the other side so that the scanning machine, of course, reads each sheet at one pass, regardless of which page (side) the answers are marked on.]

4.

About Your Supervisor

These next questions are about your supervisor. Remember, your supervisor is that person you report to directly.

To What Extent:

Rating scale (1–7):
Not At All — To A Very Little Extent — To A Little Extent — To Some Extent — To A Great Extent — To A Very Great Extent — Completely

20. Is your supervisor accurate in predicting what's going to happen next around here? .... ① ② ③ ④ ⑤ ⑥ ⑦

21. Does your supervisor provide you with the information you need to schedule work ahead of time? ...... ① ② ③ ④ ⑤ ⑥ ⑦

22. Does your supervisor set an example by working hard himself? .. ① ② ③ ④ ⑤ ⑥ ⑦

23. Does your supervisor encourage people who work for him to exchange their opinions and ideas? .... ① ② ③ ④ ⑤ ⑥ ⑦

Your Work Group

The questions below are about your work group. Remember, your work group consists of all the people who report to the same supervisor you do.

To What Extent:

Rating scale (1–7):
Not At All — To A Very Little Extent — To A Little Extent — To Some Extent — To A Great Extent — To A Very Great Extent — Completely

32. Are the persons in your work group friendly and easy to approach? ..... ① ② ③ ④ ⑤ ⑥ ⑦

33. Does your work group pay attention to what you are saying? .... ① ② ③ ④ ⑤ ⑥ ⑦

34. Does your work group maintain high standards of performance? ... ① ② ③ ④ ⑤ ⑥ ⑦

35. Do persons in your work group help you find ways to do a better job? .... ① ② ③ ④ ⑤ ⑥ ⑦

36. Does your work group offer new ideas for solving job-related problems? .... ① ② ③ ④ ⑤ ⑥ ⑦

[These two pages show page 4 of the original.]

24. Does your supervisor insist that he be kept informed on decisions made by persons under him? ...... ① ② ③ ④ ⑤ ⑥ ⑦

25. Is your supervisor willing to listen to your problems? .... ① ② ③ ④ ⑤ ⑥ ⑦

26. Does your supervisor refuse to change his mind once he's made it up? ...... ① ② ③ ④ ⑤ ⑥ ⑦

27. Is your supervisor quick to adopt new ideas? .... ① ② ③ ④ ⑤ ⑥ ⑦

28. Does your supervisor try out his own ideas in your work group? ..... ① ② ③ ④ ⑤ ⑥ ⑦

29. Does your supervisor hold meetings with your work group at certain regularly scheduled times? .... ① ② ③ ④ ⑤ ⑥ ⑦

30. Does your supervisor ask for sacrifices from people under him for the good of the entire work group? ..... ① ② ③ ④ ⑤ ⑥ ⑦

31. Does your supervisor see to it that persons under him are giving a fair day's work? ...... ① ② ③ ④ ⑤ ⑥ ⑦

37. Do members of your work group have trust and confidence in each other? .... ① ② ③ ④ ⑤ ⑥ ⑦

38. Does your work group encourage the people in it to work as a team? ... ① ② ③ ④ ⑤ ⑥ ⑦

39. Does your work group plan together and coordinate its efforts? .... ① ② ③ ④ ⑤ ⑥ ⑦

40. Is your work group able to respond successfully to unusual work demands placed upon it? ...... ① ② ③ ④ ⑤ ⑥ ⑦

41. Do persons in your work group know what their jobs are and how to do them well? .... ① ② ③ ④ ⑤ ⑥ ⑦

42. Are the purposes or goals of your work group clear to you? .... ① ② ③ ④ ⑤ ⑥ ⑦

43. Do you accept the goals of your work group? .... ① ② ③ ④ ⑤ ⑥ ⑦

44. Is your work group effective in meeting schedules with high quality results? .... ① ② ③ ④ ⑤ ⑥ ⑦

Your Job

The following questions are about your present job and how you feel about it.

To What Extent:

	Not At All	To A Very Little Extent	To A Little Extent	To Some Extent	To A Great Extent	To A Very Great Extent	Completely

45. Does your job allow you to make major decisions that affect your work? ⑦ ⑥ ⑤ ④ ③ ② ①

46. Does your job give you a chance to use your own ideas? ⑦ ⑥ ⑤ ④ ③ ② ①

47. Are your job duties related to what you expected to be doing? ⑦ ⑥ ⑤ ④ ③ ② ①

48. Does your job provide variety? ⑦ ⑥ ⑤ ④ ③ ② ①

49. Are you always working on "rush" jobs? ⑦ ⑥ ⑤ ④ ③ ② ①

50. Do you want more opportunity in your job to assume more important responsibilities? ⑦ ⑥ ⑤ ④ ③ ② ①

Satisfaction

Considering everything, how satisfied are you:

	Very dissatisfied	Dissatisfied	Neither satisfied nor dissatisfied	Satisfied	Very satisfied

53. With your job? ⑤ ④ ③ ② ①

54. With your opportunities to get a better job in this organization? ⑤ ④ ③ ② ①

55. With your pay? ⑤ ④ ③ ② ①

56. With the information you receive on what is going on in your organization? ⑤ ④ ③ ② ①

57. With the training you received for your present job? ⑤ ④ ③ ② ①

58. With your supervisor? ⑤ ④ ③ ② ①

59. With the people in your work group? ⑤ ④ ③ ② ①

60. Considering everything, how would you rate your overall satisfaction in this GM organization at the present time? ⑤ ④ ③ ② ①

[These two pages show page 5 of the original.]

51. Do you want more opportunity in your job to select and evaluate the methods you use to do your job? .... ⑦⑥⑤④③②①

52. We all do some things because we have to. We do other things because we really enjoy them, they really interest and challenge us. Compared to the amount of effort you put into doing those things which really interest and challenge you, how much effort do you find yourself putting into your job?

More effort into my job than any other thing ...... ⑦

Just as much effort into my job ...... ⑥

Almost as much (80-85%) effort into my job ...... ⑤

About 75% as much effort into my job as I put into things that really interest me ...... ④

A little more than half – (60-70%) of what I put into things that really interest me ...... ③

Somewhat less effort – about half (50%) of what I put into things that really interest me ...... ②

A great deal less effort – less than half the effort I put into things that really interest me ...... ①

About Yourself

These next questions relate most closely to you, your experiences, and how you feel about certain things. These questions will not be used to identify anyone. They are included to relate what effect your experiences may have on your answers to other items in this questionnaire.

How much importance do you place on each of the following in considering how satisfied you are with a job:

| | Not important | Fairly unimportant | Of some importance | Fairly important | Very important |

61. Geographical location where you work.. ⑤④③②①

62. Good working conditions (space, little noise, clean, etc.) ...... ⑤④③②①

63. Security...... ⑤④③②①

64. Sex:

① Male

② Female

6.

About Yourself (continued)

59. While you were growing up – until you were about eighteen - what kind of community did you generally live in?

○ Rural or farm

○ Town or small city not near large city

○ Suburban area near large city

○ Large city

60. How long have you worked for GM?

○ Less than 1 year   ○ 5 years to less than 10 years

○ 1 to less than 2 years   ○ 10 years to less than 15 years

○ 2 years to less than 3 years ○ 15 years to less than 25 years

○ 3 years to less than 4 years ○ 25 years or more

○ 4 years to less than 5 years

61. How long have you worked in this organization?

64. Not counting paid vacations, holidays or formal leaves, how often would you estimate you are absent from work during the year?

○ Less than one day a year   ○ 10–15 days

○ 1–5 days   ○ Over 15 days

○ 6–10 days

65. Within the past year did you ever have thoughts of leaving this organization?

○ Yes, many times   ○ Yes, but never seriously

○ Yes, once or twice   ○ No

66. How would you feel about working on a job where the ways of doing things were always being changed?

○ Would never feel at ease   ○ Would like it somewhat

○ Would seldom feel at ease ○ Would like it very much

○ Would not bother me

[These two pages show page 6 of the original.]

Satisfaction

Considering everything, how satisfied are you:

	Very dissatisfied	Dissatisfied	Neither satisfied nor dissatisfied	Satisfied	Very satisfied
67. With your job?	①	②	③	④	⑤
68. With your opportunities to get a better job in this organization?	①	②	③	④	⑤
69. With your pay?	①	②	③	④	⑤
70. With the information you receive on what is going on in your organization?	①	②	③	④	⑤
71. With the training you received for your present job?	①	②	③	④	⑤
72. With your supervisor?	①	②	③	④	⑤
73. With the people in your work group?	①	②	③	④	⑤
74. Considering everything, how would you rate your overall satisfaction in this GM organization at the present time?	①	②	③	④	⑤

○ Less than 1 year
○ 1 to less than 2 years
○ 2 years to less than 3 years
○ 3 years to less than 4 years
○ 4 years to less than 5 years
○ 5 years to less than 10 years
○ 10 years to less than 15 years
○ 15 years to less than 25 years
○ 25 years or more

62. Your job would be classified in which of the following levels?

○ Do not know
○ Hourly—Skilled trades
○ Hourly—all others
○ Second or third level
○ Fourth or fifth level
○ Sixth level
○ Seventh level
○ Eighth level
○ Unclassified

63. How many times during the last five years have you held a position as president, captain, or chairman of any clubs, teams or committees?

○ Five or more
○ Four
○ Three
○ Two
○ One
○ None

7.

75. How well do you feel this questionnaire allowed you to describe your organization?

⑤ All of the questions were "on target"

④ Almost all of the questions were "on target"

③ Most of the questions were "on target"

② Some of the questions were "on target"

① Not at all well, didn't ask the right questions

ON SEPARATE SHEETS YOU WILL FIND ADDITIONAL QUESTIONS.
PLEASE ANSWER THEM IN THE SPACES PROVIDED BELOW.

#	①	②	③	④	⑤		#	①	②	③	④	⑤		#	①	②	③	④	⑤
76.	①	②	③	④	⑤		96.	①	②	③	④	⑤		116.	①	②	③	④	⑤
77.	①	②	③	④	⑤		97.	①	②	③	④	⑤		117.	①	②	③	④	⑤
78.	①	②	③	④	⑤		98.	①	②	③	④	⑤		118.	①	②	③	④	⑤
79.	①	②	③	④	⑤		99.	①	②	③	④	⑤		119.	①	②	③	④	⑤
80.	①	②	③	④	⑤		100.	①	②	③	④	⑤		120.	①	②	③	④	⑤
81.	①	②	③	④	⑤		101.	①	②	③	④	⑤		121.	①	②	③	④	⑤

[These two pages show page 7 of the original.]

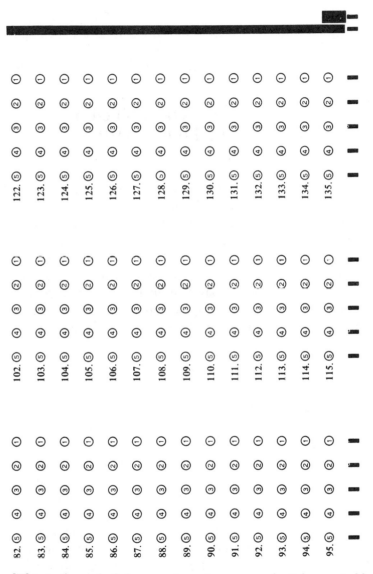

[This is the end of the questionnaire proper; the 8th page is blank (see caption, page 220).]

Appendix B:

CASE HISTORY OF A STUDY USING QUESTIONNAIRES

Reviewing an actual case history of a study that used question-naires should point out valuable insights and prevent costly oversights on the part of those who will conduct future studies using questionnaires. With this in mind, we have included the case history below based on a study [10] of graduate assistants at the University of Minnesota. This study is candidly presented with the hope that readers may benefit from our blunders as well as our successful tactics. Supplementary materials actually used in the study are located in the exhibits at the end of this appendix.

Origin of the Study

In March 1971, members of a graduate assistant association met with University of Minnesota administrators to discuss issues relevant to the roles and functions of graduate assistants. A decision was made at this meeting to conduct a study of graduate assistants at the University. This study was to be coordinated by a presidential task force.

The task force met regularly throughout the summer of 1971. Members discussed the kinds of information that would be useful to gather and assembled an outline of suggested items that might be asked of people surveyed in the study. Task force members expressed the desire to gather a variety of information, including 1) administrative descriptive data (distributions of graduate assistants by rank, college, etc.); 2) demographic and personal information pertinent to graduate assistants; 3) perceptions of graduate assistant roles; 4) descriptions of personnel policies and practices regarding graduate assistants; and 5) position duties, orientation, training, and evaluation of graduate assistants.

In October 1971, the University Measurement Services Center (MSC) was asked if they would conduct the study. MSC agreed to conduct the study and staff members prepared a research proposal that was presented to and approved by the task force. The goals of the study as developed by MSC were these:

1. To describe roles and functions of graduate assistants at the University of Minnesota.

2. To describe attitudes toward graduate assistants held by specified groups within the University.

3. To describe how various groups believe the University should administer graduate assistantships.

4. To discuss problematic situations relevant to graduate assistants as seen by various groups within the University.

5. To make recommendations regarding policies relevant to graduate assistants.

A sample of one outline of information desired by the task force is shown [recomposed] in Exhibit 1. This outline, together with others like it, provided the starting point from which MSC staff were able to design the study and construct the six questionnaires used in the study.

Designing the Study

After looking at the information desired by the task force, MSC staff members decided this information could best be obtained from college deans, department chairmen, university administrators, faculty members, graduate assistants, and undergraduate students. The decision was made to survey all the graduate assistants and department chairmen because MSC believed the risk of missing unique individual cases could be avoided by surveying these entire populations. Due to the large number of people from whom information was desired, questionnaires were considered the most feasible method of obtaining this information.

Determining who should be sent questionnaires was no easy task. More than a month was needed to update a list of who were actually graduate assistants at the time of the study. This updating was accomplished by comparing a computer print-out of the university payroll to lists of names obtained from the individual departments and units at the university. Because questionnaires were initially mailed to the separate departments employing graduate assistants, we enclosed the instruction sheet displayed [recomposed] in Exhibit 2 as a further check of who the graduate assistants really were. The MSC project directors also personally travelled to a coordinate campus to inform administrators there of the study and to further check the names of both graduate assistants and faculty at that campus. Similar problems existed for defining the other five groups that were surveyed. The lesson to be learned is that usually a population is not defined initially in a clear-cut way. Sufficient time should always be allowed to decide how to determine exactly whom you wish to complete questionnaires.

Designing the Questionnaire

The items suggested for the questionnaire that were received from the task force were reorganized so that the information requested could be obtained from people best qualified to give accurate answers. Questionnaire items were drafted and re-drafted (a total of 13 times) while striving for both clarity of meaning and formats that would be easy to understand. During this stage of the questionnaire construction, suggested drafts were circulated among seven or eight MSC staff members for criticism. The person responsible for the technical aspects of data analysis (computer programming, keypunching, etc.) was actively involved at this stage and suggested formats that would facilitate later data analysis. Exhibit 3 [recomposed] shows one of the early versions of the questionnaire for obtaining information from department chairmen.

The thirteenth draft of the questionnaire was pretested by mailing copies to samples of people who were actually members of the population under study. Exhibit 4 shows the cover letter and questionnaire [both recomposed] that were mailed to department chairmen during the pretest. Additional copies of the questionnaire also were sent to selected "questionnaire experts" on the university campus. After considering the comments of these "experts" and those receiving the pretest questionnaires, and after analyzing the results from these questionnaires, the final questionnaires were drafted. The final department chairmen questionnaire [i.e., the original] appears in Exhibit 5. An MSC artist helped design all questionnaire formats in a manner thought to be most appealing to respondents.

Mailing and Follow-up of Questionnaires

Before the actual questionnaires were mailed, a pre-letter was sent to each person who would be sent a questionnaire. This pre-letter announced the study and informed the recipient of the study purpose. A copy of this pre-letter [i.e., the original] is shown as Exhibit 6. The questionnaires were mailed with the [original] cover letter shown as Exhibit 7 and with a self-addressed return envelope with postage stamp attached.

A series of follow-up tactics were used to stimulate the return of questionnaires. The originals of some of these follow-ups are shown as Exhibit 8. Table 1 (below) shows the mailing dates of all correspondence sent to subjects throughout the study and should give the reader a rough estimate of the time it takes to mail and follow-up a large number of questionnaires. Between the mailing of the "Eyes" follow-up and the Letter of April 10, telephone calls were made to nonrespondents as a further way of eliciting their cooperation and to find out why they had not returned a questionnaire. Exhibit 9 shows two examples [originals] of personalized letters sent by the project directors in response to specific problems expressed by subjects. The project directors made personal visits to certain subjects who expressed unusual hostility toward the study and, in most cases, these subjects were willing to cooperate after they had been contacted personally (see Exhibit 10). Original copies of several examples of subjects' reactions to several of the follow-ups used are included as Exhibit 11.

Table 2 (below) shows the final response rates from each of the six groups surveyed. We believe the reason the faculty re-

Table 1:

MAILING DATES (all 1972) FOR THE 6 STUDY GROUPS

	GA[a]	DC[b]	Fac[c]	Und[d]	Ds[e]	Adm[f]
Pre-letter	1/19	1/19	1/19	1/19	1/19	1/19
Questionnaire	2/10	2/10	2/10	2/8	2/10	2/10
Valentine				2/12		
Violin	2/28	2/28	2/28	2/28	2/28	2/28
Rhino	3/10	3/10	3/10	3/10	3/10	3/10
Eyes	3/22	3/22	3/22	3/22	3/22	3/22
Letter	4/10	4/10	4/10	4/10	4/10	4/10
Mailbox	4/17	4/17	4/17	4/17	4/17	4/17
Raffle	4/24	4/24	4/24	4/24	4/24	4/24

[a]GA = Graduate Assistants;   [b]DC = Department Chairmen;   [c]Fac = Faculty;   [d]Und = Undergraduates;   [e]Ds = Deans;   [f]Adm = Administrators.

Table 2:

RESPONSE RATES BY STUDY GROUPS

Study Groups	Total N of Group	Usable Responses N	Usable Responses %
Administrators	18	17	94
College Deans	24	22	92
Graduate Assistants	2288	2043	89
Undergrad. Students	785	700	89
Department Chairmen	168	145	86
Faculty	344	281	82
Total	3627	3208	88*

*Percent returned of total N for all groups.

sponse rate was "only" 82 percent is largely attributable to oversights in the cover letter. The cover letter failed to list faculty members as one of the groups being surveyed. Also, the cover letter failed to make clear to either faculty or undergraduates that their participation was desired even if they had had no direct experience with graduate assistants.

Cost Considerations

The following is a list of items that cost money for this study. It will remind the reader of cost factors that typically occur in studies using questionnaires.

A. Pilot pre-test of Questionnaires
   1. Printing and copying costs of questionnaires and cover letters
   2. Postage (2 ways)
   3. Envelopes (2 ways)
   4. Clerical help (typing and mailing)
   5. Salaries

B.   Main Survey and Follow-ups
1.   Printing and copying costs of question-
      naires, pre-letters, cover letters, and fol-
      low-ups
2.   Postage (2 ways for questionnaire plus fol-
      low-ups)
3.   Envelopes (2 ways for questionnaire plus
      follow-ups)
4.   Clerical help (typing and mailing)
5.   Salaries
6.   Keypunch costs (cards, keypunching, and
      verifying)
7.   Computer costs
8.   Telephone bills for long-distance
      follow-ups
9.   Mailing labels
10.   Art materials for questionnaire format work
      and follow-ups
11.   Printing of final report
12.   Mail distribution of final report

EXHIBIT 1

Subject: Position Duties

QUESTIONS TO BE ANSWERED BY DEPARTMENT HEADS:

1. Note average number of hours for position duties contributed weekly by a teaching assistant or research
assistant on 50% time appointment.

    a. Less than 15 ____
    b. 15 - 20   ____
    c. 20 - 25   ____
    d. More than 25 ____
    e. Other. Please elaborate.

2. Do assistants in your department independently or under
limited supervision ever design courses in their entirety
(objectives, content, evaluation)?

	T. A.	T. A. I	T. A. II
a. Never			
b. On occasion			
c. As regular procedure			

3. Do assistants in your department provide the principal
instruction for a departmental course (a majority of the
lectures, conduct of evaluation, etc.)?

	T. A.	T. A. I	T. A. II
a. Never			
b. On occasion			
c. As a regular procedure			

4. What roles do assistants of your department play in
student evaluation?

    a. Have complete responsibility for designing and administering tests and determining grades.

241

	T. A.	T. A. I	T. A. II
1. Never			
2. On occasion			
3. As a regular procedure			

b. Assist senior staff members in developing and administering tests and determining grades.

	T. A.	T. A. I	T. A. II
1. Never			
2. On occasion			
3. As a regular procedure			

5. Do assistants in your department actively assist in the development of (creation of) instructional materials for use in departmental courses?

	T. A.	T. A. I	T. A. II
a. Never			
b. On occasion			
c. As a regular procedure			

6. Do teaching associates and assistants in your department maintain regularly defined or specified office hours?

Yes_____ No_____.

7. Do most teaching assistants in your department serve as student advisers?

a. On matters specific to designated courses

CIRCLE ONE

Never   On occasion   As a regular procedure

b. On general program of the department

Never   On occasion   As a regular procedure

c. In the general sense (as junior staff adviser)

Never   On occasion   As a regular procedure

8. Can you estimate the distribution of the time of assistants in your department among the various levels of instruction:

Level	T. A.	T. A. I	T. A. II	Percent of total time
Prefix 1	___	___	___	_____
3	___	___	___	_____
5	___	___	___	_____
8	___	___	___	_____
				100%

9. Does your department have a well-defined policy that provides for teaching opportunities for T. A. 's?

    a. Yes, well-defined   _____
    b. Informal program,   _____
       reasonably common
       in application
    c. No   _____

10. Please describe your department's policy if you have one.

[EXHIBIT 1 cont.]

Subject: Orientation, Training and Evaluation of Graduate Assistants

VIII. Orientation, Training, and Evaluation of Graduate Assistants

1. Initial Orientation

    1. 1 Is there departmental printed material available orienting T. A. 's and R. A. 's towards:

        1. 11 position duties?
        1. 12 recommended teaching/research/counseling techniques?
        1. 13 personnel policies and practices (i. e. promotion, retention, etc.)?
        1. 14 available support resources (i. e. secre-

tarial, audio-visual, etc.)?
1. 15 cultural affairs (University and community)?
1. 16 evaluation of job performance?

1. 2   Have you received departmental printed material orienting you on the following:

(1. 11 through 1. 16 above)

1. 3   Is there pre-service instruction to orient
T. A. 's and R. A. 's towards:

1. 11 through 1. 16 above, and

1. 17 briefly describe any other types of orientation available.

(These questions should be asked of T. A. 's,
R. A. 's, department heads, deans (college and
Graduate School).)

2.   Instruction (same as training on outline)

2. 1   Is continual in-service instruction offered?
(i. e. seminars--credit or non-credit, periodic
meetings, lecture series, etc.)

2. 2   Is there advanced in-service instruction appropriate to course level taught?

3.   Evaluation

3. 1   Describe in detail the formal and informal
evaluation of T. A. and R. A. teaching/re-
search counseling responsibilities in your department including such things as the technique
and frequency.

3. 11 Are results discussed with the T. A. or
R. A. ?   How?
3. 12 Does the evaluation provide for T. A. or
R. A. rebuttal?   How?
3. 13 What use is made of T. A. job evaluation
data?
3. 14 Is T. A. or R. A. retention based pri-
marily on:

a) performance as a graduate student,
b) performance in the position duties,
c) a combination of these, or
d) both.

(These questions should be asked of departments,
T. A. 's, R. A. 's and faculty.)

3. 2   Do T. A. 's and R. A. 's participate in the
       evaluation of other T. A. 's or R. A. 's in their
       position duties? Yes_____ No_____.

3. 3   Do undergraduates participate in the evalua-
       tion of other T. A. 's or R. A. 's in their po-
       sition duties? Yes_____ No_____.

3. 4   What is your perception of the evaluation
       process? Is it fair? Is it constructive?
       (for T. A.'s and R. A. 's)

(Department heads should be asked to furnish the
Task Force with copies of <u>any</u> printed material
relevant to evaluation.)

4.   Recognition of Job Excellence

4. 1   Describe the way excellence is rewarded.

EXHIBIT 2

This envelope contains questionnaires for the University task force study of graduate assistants. Also included is a list of all graduate assistants in your department or unit.

The following instructions should help make your participation simpler and minimize the time you spend handling materials:

1. Give the list of graduate assistants to someone who would know whether or not they are currently employed. Usually this is the budget secretary.

2. Since this list may not be accurate, please update it by using the following definition of a graduate assistant:

   a) a graduate student who is a teaching associate I (9501), teaching associate II (9502), teaching assistant (9511), or research assistant (9521) and;

   b) a graduate student who was on the payroll during fall quarter and is also on the present winter quarter payroll. (Do not include undergraduate assistants).

3. Distribute questionnaires to those students fitting the above definition and return all others to us with the updated list.

If you have any questions, call Jack or Doug at 373-2263.
Thank you for your helpful participation.

EXHIBIT 3

_____   Name _____

QUESTIONNAIRE FOR DEPARTMENT CHAIRMEN

1. Do you know of available printed material in your department that states:

   1. The position duties of a graduate
      assistant?   Yes _____
                                           No _____

   2. Recommended techniques to be used
      by a graduate assistant in his duties? Yes _____
                                           No _____

   3. Resources that are available to the
      graduate assistant, such as secre-
      tarial and audio-visual services?   Yes _____
                                           No _____

   4. The personnel policies and practices
      of your department regarding promo-
      tion and retention of graduate
      assistants?   Yes _____
                                           No _____

   5. The ways in which a graduate assis-
      tant's job performance is evaluated? Yes _____
                                           No _____

   6. Cultural activities available to grad-
      uate assistants in the University and
      surrounding community?   Yes _____
                                         No _____

2. Of the graduate assistants in your department over the last five years, approximately what percentage were male?
                                  0-5% _____
                                  5-25% _____
                               25-50% _____
                               50-75% _____
                               75-95% _____
                              95-100% _____

3. Of the graduate assistants in your department over the last five years, approximately what percentage were

American Negroes?   0-5% _____
                                       5-25% _____
                                       25-50% _____
                                       50-75% _____
                                       75-95% _____
                                       95-100% _____

4. Of the graduate assistants in your department over the
    last five years, approximately what percentage were
    American Indian?   0-5% _____
                                       5-25% _____
                                       25-50% _____
                                       50-75% _____
                                       75-95% _____
                                       95-100% _____

5. Of the graduate assistants in your department over the
    last five years, approximately what percentage were
    Chicanos?   0-5% _____
                                       5-25% _____
                                       25-50% _____
                                       50-75% _____
                                       75-95% _____
                                       95-100% _____

6. Of the graduates assistants in your department over the
    last five years, approximately what percentage were
    foreign students?   0-5% _____
                                       5-25% _____
                                       25-50% _____
                                       50-75% _____
                                       75-95% _____
                                       95-100% _____

7. In your department, is instruction offered for graduate
    assistants throughout their appointments on areas related
    to their duties?   Yes _____
                                                 No _____

8. In your department is there advanced training for grad-
    uate assistants appropriate to the level of course being
    taught or level of research being conducted?
                                                 Yes _____
                                                 No _____

9. In your department are new graduate assistants furnished
    with a job description describing such things as rank,
    percentage and length of appointment, work hours re-

quired per week, and name of supervisor?

Yes _____
No _____

10. Does your department have a printed policy regarding the work hours and responsibilities of graduate assistants?

Yes _____
No _____

11. Do you know of a printed University policy regarding the work hours and responsibilities of graduate assistants?

Yes _____
No _____

12. Does your department follow any printed policy regarding the work hours and responsibilities of graduate assistants?

Yes _____
No _____

13. Should departmental graduate assistantships be given only to students within that department?

Yes _____
No _____

14. How many hours of work per week do you expect of a 25% appointment graduate assistant?

(whole hours) _____hrs.

15. Are available assistantships always made known to all graduate students?

Yes _____
No _____

16. Are available assistantships always made known to all applicants?

Yes _____
No _____

17. Does your department adhere to the April 15th deadline of the Council of Graduate Schools concerning graduate assistant selection procedures?

Yes _____
No _____

18. Does your department use a waiting list in the selection procedures of graduate assistants?

Yes _____
No _____

19. If your department uses a waiting list, are applicants told where they stand on the list?

Yes _____
No _____
We don't use a list _____

20. In your department, which <u>one</u> of the following is most influential in selecting teaching associates and assistants? (check <u>1</u>)
   1. Departmental chairman   1. _____
   2. Director of Graduate Students   2. _____
   3. Faculty committee   3. _____
   4. Individual faculty members   4. _____
   5. Our department has no teaching
      associates or assistants   5. _____

21. In your department, which <u>one</u> of the following is most influential in selecting research assistants? (check <u>1</u>)
   1. Departmental chairman   1. _____
   2. Director of Graduate Students   2. _____
   3. Faculty committee   3. _____
   4. Individual faculty members   4. _____
   5. Our department has no research
      assistants   5. _____

22. If you were confronted with two applicants of equal quality and status but one had experience as a graduate assistant and the other did not, would you select the applicant with experience?   Yes _____
                                                   No _____

23A (to be asked of 1/2 the pilot study subjects)
   Upon which <u>one</u> of the following does your department place <u>most</u> emphasis in the selection of graduate assistants? (check <u>1</u>)
   1. Grade point average   1. _____
   2. Test results   2. _____
   3. Recommendations   3. _____
   4. Prior experience as an assistant   4. _____
   5. Financial need   5. _____
   6. Minority status   6. _____
   7. Sex   7. _____
   8. Publications by the applicant   8. _____
   9. Other (please state) _____

23B (to be asked of those not asked 23A)
   Please rank the following in terms of criteria your department uses to select graduate assistants (place the number 1 in the space of that criterion your department considers most important, the number 2 in the space of that criterion considered second most important, etc.).
      1. Grade point average   1. _____

2. Test results   2. _____
3. Recommendations   3. _____
4. Prior experience as an assistant   4. _____
5. Financial need   5. _____
6. Minority status   6. _____
7. Sex   7. _____
8. Publications by the applicant   8. _____
9. Other (please state) _____   9. _____

24. Which of the following indicates the length of time prior to the actual beginning of their appointment that graduate assistants in your department receive specific information (other than the general nature of their assignment) regarding their appointment (information such as which textbooks will be used, specific research techniques to be used, and class time)?
    1. No advanced notice   _____
    2. Advanced notice of less than one week   _____
    3. Advanced notice of from one to two weeks   _____
    4. Advanced notice of more than two weeks   _____

25. Does an individual graduate assistant's assignment usually utilize his own special academic skills?
                                                 Yes _____
                                                 No _____

26. Does an individual graduate assistant's assignment usually utilize his own special non-academic skills?
                                                 Yes _____
                                                 No _____

27. Do the individual graduate assistants in your department usually have a choice in their assignment?
                                                 Yes _____
                                                 No _____

28. Does the seniority of a graduate assistant increase his chance of having a choice in his own assignment?
                                                 Yes _____
                                                 No _____

29. Are there graduate assistants in your department that are not majors in your department?   Yes _____
                                                 No _____

30. Do you know of students in your department that hold assistantships in other departments?   Yes _____
                                                 No _____

31.   Do you know of graduate assistants in your department
      who also hold graduate assistantships in other depart-
      ments?   Yes _____
                                                        No _____

32.   In your department, do the following participate in the
      evaluation of a given graduate assistant?
      1.   Faculty committee   1.   Yes _____
                                                        No _____
      2.   Departmental chairman   2.   Yes _____
                                                        No _____
      3.   Professor to whom assistant
           is assigned   3.   Yes _____
                                                        No _____
      4.   Other graduate assistants   4.   Yes _____
                                                        No _____
      5.   Undergraduate students   5.   Yes _____
                                                        No _____

33.   In your department, are the results of a graduate
      assistant's evaluation discussed with him? Yes _____
                                                  No _____

34.   Is there a formal procedure in your department by which
      graduate assistants may offer rebuttal to the evaluation of
      their performance?   Yes _____
                                                      No _____

35.   Which of the following is the most important factor in
      determining a graduate assistant's retention (choose
      one)?
      1.   Performance of job duties   1. _____
      2.   Success in graduate studies   2. _____

36.   In your department, to whom are the results of graduate
      assistant evaluations made available?
      1.   Departmental faculty   1.   Yes _____
                                                        No _____
      2.   Any University faculty member   2.   Yes _____
                                                        No _____
      3.   The graduate assistant who
           was evaluated   3.   Yes _____
                                                        No _____
      4.   Prospective employers of the
           graduate assistant who was
           evaluated   4.   Yes _____
                                                        No _____

5. Other students   5. Yes _____
                                                No _____
6. Anyone   6. Yes _____
                                                No _____

37. In your opinion, is the evaluation procedure used by your
     department for evaluating graduate assistants a fair one?
                                                Yes _____
                                                No _____

38. In your department, is excellence in performance as a
     graduate assistant given any substantial reward other
     than retention, such as tuition waivers, honor awards,
     etc. ?   Yes _____
                                                No _____

39. Does the initial appointment of graduate assistants in
     your department usually carry an implicit or explicit
     promise of continued financial support for the length of
     time required to complete the degree?   Yes _____
                                                No _____

40. Does your department have a limit on the number of
     years an individual can hold a graduate assistantship?
                                                Yes _____
                                                No _____

41. Check which of the below criteria for promotion you
     consider to be the most important for graduate assis-
     tants in your department. (check 1)
     1. Seniority at the University of Minnesota   1. ____
     2. Seniority in total graduate assistantship
         experience   2. ____
     3. Proficiency in graduate work (as a
         student)   3. ____
     4. Proficiency as a graduate assistant
         (job duties)   4. ____
     5. There is no graduate assistant promo-
         tion in our department   5. ____

42. Does your department have a printed policy describing
     reasons for non-reappointment of graduate assistants?
                                                Yes _____
                                                No _____

43.   Are the graduate assistants in your department given the same quarter breaks as the student body?   Yes _____
                                                                        No _____

44.   Are graduate assistants in your department ever penalized for absence from their job duties?
                                                                       Yes _____
                                                                        No _____

45.   Are pregnant graduate assistants in your department required to resign because of their pregnancy (at a stated time in the pregnancy)?   Yes _____
                                                                        No _____
      Our department has no women G.A.'s _____

46.   In your department, is childbirth considered an excusable reason for graduate assistant absence?
                                                                       Yes _____
                                                                        No _____

47.   Is the average excused absence for childbirth in your department less than two weeks?   Yes _____
                                                                        No _____
                        Childbirth is not grounds
                            for excused absence _____

48.   Does your department have a faculty committee on graduate assistant affairs?   Yes _____
                                                                        No _____

49.   Are the graduate assistants in your department encouraged to attend departmental functions such as special lectures and social functions?   Yes _____
                                                                        No _____

50.   Do the graduate assistants in your department attend departmental functions such as special lectures and social functions?   Yes _____
                                                                        No _____

51.   Does your department encourage graduate assistants to join the Association of Student Teachers and Research Assistants (ASTRA)?   Yes _____
                                                                        No _____

52.   Does your department encourage graduate assistants to join the American Association of University Professors

(AAUP)?   Yes _____
                                             No _____

53. Does your department encourage graduate assistants to
     join professional organizations?   Yes _____
                                             No _____

54. Does your department encourage graduate assistants to
     join the Council of Graduate Students (COGS)?
                                             Yes _____
                                             No _____

55. Do you believe that graduate assistants' salaries are
     adequate for their needs?   Yes _____
                                             No _____

56. Do you believe graduate assistants earn their pay?
                                             Yes _____
                                             No _____

57. Do you believe the importance of graduate assistants is
     overemphasized?   Yes _____
                                             No _____

58. Do you believe that graduate assistants have legitimate
     grievances?   Yes _____
                                             No _____

59. Do you believe the majority of graduate assistants are
     satisfied in their role as graduate assistants?
                                             Yes _____
                                             No _____

60. Does your department augment the base salary of grad-
     uate assistants with the following:
     1. Budgeted departmental funds   1. Yes _____
                                             No _____
     2. Grants   2. Yes _____
                                             No _____
     3. Fellowships   3. Yes _____
                                             No _____
     4. Other (please specify)_____

61. Does your department have a system of recognition for
     graduate assistants that exhibit superior performance?
                                             Yes _____
                                             No _____

62. Does your department assist with the travel expenses of the department's graduate assistants to professional meetings?   Yes _____
                                                                        No _____

63. Would you like to see a university-wide system of recognition for superior graduate assistant performance?
                                                                        Yes _____
                                                                        No _____

64. Do the graduate assistants in your department have the following:

    1. Individual desks   1. Yes _____
                                              No _____
    2. Shared desks   2. Yes _____
                                              No _____
    3. Phone access   3. Yes _____
                                              No _____
    4. Mailbox   4. Yes _____
                                              No _____
    5. Clerical support   5. Yes _____
                                              No _____
    6. Free course textbooks   6. Yes _____
                                              No _____
    7. Office supplies   7. Yes _____
                                              No _____
    8. Other (please list) _____

65. Do you believe the following graduate assistants' needs are being adequately met?

    1. Salary   1. Yes _____
                                              No _____
    2. Recognition for superior
       performance   2. Yes _____
                                              No _____
    3. Office space   3. Yes _____
                                              No _____
    4. Office equipment   4. Yes _____
                                              No _____

66. Do graduate assistants have sufficient access to the following teaching aids:

    1. Audio visual equipment   1. Yes _____
                                              No _____
    2. Library sources   2. Yes _____
                                              No _____

3. Reproducing equipment   3. Yes _____
                                       No _____

67. Are your departmental graduate assistant grievance
     procedures published?   Yes _____
                                               No _____

68. Would you hire the following:
     1. A known homosexual   1. Yes _____
                                         No _____
     2. A convicted criminal   2. Yes _____
                                         No _____
     3. A political extremist   3. Yes _____
                                         No _____
     4. A notorious demonstrator   4. Yes _____
                                         No _____
     5. A man with shoulder-length hair 5. Yes _____
                                             No _____
     6. A woman who always wears
         blue-jeans   6. Yes _____
                                         No _____
     7. A woman who never wears a bra 7. Yes _____
                                           No _____
     8. An active women's liberationist 8. Yes _____
                                             No _____
     9. An unmarried graduate assistant
         who openly admits living with some-
         one of the opposite sex   9. Yes _____
                                         No _____

69. If already hired, would you fire or fail to reappoint a
     graduate assistant upon learning that he/she was:
     1. A known homosexual   1. Yes _____
                                         No _____
     2. A convicted criminal   2. Yes _____
                                         No _____
     3. A political extremist   3. Yes _____
                                         No _____
     4. A notorious demonstrator   4. Yes _____
                                         No _____
     5. A man with shoulder-length hair
         (grown after being originally ap-
         pointed)   5. Yes _____
                                         No _____
     6. A woman who always wears blue-
         jeans   6. Yes _____
                                         No _____

    7. A woman who never wears a bra   7. Yes _____
                                                      No _____

    8. An active women's liberationist   8. Yes _____
                                                      No _____

    9. An unmarried graduate assistant
        who openly admits living with some-
        one of the opposite sex   9. Yes _____
                                                      No _____

70.   Do you favor the establishment of a job placement office for all University of Minnesota masters and doctoral candidates?   Yes _____
                                                              No _____

71.   Does your department routinely distribute a copy of the departmental budget to graduate assistants?   Yes _____
                                                              No _____

72.   If a graduate assistant in your department by reason of good conscience refused to work on a specific project, would he be assigned to another project or forfeit his appointment?   assigned to another project _____
                                                                  forfeit his appointment _____

73.   Which of the following job placement services does your department provide for graduate assistants?

        1. Information   1. Yes _____
                                                      No _____

        2. Advice   2. Yes _____
                                                     No _____

        3. Formal placement program   3. Yes _____
                                                     No _____

        4. Actual job referral   4. Yes _____
                                                   No _____

        5. Other (please specify) _____

74.   Do you consider graduate assistants mainly as graduate students (as opposed to teachers or researchers)?   Yes _____
                                                        No _____

75.   Do you believe that graduate assistants should have full information about departmental policies and procedures?   Yes _____
                                                        No _____

76. Do you believe that graduate assistants should have a formal voice in determining departmental policies and procedures? Yes _____

No _____

77. Are graduate assistants in your department elected as voting members on departmental committees? Yes _____

No _____

78. Are graduate assistants in your department elected as non-voting members on departmental committees? Yes _____

No _____

79. Do you believe that graduate assistants should have a formal voice in determining departmental policies and procedures? Yes _____

No _____

80. Specifically, do you believe graduate assistants should have a voice in formulation of the following departmental policies:

   1. Curriculum   1. Yes _____
                                                 No _____
   2. Recruitment of senior faculty   2. Yes _____
                                                 No _____
   3. Recruitment of graduate assis-
      tants   3. Yes _____
                                                 No _____
   4. Selection of senior faculty   4. Yes _____
                                                 No _____
   5. Selection of graduate assistants   5. Yes _____
                                                 No _____
   6. Promotion of senior faculty   6. Yes _____
                                                 No _____
   7. Promotion of graduate assistants   7. Yes _____
                                                 No _____
   8. Instructional techniques   8. Yes _____
                                                 No _____

81. Do all graduate assistants in your department receive equal information regarding available job opportunities? Yes _____

No _____

82A (to be asked of those asked 23B)
Upon which <u>one</u> of the following does your department
place <u>most</u> emphasis when deciding which graduate assistants to reappoint? (check <u>1</u>)
1. Grade point average   1. ____
2. Test results   2. ____
3. Recommendations   3. ____
4. Prior experience as an assistant   4. ____
5. Financial need   5. ____
6. Minority status   6. ____
7. Sex   7. ____
8. Publications by the applicant   8. ____
9. Other (please state)_____

82B (to be asked of those asked 23A)
Please rank the following in terms of criteria your department uses when deciding which graduate assistants
to reappoint (place the number 1 in the space of that
criterion your department considers most important, the
number 2 in the space of that criterion considered
second most important, etc.).
1. Grade point average   1. ____
2. Test results   2. ____
3. Recommendations   3. ____
4. Prior experience as an assistant   4. ____
5. Financial need   5. ____
6. Minority status   6. ____
7. Sex   7. ____
8. Publications by the applicant   8. ____
9. Other (please state)_____   9. ____

83. Does your department use the following graduate assistant
levels:
1. Teaching assistant   1. Yes ____
                  No ____
2. Research assistant   2. Yes ____
                  No ____
3. Teaching associate I   3. Yes ____
                  No ____
4. Teaching associate II   4. Yes ____
                  No ____

84. Are all newly appointed graduate assistants in your department hired at the same rank regardless of previous
education or experience?   Yes ____
                                    No ____

85.   In your department, are all graduate assistants of the
      same rank and the same percentage appointment paid
      the same salary?   Yes _____
                                                No _____

86.   Does your department ever fire a graduate assistant
      before the completion of his appointment? Yes _____
                                                No _____

EXHIBIT 4

UNIVERSITY OF *Minnesota*

November 22, 1971

UNIVERSITY MEASUREMENT SERVICES CENTER
MINNEAPOLIS, MINNESOTA 55414

In the spring of 1971, President ____ appointed a task force to organize a study of graduate assistants at the University of Minnesota. This task force met throughout the summer of 1971 and drew up guidelines for the study. This fall, the Measurement Services Center was asked to design and implement this study.

We are asking you to participate in a pilot-survey to help us improve our questionnaire before we undertake the final study. Please complete the enclosed questionnaire and return it via campus mail to the Measurement Services Center in the enclosed self-addressed envelope. Because the enclosed questionnaire is a preliminary draft of the final form, we hope you will indicate ways of improving it. Please indicate on the questionnaire those questions you believe are poorly worded, ambiguous, or unanswerable. Specify changes that you believe would correct any problems you discover in the questionnaire. Also, feel free to write in questions that you believe are relevant to a study of graduate assistants that we have not asked.

Please return the questionnaire by November 29, 1971. We anticipate the value of your suggestions. Thank-you for your helpful participation!

Sincerely,

Doug Berdie

Jack Anderson

DEPARTMENT CHAIRMAN QUESTIONNAIRE

Dept. _____

GENERAL INSTRUCTIONS

Please respond to each item on this questionnaire.
Please read each question carefully and indicate your
response to each item with a checkmark.   Please
follow CAREFULLY the instructions provided for each
question.

I. POLICIES

1. Do you know of printed material in your department that
    describes: (check one in each row)
    1. The duties of a graduate assistant? Yes__ No__ (10)
    2. Recommended teaching and research
        techniques to be used by a graduate
        assistant in his duties?   Yes__ No__ (11)
    3. Resources that are available to the
        graduate assistant, such as secre-
        tarial and audio-visual services?   Yes__ No__ (12)
    4. The personnel policies and prac-
        tices of your department regarding
        promotion and retention of graduate
        assistants?   Yes__ No__ (13)
    5. The ways in which a graduate
        assistant's job performance is
        evaluated?   Yes__ No__ (14)
    6. Cultural activities available to
        graduate assistants in the Univer-
        sity and surrounding community?   Yes__ No__ (15)
    7. Procedures for handling graduate
        assistants' grievances?   Yes__ No__ (16)

2. Does your department follow any printed policy regarding
    the work hours and responsibilities of graduate assis-
    tants?   Yes__ No__ (17)

3. Do you know of a printed University policy regarding the
    work hours and responsibilities of graduate assistants?
                                              Yes__ No__ (18)

4. Do you believe that graduate assistants should have
    complete information about departmental policies and

procedures?   Yes__No__(19)

5. Does your department have "pre-service" seminars or classes specifically designed to assist graduate assistants in the performance of their duties?   Yes__No__(20)

6. Is in-service instruction on teaching and/or research techniques to aid graduate assistants offered by your department regularly (at least once a month)?
                                               Yes__No__(21)

7. Does your department ever offer in-service instruction for graduate assistants?   Yes__No__(22)

8. In your department, are all graduate assistants of the same rank and percentage appointment paid the same salary?   Yes__No__(23)

9. Does your department have a limit on the number of years an individual can hold a graduate assistantship?
                                               Yes__No__(24)

10. Does the initial appointment of graduate assistants in your department imply continued financial support for the length of time required to complete the degree?
                                               Yes__No__(25)

11. Are married pregnant graduate assistants in your department required to resign because of their pregnancy (at a stated time in the pregnancy)?   Yes__No__(26)
        Our dept. has no female graduate assistants ____

12. Are unmarried pregnant graduate assistants in your department required to resign because of their pregnancy (at a stated time in the pregnancy)?   Yes__No__(27)
        Our dept. has no female graduate assistants ____

13. In your department, is childbirth considered an acceptable reason for graduate assistant absence: (check one in each row)
        1. For the mother   Yes__No__(28)
        2. For the father   Yes__No__(29)

14. In your department, is the average excused absence for childbirth for graduate assistants less than two weeks: (check one in each row)

      1. For the mother   Yes__No__(30)
             Absence is not excused__
      2. For the father   Yes__No__(31)
             Absence is not excused__

15. Does your department encourage graduate assistants: (check one in each row)
    1. To attend departmental special lectures and social functions?   Yes__No__(32)
    2. To join the Association of Student Teachers and Research Assistants (ASTRA)?   Yes__No__(33)
    3. To join the American Association of University Professors (AAUP)?   Yes__No__(34)
    4. To join professional organizations? Yes__No__(35)
    5. To join the Council of Graduate Students (COGS)?   Yes__No__(36)

16. Can graduate assistants in your department be elected to departmental committees as voting members?   Yes__No__(37)

17. Are graduate assistants in your department elected to departmental committees as voting members?   Yes__No__(38)

18. Are graduate assistants in your department elected to departmental committees as non-voting members?   Yes__No__(39)

19. Does your department have a faculty committee on graduate assistant affairs?   Yes__No__(40)

20. Are graduate assistants in your department informed of how the projects on which they work are funded?   Yes__No__(41)

21. Does your department follow the April 15th deadline of the Council of Graduate Schools concerning graduate assistant selection procedures?   Yes__No__(42)
                         Never heard of it__

22. Are all available graduate assistantships in your department always made known to all graduate students in your department?   Yes__No__(43)

23. If your department uses a waiting list in the selection of graduate assistants, are applicants told where they

stand on the list?   Yes__No__(44)
                                          We use no list____

24. Would your department hire a qualified applicant that was
     not a major in your department for a graduate assistant
     position?   Yes__No__(45)

25. If you were confronted with two applicants for a graduate
     assistant position, equal in all respects except that one
     had experience as a graduate assistant and the other did
     not, would you select the applicant with prior experi-
     ence?   Yes__No__(46)

26. In your department, are all newly appointed graduate
     assistants hired at the same rank regardless of previous
     education or experience?   Yes__No__(47)

II. HIRING PRACTICES

1.   Would you hire the following as a graduate assistant:
     (check one in each row)
     1. A known homosexual .... 1. Yes__No__(48)
     2. A convicted criminal .... 2. Yes__No__(49)
     3. A political extremist .... 3. Yes__No__(50)
     4. A man with shoulder-length hair . 4. Yes__No__(51)
     5. A woman who usually wears
        blue jeans .... 5. Yes__No__(52)
     6. A woman who rarely wears a bra. 6. Yes__No__(53)
     7. An active women's liberationist .. 7. Yes__No__(54)
     8. An unmarried female who openly
        admits living with a male....... 8. Yes__No__(55)
     9. An unmarried male who openly
        admits living with a female ..... 9. Yes__No__(56)
    10. A heavy social drinker ....10. Yes__No__(57)
    11. A drug user ....11. Yes__No__(58)

2.   In your department or unit, which one of the following,
     in your opinion, is most influential in selecting teaching
     associates and assistants? (check one only)
     1. Other graduate assistants .... 1. ____
     2. Faculty committee .... 2. ____
     3. Departmental chairman or director of unit 3. ____
     4. Individual faculty member.............. 4. ____(59)
     5. Director of Graduate Students .... 5. ____
     6. Our department has no teaching
        associates or assistants .... 6. ____

7. Other (please specify) _____ .... 7. ____

3. In your department or unit, which <u>one</u> of the following, in your opinion, is most influential in selecting <u>research</u> <u>assistants</u>? (check <u>one</u> only)
   1. Other graduate assistants .... 1. ____
   2. Faculty committee .... 2. ____
   3. Departmental chairman or director of unit .... 3. ____
   4. Individual faculty members .... 4. ____ (60)
   5. Director of Graduate Students .... 5. ____
   6. Our department has no research assistants .... 6. ____
   7. Other (please specify)_____ .. 7. ____

4. From the following list, select the **THREE MOST IM-PORTANT** criteria your department uses in selecting graduate assistants. (Place the number 1 in the space of that criterion considered most important by your department, the number 2 in the space of that criterion considered second most important, and the number 3 in the space of that criterion considered third most important.) REMEMBER, 1ᵃ most important, 2 = second most important, and 3 = third most important).
   1. Grade point average .... 1. ____
   2. Scholastic test results such as Graduate Record Examination and Miller Analogies Test .... 2. ____
   3. Recommendations................. 3. ____
   4. Prior experience as an assistant ... 4. ____ (61-
   5. Financial need .... 5. ____   63)
   6. Minority status.................. 6. ____
   7. Sex .... 7. ____
   8. Publications by the applicant .... 8. ____
   9. Other (please specify)_____.... 9. ____

5. Which of the criteria for promotion listed below do you consider to be the **MOST IMPORTANT** for graduate assistants in your department? (check <u>one</u> only)
   1. Seniority at the University of Minnesota.................... 1. ____
   2. Seniority in total graduate assistant experience .... 2. ____
   3. Proficiency in graduate work (as a student)................. 3. ____
   4. Proficiency as a graduate   (64) assistant (job duties) .... 4. ____

     5. There is no graduate assistant
        promotion in our department .... 5. __
     6. Other (please specify) .... 6. __

6. In your department, which is generally the MOST IM-
   PORTANT factor in determining a graduate assistant's
   retention? (check only one)
       1. Performance of job duties .... 1. __
       2. Success in graduate studies............. 2. __(65)

7. Does your department ever dismiss a graduate assistmt
   before the completion of his appointment? Yes__ No__(66)

8. Does your department use the following graduate assistant
   levels? (check one in each row)
       1. Teaching assistant .... 1. Yes__ No__(67)
       2. Research assistant............. 2. Yes__ No__(68)
       3. Teaching associate I .... 3. Yes__ No__(69)
       4. Teaching associate II .... 4. Yes__ No__(70)

9. How long before actually beginning their duties do graduate assistants in your department receive specific information regarding their appointment (information such as
   which textbooks will be used, specific research techniques
   to be used, class time, etc.)? (check only one)
       1. No advance notice .... 1. __
       2. Advance notice of less than one week..... 2. __
       3. Advance notice of from one to two weeks .. 3. __ (71)
       4. Advance notice of more than two weeks.... 4. __

10. Do the graduate assistants in your department play an
    active role in deciding their job assignments?
                                              Yes__ No__ (72)

11. Does the seniority of a graduate assistant increase his
    chance of having a choice in his own assignment?
                                              Yes__ No__ (73)

12. Are the graduate assistants in your department given job
    assignments in which they use their academic skills?
                                              Yes__ No__ (74)

13. Are the graduate assistants in your department given job
    assignments in which they use their non-academic skills?
                                              Yes__ No__ (75)

14. In your department, are new graduate assistants furnished with a job description that describes such items as rank, percentage and length of appointment, work hours required per week, and name of supervisor?
Yes__No__(76)

15. If a graduate assistant in your department, by reason of conscience, refused to work on a specific project, would he be assigned to another project or forfeit his appointment? (check one)   Assigned to another project___
Forfeit his appointment   ___(77)

III. GRADUATE ASSISTANT DUTIES

1. How many hours per week does your department require of a 25% appointment graduate assistant? (please check one)   less than 10 hrs. ___
10 hrs. ___
11 hrs. ___
12 hrs. ___
13 hrs. ___ (78)
14-19 hrs. ___
20-29 hrs. ___
30-39 hrs. ___
40 or more hrs. ___

2. Do graduate assistants in your department work at all on job duties during quarter breaks?   Yes__No__(79)

3. Are graduate assistants in your department ever penalized for absence from their job duties?   Yes__No__(80)

4. In your department, do the teaching assistants and/or teaching associates maintain regularly defined office hours?   Yes__No__(6)
We have no teaching assistants or associates _____

5. Do graduate assistants in your department have the following: (check one in each row)
1. Individual offices .... 1. Yes__No__(7)
2. Shared offices .... 2. Yes__No__(8)
3. Access to a phone .... 3. Yes__No__(9)
4. Individual desks .... 4. Yes__No__(10)
5. Shared desks .... 5. Yes__No__(11)
6. Mailbox .... 6. Yes__No__(12)
7. Clerical support .... 7. Yes__No__(13)

8. Free course textbooks .... 8. Yes__No__(14)
9. Office supplies .... 9. Yes__No__(15)
10. Other (please specify)_____ ...10. Yes__No__(16)

6. Do graduate assistants in your department have sufficient
access to the following teaching aids: (check one in each
row)
   1. Audio-visual equipment .... 1. Yes__No__(17)
   2. Library sources .... 2. Yes__No__(18)
   3. Reproducing equipment (Xerox,
      ditto, mimeograph, etc.) .... 3. Yes__No__(19)

DIFFERENCES BETWEEN TEACHING ASSISTANTS
AND TEACHING ASSOCIATES

The next 9 items deal with the differences in the duties of
teaching assistants and teaching associates. If your department has no teaching assistants please check the space "not
applicable" each time a question is asked about teaching
assistants. Similarly, if your department has no teaching
associates I or teaching associates II, indicate this by checking the space "not applicable" each time these titles appear.

1-6. How often do graduate assistants in your department:
(check one in each row)

	Never	Some- times	Often	Not Applicable

1. Independently or under
limited supervision, de-
sign courses in their en-
tirety (objectives, content,
evaluation, etc.)?
   Teaching assistants   ___ ___ ___ ___ (20)
   Teaching associates I ___ ___ ___ ___ (21)
   Teaching associates II ___ ___ ___ ___ (22)

2. Provide the principal instruction for a depart-
mental course (majority
of lectures, evaluation,
etc.)?
   Teaching assistants   ___ ___ ___ ___ (23)
   Teaching associates I ___ ___ ___ ___ (24)
   Teaching associates II ___ ___ ___ ___ (25)

	Never	Some-times	Often	Not Applicable

3. Have complete responsibility for constructing and
administering tests, and
determining grades?
Teaching assistants ____ ____ ____ ____(26)
Teaching associates I ____ ____ ____ ____(27)
Teaching associates II ____ ____ ____ ____(28)

4. Assist senior staff members in constructing and
administering tests, and
determining grades?
Teaching assistants ____ ____ ____ ____(29)
Teaching associates I ____ ____ ____ ____(30)
Teaching associates II ____ ____ ____ ____(31)

5. Assist in the development
of instructional materials
for use in courses?
Teaching assistants ____ ____ ____ ____(32)
Teaching associates I ____ ____ ____ ____(33)
Teaching associates II ____ ____ ____ ____(34)

6. Serve as officially assigned
student advisors?
Teaching assistants ____ ____ ____ ____(35)
Teaching associates I ____ ____ ____ ____(36)
Teaching associates II ____ ____ ____ ____(37)

7. In your department, do teaching associates teach higher
level classes than teaching assistants? Yes__No__(38)
Not applicable____

8. In your department, do teaching associates have more
teaching experience than teaching assistants?
Yes__No__(39)
Not applicable ____

9. In your department, is salary the only difference between
teaching associate I and teaching associate II?
Yes__No__(40)
Not applicable ____

1. Does your department have a formal procedure for evaluating the job performance of graduate assistants?
                                            Yes__No__(41)

2. In your department, do the following participate in the formal or informal evaluation of each graduate assistant? (check one in each row)
   1. Faculty committee .... 1. Yes__No__(42)
   2. Undergraduate students......... 2. Yes__No__(43)
   3. Departmental chairman......... 3. Yes__No__(44)
   4. Faculty member to whom the assistant is assigned .... 4. Yes__No__(45)
   5. Other graduate assistants....... 5. Yes__No__(46)
   6. The graduate assistant being evaluated.................. .... 6. Yes__No__(47)
   7. Other (please specify)_____.. 7. Yes__No__(48)

3. Is there a formal procedure in your department by which graduate assistants may offer rebuttal to the evaluation of their performance?   Yes__No__(49)

4. In your opinion, is the evaluation procedure used by your department for evaluating graduate assistants a fair one?
                                            Yes__No__(50)

5. In your department, are the results of graduate assistant evaluations made available to the following: (check one in each row)
   1. Departmental faculty........... 1. Yes__No__(51)
   2. Any University faculty member... 2. Yes__No__(52)
   3. The graduate assistant who was evaluated.................. 3. Yes__No__(53)
   4. Prospective employers of the graduate assistant who was evaluated..................... 4. Yes__No__(54)
   5. Other students in the department 5. Yes__No__(55)
   6. U of M Graduate School .... 6. Yes__No__(56)
   7. Other (please specify)_____ .. 7. Yes__No__(57)

6. If a graduate assistant in your department were to perform his duties inadequately, do you believe the following are reasonable ways of handling the situation? (check one in each row)
   1. Dismissal from appointment .... 1. Yes__No__(58)
   2. Non-reappointment .... 2. Yes__No__(59)

3. Closer supervision .... 3. Yes__No__(60)
4. Counseling and advice .... 4. Yes__No__(61)
5. Tolerate it .... 5. Yes__No__(62)
6. Extra work assignments .... 6. Yes__No__(63)
7. Other (please specify) .... 7. Yes__No__(64)

7. How are the grievances of graduate assistants handled in your department? (check one)
    1. Special grievance committee (faculty only) .. 1.____
    2. Special grievance committee (faculty and graduate assistants)....................... 2.____
    3. No standard policy....................... 3.____
    4. Don't know.............................. 4.__(65)
    5. Our graduate assistants don't have grievances .... 5.____
    6. Grievances are ignored .... 6.____

8. Do all graduate assistants in your department receive equal information regarding available job opportunities?
                                     Yes__No__(66)

9. In your department, is excellence in performance as a graduate assistant given any reward other than retention (such as tuition waivers, honor awards, etc.)?
                                     Yes__No__(67)

10. Does your department have a system of recognition for graduate assistants that exhibit superior performance in their duties?   Yes__No__(68)

11. Does your department assist with the travel expenses (i. e., pay more than 50%) of the department's graduate assistants to professional meetings?   Yes__No__(69)

12. Does your department augment the base salary of graduate assistants with the following: (check one in each row)
    1. Budgeted departmental funds.... 1. Yes__No__(70)
    2. Grants .... 2. Yes__No__(71)
    3. Fellowships................... 3. Yes__No__(72)
    4. Other (please specify)_____ .. 4. Yes__No__(73)

13. Do you consider graduate assistants mainly as graduate students (as opposed to teachers or researchers)?
                                     Yes__No__(74)

V. OPINIONS

The following list contains a series of statements about graduate assistants (teaching assistants, research assistants, teaching associates I, and teaching associates II).   Please indicate your degree of agreement or disagreement with each statement by checking how you ACTUALLY feel about graduate assistants at the University of Minnesota.   Do not answer in terms of how you think you should feel.

HOW YOU ACTUALLY FEEL

	Strongly Agree	Agree	Neutral	Disagree	Strongly Disagree	
1. Graduate assistants make a valuable contribution to the educational function of the University.	___	___	___	___	___	(75)
2. Graduate assistants are paid too much.	___	___	___	___	___	(76)
3. The University sees graduate assistants as a cheap source of labor.	___	___	___	___	___	(77)
4. Graduate assistants are more effective in working with undergraduate students than are professors.	___	___	___	___	___	(78)
5. Graduate assistants should be paid more.	___	___	___	___	___	(79)
6. Graduate assistantships should be eliminated.	___	___	___	___	___	(80)
7. Graduate assistants are creative.	___	___	___	___	___	(6)
8. Graduate assistants who do not hold fellowships are less capable than graduate assistants holding fellowships.	___	___	___	___	___	(7)

HOW YOU ACTUALLY FEEL

	Strongly Agree	Agree	Neutral	Disagree	Strongly Disagree

9. Graduate assistants have legitimate grievances about their roles and functions. ___ ___ ___ ___ ___(8)

10. Undergraduate classes should not be taught by graduate assistants. ___ ___ ___ ___ ___(9)

11. Most graduate assistants are satisfied with their role. ___ ___ ___ ___ ___(10)

12. Graduate assistants are the most capable students on the campus. ___ ___ ___ ___ ___(11)

13. The Association of Student Teachers and Research Assistants (ASTRA) is a vocal minority of graduate assistants. ___ ___ ___ ___ ___(12)

14. Graduate assistants are more concerned with their own course work than with their responsibilities as graduate assistants. ___ ___ ___ ___ ___(13)

15. Departmental graduate assistantships should be given only to students within that department. ___ ___ ___ ___ ___(14)

16. Graduate assistants should have an active role in determining their job assignments. ___ ___ ___ ___ ___(15)

17. Graduate assistants' salaries are adequate for their needs. ___ ___ ___ ___ ___(16)

18. The University should establish a job placement office for all masters and doctoral candidates. ___ ___ ___ ___ ___(17)

HOW YOU ACTUALLY FEEL

	Strongly Agree	Agree	Neutral	Disagree	Strongly Disagree

19. The importance of graduate
    assistants is overemphasized.   ___ ___ ___ ___ ___(18)

20. The work graduate assistants
    do justifies their pay.   ___ ___ ___ ___ ___(19)

21. If a graduate assistant, by rea-
    son of conscience, refused to
    work on a specific project, he
    should forfeit his appointment.   ___ ___ ___ ___ ___(20)

22. Graduate assistants should not
    be required to work at all dur-
    ing quarter breaks.   ___ ___ ___ ___ ___(21)

23. There should be a university-
    wide system of recognition for
    superior graduate assistant
    performance.   ___ ___ ___ ___ ___(22)

24. Each department should have a
    system of recognition for superior
    graduate assistant performance.   ___ ___ ___ ___ ___(23)

25. The most important factor in de-
    termining graduate assistant re-
    tention should be how the graduate
    assistant performs his duties.   ___ ___ ___ ___ ___(24)

26. The University could not function
    without graduate assistants.   ___ ___ ___ ___ ___(25)

27. Excellence in performance as a
    graduate assistant should be given
    special reward such as tuition
    waivers, honor awards, etc.   ___ ___ ___ ___ ___(26)

28. Graduate assistants are exploited
    by the University as a source of
    cheap labor.   ___ ___ ___ ___ ___(27)

HOW YOU ACTUALLY FEEL

29. Graduate assistants should play an active role in the formulation of the following departmental policies: (check one in each row)

	Strongly Agree	Agree	Neutral	Disagree	Strongly Disagree	
1. Curriculum	1. __	__	__	__	__	(28)
2. Recruitment of faculty	2. __	__	__	__	__	(29)
3. Recruitment of graduate assistants	3. __	__	__	__	__	(30)
4. Selection of faculty	4. __	__	__	__	__	(31)
5. Selection of graduate assistants	5. __	__	__	__	__	(32)
6. Promotion of faculty	6. __	__	__	__	__	(33)
7. Promotion of graduate assistants	7. __	__	__	__	__	(34)
8. Instructional techniques	8. __	__	__	__	__	(35)

EXHIBIT 5

TASK FORCE ON GRADUATE ASSISTANTS

This questionnaire is about graduate assistants. Please respond only in terms of teaching assistants, research assistants, and teaching associates I and II. Read each question carefully and indicate your response by circling the appropriate alternative or supplying the appropriate information.

POLICIES

1. Do you know of printed (mimeographed, dittoed, etc.) material in your department that describes: (circle one in each column)

	Teaching Assistant	Research Assistant	Teaching Associate I	Teaching Associate II	
A. the duties of:					
Yes	Y	Y	Y	Y	
No	N	N	N	N	
Not Applicable	NA	NA	NA	NA	(16-19)
B. recommended techniques to be used by:					
Yes	Y	Y	Y	Y	
No	N	N	N	N	
Not Applicable	NA	NA	NA	NA	(20-23)
C. available resources such as secretarial and audio-visual services for:					
Yes	Y	Y	Y	Y	
No	N	N	N	N	
Not Applicable	NA	NA	NA	NA	(24-27)
D. the policies of your department on promotion and retention of:					
Yes	Y	Y	Y	Y	
No	N	N	N	N	
Not Applicable	NA	NA	NA	NA	(28-31)

[At 75% of real size the following 16 pages, in pairs, show the eight pages (unpaginated) of the original questionnaire sent to department chairmen.]

E. the ways in which job performance is evaluated for:

   Yes   Y   Y   Y   Y

   No   N   N   N   N

   Not Applicable   NA (32–35)   NA   NA   NA

F. procedures for handling the grievances of:

   Yes   Y   Y   Y   Y

   No   N   N   N   N

   Not Applicable   NA (36–39)   NA   NA   NA

2. Does your department follow any printed policy on work hours and responsibilities of:

   Yes   Y   Y   Y   Y

   No   N   N   N   N

   Not Applicable   NA (40–43)   NA   NA   NA

3. Do you know of a printed University policy regarding work hours and responsibilities of:

   Yes   Y   Y   Y   Y

   No   N   N   N   N

   Not Applicable   NA (44–47)   NA   NA   NA

4. Does your department offer "pre-service" meetings (specifically designed to assist graduate assistants in the performance of their duties) for:

   Yes   Y   Y   Y   Y

   No   N   N   N   N

   Not Applicable   NA (48–51)   NA   NA   NA

5. Is in-service instruction on teaching and/or research techniques to aid graduate assistants offered by your department regularly (at least once a month) for:

   Yes   Y   Y   Y   Y

   No   N   N   N   N

   Not Applicable   NA (52–55)   NA   NA   NA

[The four original leaves of this eight-page questionnaire were brownish-beige, heavy stock, 8½" x 11" paper.]

6. Does the initial appointment of graduate assistants in your department imply continued financial support for the length of time required to complete the degree for:

	TA	RA	TA I	TA II
Yes	Y	Y	Y	Y
No	N	N	N	N
Not Applicable	NA	NA	NA	NA (56-59)

7. Does your department have a faculty committee on graduate assistant affairs for:

	TA	RA	TA I	TA II
Yes	Y	Y	Y	Y
No	N	N	N	N
Not Applicable	NA	NA	NA	NA (60-63)

8. In your department, are all graduate students informed of available positions as:

	TA	RA	TA I	TA II
Yes	Y	Y	Y	Y
No	N	N	N	N
Not Applicable	NA	NA	NA	NA (64-67)
Don't know	DK	DK	DK	DK

9. If your department uses a waiting list in the selection procedures of graduate assistants, are applicants told where they stand on the list?

	TA	RA	TA I	TA II
Yes	Y	Y	Y	Y
No	N	N	N	N
Not Applicable	NA	NA	NA	NA
We Use No List	NL	NL	NL	NL (68-71)

10. Do you believe that graduate assistants should have complete information about departmental policies?

Yes   No   Uncertain   (1)

11. In your department, are all graduate assistants of the same rank and percentage appointment paid the same salary?

Yes   No   (2)

[These two pages show page 2 of the original.]

12. Would a married pregnant graduate assistant in your department be required to resign at a stated time in her pregnancy? Yes No (3)

13. Would an unmarried pregnant graduate assistant in your department be required to resign at a stated time in her pregnancy? Yes No (4)

14. In your department, would the average excused absence for childbirth for graduate assistants be less than two weeks:

    For the mother Yes No Absence Not Excused (5)

    For the father Yes No Absence Not Excused (6)

15. Can graduate assistants in your department sit on departmental committees as voting members? Yes No (7)

16. Do graduate assistants in your department sit on departmental committees as voting members? Yes No (8)

17. Do graduate assistants in your department sit on departmental committees as non-voting members? Yes No (9)

18. Are graduate assistants in your department informed of how the projects on which they work are funded? Yes No Only If They Ask (10)

19. Does your department notify graduate assistants of re-appointment by April 1? Yes No (11)

20. Does your department follow the April 15th deadline of the Council of Graduate Schools concerning initial graduate assistant appointment procedures? Yes No Don't Know (12)

21. Would your department hire a qualified applicant who is not majoring in your field for a graduate assistant position? Yes No (13)

22. In your department, are all newly appointed graduate assistants hired at the same rank regardless of previous education or experience? Yes No (14)

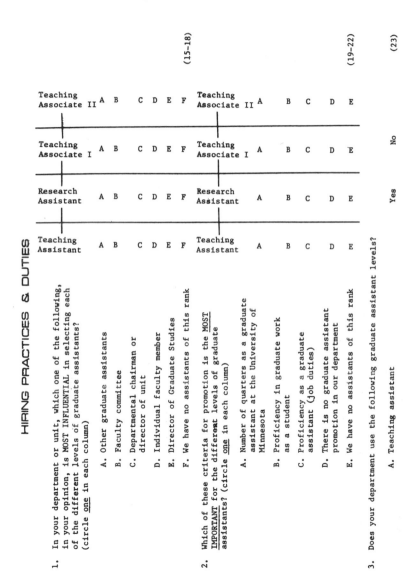

HIRING PRACTICES & DUTIES

(15-18)   (19-22)   (23)

													Yes	No
Teaching Associate II	A	B	C	D	E	F	Teaching Associate II	A	B	C	D	E		
Teaching Associate I	A	B	C	D	E	F	Teaching Associate I	A	B	C	D	E		
Research Assistant	A	B	C	D	E	F	Research Assistant	A	B	C	D	E		
Teaching Assistant	A	B	C	D	E	F	Teaching Assistant	A	B	C	D	E		

1. In your department or unit, which one of the following, in your opinion, is MOST INFLUENTIAL in selecting each of the different levels of graduate assistants? (circle one in each column)

   A. Other graduate assistants

   B. Faculty committee

   C. Departmental chairman or director of unit

   D. Individual faculty member

   E. Director of Graduate Studies

   F. We have no assistants of this rank

2. Which of these criteria for promotion is the MOST IMPORTANT for the different levels of graduate assistants? (circle one in each column)

   A. Number of quarters as a graduate assistant at the University of Minnesota

   B. Proficiency in graduate work as a student

   C. Proficiency as a graduate assistant (job duties)

   D. There is no graduate assistant promotion in our department

   E. We have no assistants of this rank

3. Does your department use the following graduate assistant levels?

   A. Teaching assistant

[These two pages show page 3 of the original.]

B. Research assistant   Yes   No   (24)

C. Teaching associate I   Yes   No   (25)

D. Teaching associate II   Yes   No   (26)

4. In your department, are new graduate assistants furnished with a job description including such items as rank, percentage and length of appointment, work hours required, and name of their supervisor?   Yes   No   (27)

5. From the following list, select the THREE MOST IMPORTANT criteria your department uses in hiring new graduate assistants. (Place the number 1 by the most important, number 2 by the second most important, and the number 3 in the space of that criterion considered third most important.)

   A. Academic record (GPA, courses taken, etc.)   _____   (28)

   B. Scholastic test results (GRE, Miller Analogies, etc.)   _____   (29)

   C. Recommendations   _____   (30)

   D. Prior experience and/or special skills   _____   (31)

   E. Financial need   _____   (32)

   F. Sex or race   _____   (33)

   G. Interests of applicant   _____   (34)

   H. Publications by the applicant   _____   (35)

6. Has your department ever dismissed a graduate assistant before his appointment expired?   Yes   No   (36)

7. Are the teaching assistants and/or teaching associates in your department required to maintain scheduled office hours?   Yes   No   Not Applicable   (37)

8. How many hours of work per week does your department require of a:

A. 25% teaching assistant	_____ hrs. We have none	(38–39)
B. 25% teaching associate I	_____ hrs. We have none	(40–41)
C. 25% teaching associate II	_____ hrs. We have none	(42–43)
D. 25% research assistant	_____ hrs We have none	(44–45)
E. 50% teaching assistant	_____ hrs. We have none	(46–47)
F. 50% teaching associate I	_____ hrs. We have none	(48–49)
G. 50% teaching associate II	_____ hrs. We have none	(50–51)
H. 50% research assistant	_____ hrs. We have none	(52–53)

9. Do you believe graduate assistants in your department have sufficient access to the following teaching aids:

A. Audio-visual equipment	Yes	No	(54)
B. Library sources	Yes	No	(55)
C. Reproducing equipment (xerox, ditto, mimeograph, etc.)	Yes	No	(56)
D. Office supplies (pencils, pens, paper, etc.)	Yes	No	(57)

How often do graduate assistants in your department: (circle one in each row)

10. Independently or under limited supervision, design courses in their entirety (objectives, content, evaluation, etc.)?

	Never	Sometimes	Often	Not Applicable	
Teaching assistants	N	S	O	NA	(58)
Teaching associates I	N	S	O	NA	(59)
Teaching associates II	N	S	O	NA	(60)

[These two pages show page 4 of the original.]

11. Provide the principal _instruction_ for a departmental course (majority of lectures, evaluation, etc.)?

	N	S	O	NA	
Teaching assistants	N	S	O	NA	(61)
Teaching associates I	N	S	O	NA	(62)
Teaching associates II	N	S	O	NA	(63)

12. Have complete responsibility for constructing and administering tests, and determining grades?

	N	S	O	NA	
Teaching assistants	N	S	O	NA	(64)
Teaching associates I	N	S	O	NA	(65)
Teaching associates II	N	S	O	NA	(66)

13. Assist senior staff members in constructing and administering tests, and determining grades?

	N	S	O	NA	
Teaching assistants	N	S	O	NA	(67)
Teaching associates I	N	S	O	NA	(68)
Teaching associates II	N	S	O	NA	(69)

14. Assist in the development of instructional materials for use in courses?

	N	S	O	NA	
Teaching assistants	N	S	O	NA	(70)
Teaching associates I	N	S	O	NA	(71)
Teaching associates II	N	S	O	NA	(72)

15. Serve as officially assigned student advisors?

	N	S	O	NA	
Teaching assistants	N	S	O	NA	(1)
Teaching associates I	N	S	O	NA	(2)
Teaching associates II	N	S	O	NA	(3)

EVALUATION

1. Does your department have a formal procedure for evaluating the job performance of:

	Teaching Assistant			Research Assistant			Teaching Associate I			Teaching Associate II		
	Y	N	NA	Y	N	NA	Y	N	NA	Y	N	NA
Yes / No / Not Applicable	Y	N	NA	Y	N	NA	Y	N	NA	Y	N	NA (4–7)

2. In your department, do the following participate in the formal or informal evaluation of each rank of graduate assistant?

	Teaching Assistant			Research Assistant			Teaching Associate I			Teaching Associate II		
	Y	N	NA	Y	N	NA	Y	N	NA	Y	N	NA
A. Faculty committee · · · · · · · · · · · · · · · (Yes / No / Not Applicable)	Y	N	NA	Y	N	NA	Y	N	NA	Y	N	NA (8–11)
B. Undergraduate students · · · · · · · · (Yes / No / Not Applicable)	Y	N	NA	Y	N	NA	Y	N	NA	Y	N	NA (12–15)
C. Departmental chairman or director of unit · · · · · · · · · · (Yes / No / Not Applicable)	Y	N	NA	Y	N	NA	Y	N	NA	Y	N	NA (16–19)
D. Faculty member to whom the assistant is assigned · · · · · · (Yes / No / Not Applicable)	Y	N	NA	Y	N	NA	Y	N	NA	Y	N	NA (20–23)

[These two pages show page 5 of the original.]

7. Is there a formal procedure in your department by which
   graduate assistants may offer rebuttal to the evaluation
   of their performance?   Yes   No   (42)

8. In your department, are the results of graduate assistant
   evaluations made available to the following upon request:

   A. Departmental faculty . . . .   Yes   No   (43)

   B. The graduate assistant's major advisor . . . .   Yes   No   (44)

   C. The graduate assistant who was evaluated . . . .   Yes   No   (45)

   D. Prospective employers of the graduate assistant
      who was evaluated (excluding letters of recommendation)   Yes   No   (46)

   E. Other students in the department . . . .   Yes   No   (47)

   F. U of M Graduate School . . . .   Yes   No   (48)

9. If a graduate assistant in your department were to perform his duties
   inadequately, do you believe the following are reasonable methods of
   handling the situation?

   A. Dismissal from appointment . . . .   Yes   No   (49)

   B. Non-reappointment . . . .   Yes   No   (50)

   C. Closer supervision . . . .   Yes   No   (51)

   D. Counseling and advice . . . .   Yes   No   (52)

   E. Tolerate it . . . .   Yes   No   (53)

E. Other graduate assistants . . . . Yes   Y   Y   Y   Y

No   N   N   N   N

Not Applicable   NA   NA   NA   NA (24–27)

F. The graduate assistant being evaluated . . . . Yes   Y   Y   Y   Y

No   N   N   N   N

Not Applicable   NA   NA   NA   NA (28–31)

3. Does your department have a system of recognition for superior performance of duties by:

Yes   Y   Y   Y   Y

No   N   N   N   N

Not Applicable   NA   NA   NA   NA (32–35)

4. Are graduate assistants in your department required to work on job duties during quarter breaks (last day of finals week until first day of classes)?

Yes   Y   Y   Y   Y

No   N   N   N   N

Not applicable   NA   NA   NA   NA (36–39)

5. How are the grievances of graduate assistants handled in your department? (circle only one)

1. Committee of faculty only
2. Committee of faculty and graduate assistants
3. Conference with department chairman or director of unit
4. No standard policy
5. Our graduate assistants don't have grievances
6. Grievances are ignored
7. Don't know

(40)

6. In your opinion, is the evaluation procedure used by your department for evaluating graduate assistants a fair one?

Yes   No   (41)

[These two pages show page 6 of the original.]

F. Extra work assignments . . . . Yes   No   (54)

G. Reassignment . . . . Yes   No   (55)

10. Does your department augment the salary of graduate assistants with the following:

    A. Budgeted departmental funds . . . . Yes   No   (56)

    B. Grants . . . . Yes   No   (57)

    C. Fellowships . . . . Yes   No   (58)

    D. Other (specify) _____ Yes   No   (59)

11. Does your department assist with the travel expenses (e.g., pay more than 50%) of the department's graduate assistants to professional meetings?

    Yes   No   On occasion   (60)

12. What do you believe are the greatest job needs of the graduate assistants in your department? (please discuss below)

TASK FORCE ⌂⌂⌂ ON GRADUATE ASSISTANTS

OPINIONS

Please indicate your degree of agreement with each of the following statements by circling how you feel about graduate assistants at the University of Minnesota.

	Strongly Agree	Agree	Neutral	Disagree	Strongly Disagree	
1. Most graduate assistants make a valuable contribution to the educational function of the University.	SA	A	N	D	SD	(40)
2. In most cases, graduate assistant are more effective in working with undergraduate students than are professors.	SA	A	N	D	SD	(41)
3. Graduate assistants should be paid more.	SA	A	N	D	SD	(42)
4. Graduate assistantships should be eliminated.	SA	A	N	D	SD	(43)
5. The majority of job grievances expressed by graduate assistants are justified.	SA	A	N	D	SD	(44)
6. Undergraduate classes should <u>not</u> be taught by graduate assistants.	SA	A	N	D	SD	(45)

[These two pages show page 7 of the original.]

7. The Association of Teaching and Research Assistants (ASTRA) is a worthwhile organization.　　SA　A　N　D　SD　(46)

8. Graduate assistants are more concerned with their own course work than with their responsibilities as graduate assistants.　　SA　A　N　D　SD　(47)

9. Departmental graduate assistantships should be given only to students within that department.　　SA　A　N　D　SD　(48)

10. Graduate assistants should have an active role in determining their job assignments.　　SA　A　N　D　SD　(49)

11. Graduate assistants' salaries are adequate for their needs.　　SA　A　N　D　SD　(50)

12. The University should maintain a job placement office for all masters and doctoral graduates.　　SA　A　N　D　SD　(51)

13. Research projects should not be directed by graduate assistants.　　SA　A　N　D　SD　(52)

14. Most people overemphasize the importance of graduate assistants.　　SA　A　N　D　SD　(53)

15. The work graduate assistants do justifies their pay.　　SA　A　N　D　SD　(54)

16. If a graduate assistant, by reason of conscience, refused to work on a specific project, his appointment should be terminated.　　SA　A　N　D　SD　(55)

17. Graduate assistants should not be required to work at all during quarter breaks (last day of finals week until first day of classes).　　SA　A　N　D　SD　(56)

(over)

	Strongly Agree	Agree	Neutral	Disagree	Strongly Disagree	
18. There should be a university-wide system of recognition for superior graduate assistant performance.	SA	A	N	D	SD	(57)
19. Each department should have a system of recognition for superior graduate assistant performance.	SA	A	N	D	SD	(58)
20. The _most_ important factor in determining job retention should be how the graduate assistant performs his duties.	SA	A	N	D	SD	(59)
21. Excellence in performance as a graduate assistant should be given special reward such as tuition waivers, honor awards, etc.	SA	A	N	D	SD	(60)
22. Graduate assistants are exploited by the University as a source of cheap labor.	SA	A	N	D	SD	(61)
23. Each department should have orientation or "pre-service" meetings specifically designed to assist graduate assistants in the performance of their duties.	SA	A	N	D	SD	(62)
24. Each department should have regular (at least once a month) in-service instruction on teaching and/or research techniques to aid graduate assistants.	SA	A	N	D	SD	(63)

[These two pages show page 8 of the original.]

25. Graduate assistants should play an active role in:

	Always	Often	Sometimes	Seldom	Never	
1. Selection of faculty	1	2	3	4	5	(64)
2. Selection of graduate assistants	1	2	3	4	5	(65)
3. Promotion of faculty	1	2	3	4	5	(66)
4. Promotion of graduate assistants	1	2	3	4	5	(67)
5. Development of curriculum	1	2	3	4	5	(68)
6. Development of instructional techniques	1	2	3	4	5	(69)
7. Development of research projects and/or techniques	1	2	3	4	5	(70)

EXHIBIT 6

m **SC** university measurement services center
9 clarence avenue s.e. minneapolis, minnesota 55414

TASK FORCE ▷ ▷ ▷ ▷
◁ ◁ ON GRADUATE ASSISTANTS

January 15, 1972

Lloyd Lofquist, Co-Chairman
  Assistant Vice-President
  of Academic Administration
Jodi Wetzel, Co-Chairman
  Former ASTRA President
Norene Bagnall
  ASTRA President
Francis Boddy
  Associate Dean of Graduate
  School
Scott Erickson
  Freshman Advisor, CLA
Eville Gorham
  Chairman
  Department of Botany
Siegfried Grosser
  Assistant Professor of
  Mathematics
Marian Hall
  Director, School Psychology
Bo Hedlund
  Teaching Assistant
Tim Jollymore
  Teaching Assistant
Keith McFarland
  Acting Dean, College
  of Home Economics
Toni McNaron
  Associate Professor of
  English
Patrick Norris
  Scholastic Committee, CLA
Roy Schuessler
  Chairman, Department of
  Music & Music Education
John Turnbull
  Associate Dean, CLA
David Vose
  Vice Provost for
  Academic Administration
  (Duluth)
Ronald Zillgitt
  Coordinator for Admissions
  Systems Development

Dear University Community Member:

We need your help! We are conducting a study
of graduate assistants at the University of
Minnesota. Our study is the result of discussions between the Association of Teaching and
Research Assistants (ASTRA), President Moos
and a Task Force on the role of graduate assistants in which it was determined that more
information is needed regarding graduate assistants.

In the next few weeks you will be receiving a
questionnaire designed to gather useful information regarding graduate assistants at the
University. The data from the survey will be
used to more wisely evaluate the roles and
functions of graduate assistants, and related
policies.

The status of graduate assistants should be of
concern to all members of the University community. So that this study will most accurately
reflect the opinions of all, we urgently request
your participation in the study by promptly returning the forthcoming questionnaire.

We thank you in advance for your time and
cooperation.

Sincerely,

Patricia S. Faunce

Patricia S. Faunce
Director, UMSC

Jack Anderson
Research Fellow

Doug Berdie
Research Sepcialist

[Reproduced here at 60% of original size.]

294

EXHIBIT 7

University measurement services center
9 clarence avenue s.e. minneapolis, minnesota 55414

TASK FORCE ▷ ▷ ▷ ▷ ▷
◁◁ ON GRADUATE ASSISTANTS

Lloyd Lofquist, Co-Chairman
  Assistant Vice-President
  of Academic Administration
Jodi Wetzel, Co-Chairman
  Former ASTRA President
Norene Bagnall
  ASTRA President
Francis Boddy
  Associate Dean of Graduate
  School
Scott Erickson
  Freshman Advisor, CLA
Eville Gorham
  Chairman
  Department of Botany
Siegfried Grosser
  Assistant Professor of
  Mathematics
Marian Hall
  Director, School Psychology
Bo Hedlund
  Teaching Assistant
Tim Jollymore
  Teaching Assistant
Keith McFarland
  Acting Dean, College
  of Home Economics
Toni McMaron
  Associate Professor of
  English
Patrick Norris
  Scholastic Committee, CLA
Roy Schuessler
  Chairman, Department of
  Music & Music Education
John Turnbull
  Associate Dean, CLA
David Voss
  Vice Provost for
  Academic Administration
  (Duluth)
Ronald Zillgitt
  Coordinator for Admissions
  Systems Development

January 21, 1972

Dear Friend,

As you recall from our letter of January 15, 1972, we
are conducting a study of the roles and functions of
graduate assistants at the University of Minnesota. We
are now sending appropiate questionnaires to graduate
assistants, department chairman, undergraduate students,
college deans, and administrators.

Since situations may differ greatly, and since we wish
the results of the study to be as accurate as possible,
we cannot overemphasize the importance of receiving your
completed questionnaire. Please limit your responses to
graduate students who are teaching assistants, research
assistants and teaching associates I and II. In those
instances in the questionnaire where no response category
accurately reflects your situation, mark the best answer
available and then qualify your response in the margin.

A NOTE ON CONFIDENTIALITY

A vital concern of the Measurement Services Center
is the importance of confidentiality in research.
You will notice a code number on your questionnaire.
This code number will only be used to facilitate
our follow-up techniques and to prevent you from
receiving bothersome reminder letters. At no time
will questionnaires be identified by respondent.

If you have any questions, please call Doug or Jack at
373-2263. We appreciate your time and cooperation and
look forward to receiving your completed questionnaire.

Sincerely,

Patricia S. Faunce
Director USMC

[Reproduced here at 60% of original size.]

295

EXHIBIT 8

we don't just send
out questionnaires····

HAPPY

VALENTINES DAY

Pat, Doug & Jack
measurement services center

[Reproduced here at 75% of original size, with the two long sides slightly trimmed. Original color: black print on loud pinkish red background.]

[Original postcard size 3¾" x 5⅜" on dark mustard-brown heavy stock paper.]

UNIVERSITY MEASUREMENT SERVICES CENTER
9 CLARENCE AVENUE S.E. · MINNEAPOLIS, MINNESOTA 55414

We've considered the possibility that
a rampaging rhino has eaten your
questionnaire on graduate assistants.

We know the questionnaires are food
for thought and can't think of any other
reason for not having received one from
you.

We are sending you another questionnaire
because we're very anxious to hear from
you. If you have any questions, call
You Know Who at 373-2263.

[Reproduced here at 52% of original size; original color, black on
grey; 8½″ x 11″ medium-weight paper.]

[Reproduced here at 75% of original size; black on brownish beige, 5″ x 8″ medium-weight paper.]

UNIVERSITY OF *Minnesota*

April 10, 1972

UNIVERSITY MEASUREMENT SERVICES CENTER
9 CLARENCE AVENUE S.E.
MINNEAPOLIS, MINNESOTA 55414

Dear John,

We are concluding the data-collecting phase of our study
on Graduate Assistants of the University of Minnesota
and have not yet received your response. We have tried
a variety of ways to remind you that we still want to
hear from you very much, but apparently none of them
has convinced you to help us out. Perhaps you have
been very busy or perhaps have just forgotten about us -
if this is the case, please take some time from your already busy schedule to help us out. We have enclosed
one last form for your convenience and urge you to complete it immediately.

If for any reason you decide not to complete the questionnaire, we would appreciate it if you would call Doug or
Jack at 373-2263.

Sincerely,

Patricia S. Faunce

Patricia S. Faunce
Director, Measurement Services Center
    and Associate Professor of Psychology

PSF/pgs

[Original on 5½″ x 8½″ white note paper.]

UNIVERSITY OF MINNESOTA | University Measurement Services Center
TWIN CITIES | 9 Clarence Avenue S.E.
| Minneapolis, Minnesota 55414

April 7, 1972

Professor _____
Chairman, Department of _____
_____

Dear Professor_____ :

We are concluding the data collection phase of our study on the roles and
functions of graduate assistants at the University of Minnesota. As of this
date, we have not received a completed questionnaire from you and are eagerly
awaiting its return.

We believe this to be an extremely valuable study in that the total position
of graduate assistants is being thoroughly evaluated and should yield useful and
insightful information for all segments of the University. We are presently
trying to establish a method (consistent with our guarantee of confidentiality
to all participants in the study) by which the results of our study will be
available to interested departments in those areas of specific concern to them.

Some of the departmental chairmen and directors of units in our study have
questioned the relevance of their participation in the study. The population
of department chairmen or directors which the study encompasses, has been defined
as "those chairmen or directors of departments or units employing at least one
'graduate assistant' (9501, 9502, 9511, 9521)." Our records show that you fit
this definition. If, however, you believe that some parts of the questionnaire
are irrelevant to your unit, please feel free to leave those sections blank.
Also, realize that we will incorporate written remarks into our report so do
not feel overly restricted by the format of the questionnaire (attach additional
sheets if you desire).

If you have any further questions or desire clarification on any aspect of the
study, please call Jack Anderson or Doug Berdie at 373-2263. Thank you for your
time and cooperation! We look forward to receiving your completed questionnaire.

Sincerely,

Patricia S. Faunce
Director, Measurement Services Center
  and Associate Professor of Psychology

PSF:hg

[Original standard letter on 8½″ by 11″ paper.]

[Original 5⅜″ x 8½″ (shown here at 75% real size), black on medium intensity red, light-weight paper.]

```
      BULLETIN!!!   $$$$$   BULLETIN!!!   $$$$$   BULLETIN!!!

 $     $ $ $ $ $ $ $ $ $ $ $ $ $ $ $ $ $ $ $ $ $ $ $ $      $

 $   ANNOUNCING THE MEASUREMENT SERVICES CENTER RESPONDENT RAFFLE    $
                       University of Minnesota
 $                                                                  $

 $      In order to show our appreciation to the many generous      $
        people who have completed our questionnaire on graduate
 $      assistants, and in order to induce you to respond, the      $
        MSC Director is personally sponsoring a $25.00 cash prize
 $      to the winner of our respondent raffle.  On May 2, 1972,    $
        one lucky person who has completed our questionnaire will
 $      be selected randomly and will receive a cash prize of $25.00. $

 $                                                                  $
                          Raffle Rules
 $                                                                  $
                  1. Only people to whom we have sent
 $                questionnaires are eligible.                      $

 $                2. Only one returned questionnaire per            $
                  person will be accepted.
 $                                                                  $
                  3. Only completed questionnaires received
 $                in our office by 4:30 p.m., May 1, 1972           $
                  will be eligible.
 $                                                                  $
                  4. The winner will be announced in the
 $                Daily and in the Brief.                           $

 $                                                                  $

 $      IMPORTANT NOTE: Some people have called and told us they    $
        haven't finished the questionnaire about graduate assistants
 $      because some items do not seem applicable.  Please feel     $
        free to omit any items you feel you cannot answer.  This is
 $      positively our last attempt to persuade you to respond, so  $
        please don't wait to see what we try next!!!!!
 $                                                                  $

 $      P.S. This reminder is not a joke--we will award the $25     $
        prize to one respondent!!!!!!
 $                                                                  $

 $      Call Doug or Jack  373-2263  if you need another questionnaire $

 $                                                                  $

 $                                                                  $
        $ $ $ $ $ $ $ $ $ $ $ $ $ $ $ $ $ $ $ $ $ $ $ $
```

[Original on standard 8½″ x 11″ paper.]

EXHIBIT 9

 UNIVERSITY OF MINNESOTA   University Measurement Services Center
TWIN CITIES   9 Clarence Avenue S.E.
Minneapolis, Minnesota 55414

February 18, 1972

Dr. _____
Department Chairman
Department of _____
University of Minnesota

Dear Dr. _____:

We have just received your returned questionnaire with attached note
indicating the inapplicability of your department in regard to our
current study of graduate assistants at the University.

We realize that throughout the   departments in the University,
graduate assistants are often classified as either teaching associates
(9501, 9502), teaching assistants (9511), or research assistants (9521)
as a form of financial assistance apart from the duties usually associated with those positions. Nevertheless, this is a part of the
"roles and functions" of graduate assistants at the University.

Because   is classified in one of the above categories,
you have been included in our department chairmen population (which
includes the chairmen, directors, and heads of all units employing at
least one graduate assistant). Although some (or most) of the questions on the questionnaire may seem inappropriate to the situation
in your department, we hope you will fill out the questionnaire to the
best of your ability and return it to us. Please feel free to comment
(either on the questionnaire or on the attached sheet) on any items in
the questionnaire you believe necessary to clarify your response.

In order to accurately reflect the situation at the University of
Minnesota in regard to graduate assistants, it is imperative that we
also hear from the situations that one might consider "borderline" in
regard to applicability.

Thank you for your time and efforts!

Sincerely,

Douglas R. Berdie
Research Specialist
UMSC

[Original standard letter on 8½" x 11" paper.]

304

March 2, 1972

Dear Mrs. ——,

We appreciate your time and effort in writing to inform us that your son Michael is overseas and, consequently, unable to respond to our questionnaire on graduate assistants at the University. We would appreciate it if you could have him complete the form upon his return home and mail it back to us.

We will not bother you with further follow-up reminders as this is obviously unnecessary

Thank-you again for your consideration!

Sincerely,

Doug Berdie
Jack Anderson

EXHIBIT 10

Response before Personal Contact

Response after Contact

Dear Friend:
   I have no intention of filling out
the form on graduate assistants. If
you should by some chance design a
reasonable one, I would be delighted to
cooperate.
                    Yours very truly,

Will send a letter describing
his views on the issues covered in the questionnaire.

*This is the second "task
force" questionnaire I received
in the mail today. We will
soon have a "task force"
on "task forces." To Hell
with you.*

"If you take the trouble to
come over here, I'll take
the trouble to answer it."

*This form is biased toward
grievances of graduate assistants.
I'm very pleased with my TA ship
and generally discuss relevant
problems with people in the
department.
Perhaps by not completing it, I'm
able to express my displeasure
of it.*

Will respond with a letter
describing her satisfaction
with her appointment.

306

EXHIBIT 11

Sorry this is so late, I tried, but I just wouldn't get the first one out of the Rhino's jaws.

Dear Pat, Doug and Jack,

I'm sorry I didn't send the questimaire in sooner. But, all your mail came to my mothers house.

Thanks for the Valentine. Mother was wondering what type service center you were. P.M.N
I.D. 353727

Candy,
Persistent aren't you! Good luck on your survey.

Harlan

Sorry about the lateness

Thanks for the Valentine

I apologize for my delay but I send this with reluctance because I would like to see what
Please indic circling how
the next level of inducement is (maybe?)
Thank...

Hey! Thanks for the Valentine! Maybe our company should start that sort of thing Just think of the good customer relations!

Love & Kisses,
"P"

DOUG + JACK

REJOICE YE

I'm turning this thing in !!........

[EXHIBIT 11, cont.]

<u>CANDY</u>   3636

Dear Survey Takers,
    Although I understand how
statistics works and your need
to receive as many of these back
as possible to get accurate
results, I still hate surveys.
This is the 3rd copy I have
received (thanks for the other 2 stamps)
and the only reason I am sending
this one back is because the
girl who did the calling for you (Candy)
had such a nice, convincing voice.
(It took her 15 min though)
Since I've decided to run a
survey myself; I think I'll do

it on voices, it would be much appreciated if somehow you could inform Candy of my need to hear her voice again. (for research reasons only, of course)

The personal touch to match your survey Sincerely yours,

3636

P.S.
You should have Candy call everyone before you send the surveys out; then maybe you would get better results.

Appendix C:

SAMPLE FOLLOW-UP LETTERS

Teachers College
COLUMBIA UNIVERSITY
New York

Dear Sir:*

We find your name among the few graduates of the ----
------ School of -------- who have not returned the questionnaire sent you recently. A new questionnaire is herewith
enclosed, in case you have mislaid the other one or if it has
been lost in the mail. We hope the following short story will
encourage you to answer this questionnaire at once.

The Merchant's Dinner

In France before the war it was the custom on a certain
holiday for thirty jovial tradesmen to meet at the home of a
popular merchant. They foregathered to renew friendships,
to have speeches, and to make merry with wine and song.
But a sad day came with the advent of the war. The good
merchant's stock of wine was exhausted and, on account of
business reverses, he had not the means to purchase more.
Great were his misgivings as the holiday approached, for he
could not think of the feast without the customary wine. The
tradesmen all shook their heads sadly, until one made the
bright suggestion that each procure a bottle of wine, to re-
plenish the good merchant's cask with thirty bottles.

The holiday came. There was no lack of merriment and
this served somewhat to dispel the host's fears. Unnoticed
by him, the tradesmen one by one proceeded to the cellar,
each withdrawing a small bottle from beneath his cloak,

310

emptying the contents into the cask, and returning to the company unnoticed. While the feast was at its height, the merchant made the sad announcement that his wine cask was empty. One of the guests spoke up: "Good friend, perhaps the last drop has not been drawn. Let us at least see the color of a good glass of wine."

The merchant went down to his cellar and was astonished beyond measure when, upon turning the faucet, his pitcher was quickly filled to the brim. He hastened up the dim stairway to his guests. When lo and behold! In place of the golden liquid which he expected to see, there was nothing but water in the pitcher. It seems that every man had said to himself; "Among so many bottles, it will not matter if I fail to furnish good wine. I will fill my bottle with water, and no one will ever know the difference."

With so many graduates of the ---------- School of --- -----, you may feel that whether or not you answer the questionnaire will make but little difference. But, as the above story so forcibly shows, it is only when every man feels responsible for a big undertaking that the undertaking succeeds. We have to have one hundred per cent of returned questionnaires. Will you please cooperate by sitting down now and filling out the answers to the questions?

Very sincerely yours,

Herbert A. Toops

---

*The above letter is taken from Herbert A. Toops, "Validating the Questionnaire Method," Journal of Personnel Research, Vol. 2, Nos. 4 & 5 (1923), 162-9. Reprinted with the permission of Personnel Journal, Costa Mesa, California; all rights reserved.

Columbus, Ohio
April 25, 1924

Dear Sir:†

All but 38 of the 110 colleges and universities to whom we sent on March 12th, a questionnaire regarding the use of

intelligence tests have replied. In a few cases the addresses
were incomplete and so did not reach the person intended.
Such addresses have been corrected to the best of our ability,
and hence we are in doubt as to the reason for our not yet
having heard from you. We have been personally "bothered"
with questionnaires in the past. It was with some misgivings
therefore that, after deliberation, we decided to "bother" busy
college people with a questionnaire. We then reduced the
work involved in replying to a minimum. You will note that
practically all of the questions can be answered with either a
check mark, a number, or a single word. That 72 colleges
should have responded with but one follow-up letter is grati-
fying. If but 37 other people, in addition to yourself, respond to this letter we shall have full returns and can then
be assured that we do not have a biased selection of colleges.

Perhaps you are not the person to whom the questionnaire should have been addressed; if so, will you please hand
the questionnaire to a colleague who is in closer touch with
such personnel work? And perhaps you have lost the former
questionnaire (sometimes they go the way of the waste paper
basket). At any rate, we are enclosing another for your
convenience in sending us a prompt reply. Let us repeat that
the tabulated results will be published for the benefit of all.
May we not have the benefits of your experience with such
tests?

Yours very sincerely,

---

†The above letter is taken from Herbert A. Toops, "The Returns from Follow-up Letters to Questionnaires," Journal of
Applied Psychology, 1926, 10, 92-101. Copyright 1926 by
the American Psychological Association. Reprinted by permission.

Teachers College
COLUMBIA UNIVERSITY
New York

Dear Sir:*

Do you know that the -------- -------- School on December 31, 1922, had enrolled 876 students since its begin-

ning five years ago? Do you know that your name is on our list of 55 of the graduates who have not yet answered the questionnaire sent them recently? We have sent you three letters; none of them have been returned by the Post Office Department; consequently we can only assume that you must have received them. Why don't you answer?

We have tried to guess what must be your objections to answering. Please read the objections below and our answers. We hope these will answer your objections and that you will send in your reply at once.

No. 1: "I HAVEN'T THE TIME. "--We have so designed the questionnaire that most of the answers are "Yes" or "No." You will find that it will take but a few minutes to answer them.

No. 2: "I DO NOT WISH TO GIVE INFORMATION REGARD-ING MY PERSONAL AFFAIRS. "--You will note that the questionnaire does not ask for the amount of your present salary, nor for your religious preferences. We are not interested in knowing who is your present employer, so that you may omit that in case you do not want to give it, if you will be specific in regard to the kind of work you are doing. The results will be held absolutely confidential.

No. 3: "I WILL NOT PROFIT BY THE ANSWERS WHICH I MAY GIVE. "--Neither may you profit by giving your seat to a lady in the street car. The whole purpose of the survey is to enable us to devise and put into effect better methods of instruction. We want to know, for instance, whether former graduates are now working at --------, and whether they secured their own positions or were aided by the -------- School. Our results will help the next student who enrolls.

No. 4: "I HAVE ONLY KICKS TO MAKE; I CANNOT RECOMMEND THE --------COURSE. "--If that is your reason, let's have it; and please go a little bit further and tell us why you have the kick. Perhaps we can have the cause of the grouch removed for the next student who comes along.

No. 5: "I AM MAKING A SUCCESS. THE INSTITUTE WILL HAVE PLENTY OF REPLIES LIKE MINE, SO WHY SHOULD I SEND ONE?"--"Yes," that may be true; BUT, the Insti-tute does not know it until it hears from you. If you have either kicks or recommendations for the --------course, please send them in along with your questionnaire.

We cannot be sure that we have an accurate picture of what the school is doing until we have one hundred per cent of replies to our questionnaire. Only 55 more answers will give us this one hundred per cent. Will you please send in your questionnaire today?

Very sincerely yours,

Herbert A. Toops

---

*The above letter is taken from Herbert A. Toops, "Validating the Questionnaire Method," Journal of Personnel Research, Vol. 2, Nos. 4 & 5 (1923), 162-9. Reprinted with the permission of Personnel Journal, Costa Mesa, California; all rights reserved.

Appendix D: SAMPLE CHECK-OFF LIST

Identifying Number	Date Pre-letter Mailed	Date Questionnaire Mailed	Date Completed Questionnaire Received	Follow-Up [F. U.]				
				F. U. 1	F. U. 2	F. U. 3.	F. U. 4	F. U. 5

INDEX TO THE BIBLIOGRAPHY
(Keyed to citation numbers, not to pages)

GENERAL INDEX
(Keyed to page numbers)